MW01400956

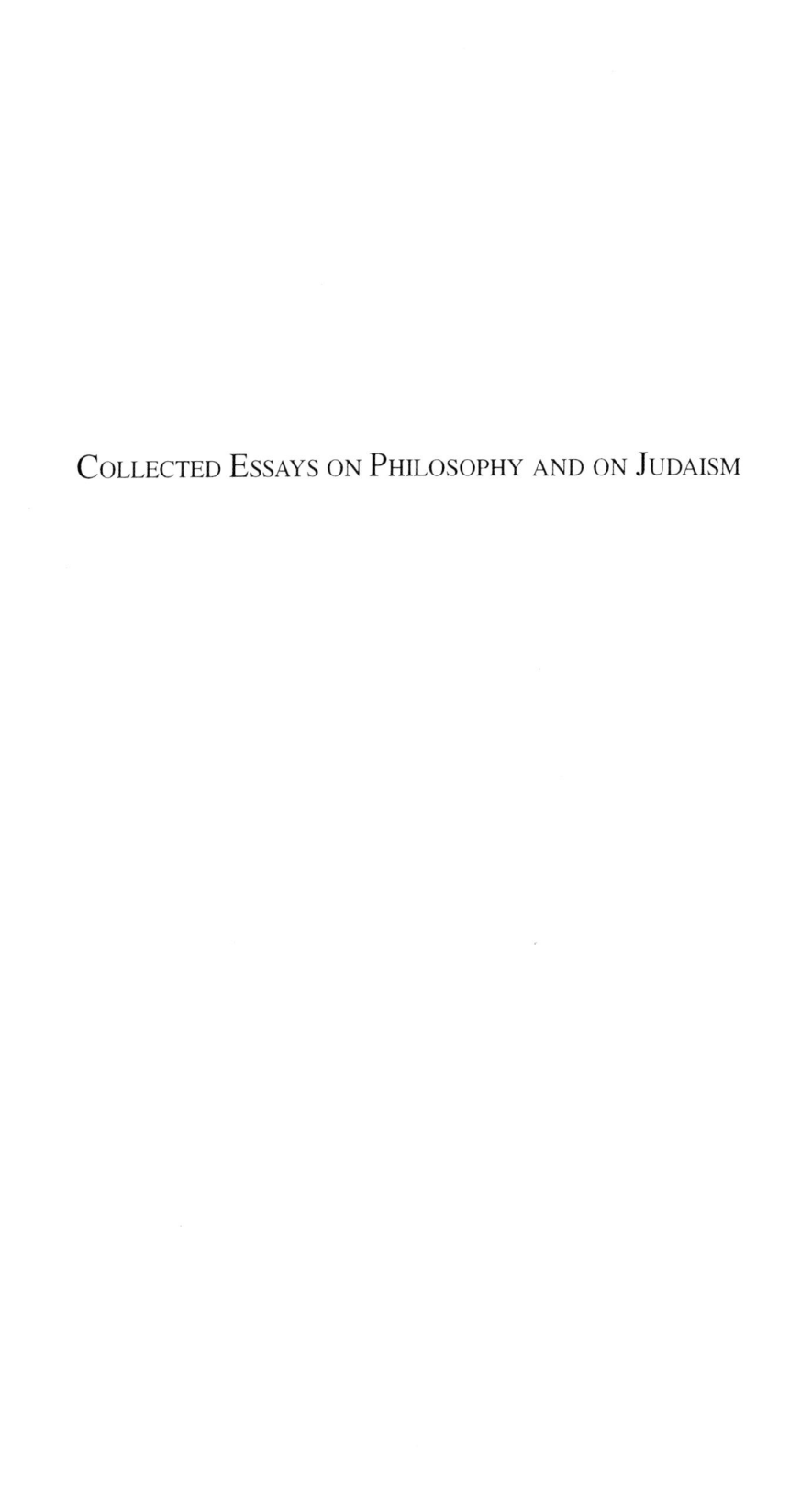

COLLECTED ESSAYS ON PHILOSOPHY AND ON JUDAISM

MARVIN FOX

COLLECTED ESSAYS ON PHILOSOPHY AND ON JUDAISM

EDITED BY JACOB NEUSNER

VOLUME ONE

GREEK PHILOSOPHY, MAIMONIDES

Academic Studies in the History of Judaism
Global Publications, Binghamton University
Binghamton, New York
2001

Copyright © 2001 by June Fox

All rights reserved. No portion of this publication may be duplicated in any way without the expressed written consent of the publisher, except in the form of brief excerpts or quotations for review purposes.

Cover artwork entitled "Torah Mantle" by Suzanne R. Neusner.

Library of Congress Cataloging-in-Publication Data:

Fox, Marvin.
  Collected essays on philosophy and on Judaism / Marvin Fox ; edited by Jacob Neusner.
    p. cm. -- (Academic studies in the history of Judaism)
  Includes bibliographical references.
  ISBN 1-58684-144-0 (v. 1 : pbk. : alk. paper) -- ISBN 1-58684-145-9 (v. 2 : pbk. : alk. paper) -- ISBN 1-58684-146-7 (v. 3 : pbk. : alk. paper)
  1. Philosophy, Jewish. 2. Judaism. 3. Maimonides, Moses, 1135-1204.
  I. Neusner, Jacob, 1932- II. Title. III. Series.
  B5800 .F69 2001
  181'.06--dc21
                                                            2001004123

Published and Distributed by:
Academic Studies in the History of Judaism
Global Publications, Binghamton University
State University of New York at Binghamton
LNG 99, Binghamton University
Binghamton, New York, USA 13902-6000
Phone: (607) 777-4495 or 777-6104; Fax: (607) 777-6132
E-mail: pmorewed@binghamton.edu
http://ssips.binghamton.edu

Dedication

This volume of Marvin Fox's Essays is dedicated to our dear children, Avrom and Debra, Daniel and Barbara, Sherry and Laurence; and our beloved grandchildren, Jeremy, Aliza, Roniel, Emunah, Eytan, Amy, Naomi, Aaron, David, Joshua, Michael and Jonathon.

All of them join me in expressing our profound gratitude to Marvin's esteemed colleague and devoted friend, Professor Jacob Neusner, whose remarkable efforts have brought about the publication of this work.

June Fox

ACADEMIC STUDIES IN THE HISTORY OF JUDAISM
Publisher: Global Publications, State University of New York at Binghamton
Address: LNG 99, SUNY-Binghamton, Binghamton, New York 13902-6000

Editor-in-Chief
Jacob Neusner, *Bard College*

Editorial Committee
Alan J. Avery-Peck, *College of the Holy Cross*
Bruce D. Chilton, *Bard College*
William Scott Green, *University of Rochester*
James F. Strange, *University of South Florida*

Preface

Professor Marvin Fox was born October 17, 1922 in Chicago, Illinois and died in Newton, Massachusetts, on February 8, 1996. Professor Marvin Fox received his B. A. in philosophy in 1942 from Northwestern University, the M. A. in the same field in 1946, and the Ph. D. at the University of Chicago in 1950 in that field as well. His education in Judaic texts was certified by rabbinical ordination as Rabbi by the Hebrew Theological College of Chicago in 1942. He served as a Jewish Chaplain in the U.S. Army Air Force during World War II in 1942-1946. He taught at Ohio State University from 1948 through 1974, rising from Instructor to Professor of Philosophy. During those years he served also as Visiting Professor of Philosophy at the Hebrew Theological College of Chicago (1955) and also at the Hebrew University of Jerusalem and Bar Ilan University (1970-1971). In 1974 he came to Brandeis University as Appleman Professor of Jewish Thought, and from 1976 onward he has held the Lown Professorship. In 1975-1982 and from 1984-1987 he was Chairman of the Department of Near Eastern and Judaic Studies at Brandeis, and from 1976 he has also served as Director of the Lown School of Near Eastern and Judaic Studies. In 1980-1981 he was Visiting Scholar in Jewish Philosophy at the Center for Jewish Studies of nearby Harvard University.

He has received numerous academic awards, a selected list of which includes the following: 1956-1957: Elizabeth Clay Howald Post-Doctoral Scholarship; 1962-1963, Fellow of the American Council of Learned Societies; 1975-1978, Director of the Association for Jewish Studies regional conferences, funded by the National Endowment for the Humanities; 1977-1980, Director of the project, "For the Strengthening of Judaic Studies at Brandeis and their Links to the General Humanities," also funded by the National Endowment for the Humanities. From 1979 he has been Fellow of the Academy of Jewish Philosophy; 1980-1981, Senior Faculty Fellow, National Endowment for the Humanities. He has served on the editorial boards of *the AJS Review, Daat, Judaism, Tradition, Journal for the History of Philosophy*, and other journals. He has lectured widely at universities and at national and international academic conferences and served as

Member of the National Endowment for the Humanities National Board of Consultants for new programs at colleges and universities. Over the years he has counseled various universities and academic publishers as well. His ties to institutions of Jewish learning under Jewish sponsorship are strong. He has served on the Advisory Committee of the Jewish Studies Adaptation Program of the International Center for University Teaching of Jewish Civilization (Israel), since 1982; International Planning Committee of the Institute for Contemporary Jewry of the Hebrew University since that same year; member of the governing council of the World Union of Jewish Studies since 1975; secretary, 1971-1972, vice president, from 1973-1975, and then president, from 1975-1978, of the Association for Jewish Studies; and he has been on the board of directors of that organization since 1970. From 1964 through 1968 he served on the Executive Committee of the Conference on Jewish Philosophy; from 1970 until his death on the Executive Committee of the Institute of Judaism and Contemporary Thought of Bar Ilan University; from 1972 as Member of the Academic Board of the Melton Research Center of the Jewish Theological Seminary of America; Member of the board of directors of the Institute for Jewish Life from 1972 through 1975; member of the board of directors of the Library of Living Philosophers, Inc., from 1948; Associate of the Columbia University Seminar on Israel and Jewish Studies from 1968 through 1974; and many other organizations.

His committee service at Brandeis University has covered these committees: Graduate School Council; Philosophy Department Advisory Committee and Reappointment and Promotions Committee; University Tenure Panels; Academic Planning Committee (Chairman, 1982-1984); Faculty Committee for the Hiatt Institute; Tauber Institute Faculty Advisory Committee and its academic policy sub-committee; Committee on University Studies in the Humanities; Faculty representative on the Brandeis University Board of Trustees (1978-1980). His professional memberships include the American Philosophical Association, the Metaphysical Society of America, the Medieval Academy of America, as well as the Association for Jewish Studies, Conference on Jewish Philosophy, and American Academy for Jewish Research.

When I taught at Brown, I called upon Professor Fox for counsel in the fifteen years after Professor Fox came to Brandeis University. And he responded, always giving his best judgment and his wisest counsel.

Preface

Professor Fox was a good neighbor, a constant counselor, and valued friend. In the sequence of eight academic conferences that I presented annually at Brown Universixty in the 1970s, Professor Fox played a leading role in the planning of the programs and in scholarly interchange. At that time, also, Brown and Brandeis Universities held a conference at which graduate students in the respective graduate programs met and engaged in shared discussion of common interests. Professor Fox moreover has taken a position on numerous dissertation committees in Brown's graduate program in the History of Judaism. His conscientious and careful reading of these dissertations give to the students the benefit not only of his learning but also of his distinct and rich perspective upon the problem of the dissertation.

I organized and edited the *festschrift* published in his honor in my series at Scholars Press, as follows:

From Ancient Israel to Modern Judaism. Intellect in Quest of Understanding. Essays in Honor of Marvin Fox. Atlanta, 1989: Scholars Press for Brown Judaic Studies. I-IV.

I. *What Is at Stake in the Judaic Quest for Understanding? Judaic Learning and the Locus of Education. Ancient Israel. Formative Christianity. Judaism in the Formative Age: Religion.*

II. *Judaism in the Formative Age: Theology and Literature. Judaism in the Middle Ages: The Encounter with Christianity. The Encounter with Scripture. Philosophy and Theology.*

III. *Judaism in the Middle Ages: Philosophers. Hasidism. Messianism in Modern Times. The Modern Age: Philosophy.*

IV. *The Modern Age: Theology, Literature, History.*

I also organized the celebration in Professor Fox's honor held by President Evelyn Handler of Brandeis University in connection with the publication of the festschrift.

This volume of his essays offers to a new generation of scholars of Jewish thought and philosophy a selection of his more important writings.

Their original publication is indicated in the bibliography of Marvin Fox that follows.

The essays collected and presented here represent the selections of Dr. June Fox in consultation with the editor.

Jacob Neusner

Research Professor of Religion and Theology
Program in Religion and Institute of Advanced Theology
Bard College
Annandale-on-Hudson, New York 12504

neusner@webjogger.net

Marvin Fox - A Memoir

Memoirs have a tendency to be less than faithful to the truth. The writer may romanticize, or rely on anecdotes, or fill in spaces when she was not present at times being recollected in the life of the memorialized. This memoir is different from most, I believe. I knew Marvin all my life—when he was a child, a teenager, a young man, and as my husband of fifty-two years, until his death. I believe that the words, which follow, faithfully describe him, the events of his life, and the goals, and aspirations which animated him, since I was privileged to observe and share them with him for so many decades.

Marvin's parents and his older brother emigrated to the United States from Russia, to escape the persecution of Jews and the turmoil of the Russian Revolution. They came to Chicago (where a number of relatives resided) in October of 1922. Marvin was born within a few days after their arrival. The early years in America were a time of great poverty for his family, which, in truth, was not alleviated for two decades. But his parents knew that a better life for their children depended upon education and study, and they inspired him to read and learn, both the culture of their new society and Jewish texts and sources, which they revered and he came to revere as well.

At a very early age, in the late 1930's, while studying at the Hebrew Theological College, he became a student at Northwestern University, and became fascinated by philosophy. I recall, vividly, listening to him formulate his dream for our future. He wanted to become a professor of philosophy, in a major secular university, and a Jewish scholar as well. It was a hopeless dream, as we well knew, at least the professor part. There were virtually no universities which employed Jews as academics, and few which welcomed them even as students. Although he was extraordinarily gifted, a kind professor in the Philosophy Department spoke to him, and told that such an aspiration for a young Jewish man was virtually impossible, and that he needed to face reality.

It took World War II to create a new reality. Marvin joined the United States Army Air Force, after his graduation from Northwestern and the end of his rabbinical studies at the Yeshiva. He served as a Jewish Chaplain for almost four years, which provided extraordinarily important insights into the many facets of America, which he had never experienced. We were married in the middle of the war. When we returned to Chicago, hundreds of thousands of young men who had served their country were descending upon the universities, subsidized by the G.I. Bill. This influx of ordinary Americans into higher education did more to undermine elitism in American society than, perhaps, any legislative action before or since in the history of our country.

The universities needed professors to teach their students, and though it may not have been their preference, they were obliged to hire as faculty, anyone qualified to teach. During the late 40's, and forward to this day, Jewish men and later women entered academia in large numbers. Marvin started and completed his Ph.D. at the University of Chicago, and in 1948 was appointed to the faculty of Philosophy at the Ohio State University, in Columbus. Here he spent twenty-six years, teaching with great distinction, writing, assuming a leadership role in faculty affairs, engaging actively as a community leader, both locally and nationally, raising our family, and achieving the first part of his dream for his future.

The second part—becoming a Jewish scholar—became a "private" occupation. Marvin wrote, published, and lectured extensively in the field of Jewish thought, at the same time as he studied and published in general philosophy. His good friends and colleagues in philosophy and the humanities at Ohio State good-naturedly referred to the "Jewish thing" as his "hobby." Judaic studies were not considered, by scholars, as worthy of inclusion in the academic curricula of the universities in America. With the exception of Harvard and Columbia, which had a few scholars of Judaica on their faculties, serious Jewish study was confined to the Seminaries, Dropsie College, and Brandeis University, which was founded in 1948.

By the 1960's, this landscape also began to change. Marvin played a significant role in bringing about the change. In the early 60's, a wonderful philanthropic member of the Columbus Jewish community, Samuel Melton, who was very interested in promoting Jewish study at Ohio State, came to Marvin to discuss the possibility of endowing a chair in Judaic studies. Marvin served as negotiator with the University administration, which was receptive to the idea. It was determined that it would be a chair in Jewish History. It was necessary to convince the members of the History Department that Jewish history was a legitimate area of study—the history of the Jews at most merited one chapter or one part of a lecture in a World History class. Marvin found an ideal candidate for the chair: a professor from the Hebrew University who had studied and taught with Salo Baron at Columbia. He was a noted scholar and a charismatic teacher. Upon meeting him, the history department was convinced that Jewish history was indeed a worthy subject for study, and Jewish Studies was instituted at Ohio State. The administration, at Marvin's urging, brought in a professor of Hebrew, acquired a Judaic library collection, employed a Judaic librarian, and a new discipline found its way in to the University in the heartland of our country.

At the same time, a small group of faculty of Judaica at seminaries, at an occasional university, and men and women who were interested in developing Jewish studies in higher education gathered at Brandeis University and founded the Association of Jewish Studies. Marvin was among the group, which grew larger

Memoir

with each passing year, until its membership has surpassed one thousand. More and more universities introduced Jewish Studies, following the Ohio State model or creating alternative models. Marvin served as president of the Association, helped launch its academic journal, and acted as consultant to numerous university administrations as they planned and adopted Judaic Studies in their institutions.

In 1974, Marvin was invited to join the Department of Near Eastern and Judaic Studies at Brandeis University, as a Professor of Jewish Philosophy. He had never taught a course in Jewish studies in his entire career as a professor of philosophy in America. (He had done so only as a visiting professor at the Hebrew University of Jerusalem in 1970.) The second part of his dream then became a reality. He joined a faculty of scholars distinguished in every aspect of Jewish study. He became and served as Chairman of the Department for many years. He was appointed Director of the Lown School of Jewish Studies, which included contemporary as well as classical Jewish Studies. He had, for the first time in his life, many doctoral students in Jewish Studies, whom he guided to degrees and saw them placed in teaching positions in universities all over the world. No longer pursuing a "hobby", he devoted his writing primarily to topics related to Jewish thought. He remained at Brandeis until his retirement in 1994, having experienced the most rewarding professional years of his life.

A final culminating experience came his way after he left Brandeis. Boston University, which occasionally appointed distinguished emeritus professors to its faculty, invited him to join the departments of Religion and Philosophy in that capacity. He enjoyed a wonderfully satisfying year with interesting new colleagues and new students, a pattern which he hoped would continue on into the future. Alas, he became mortally ill at that point and died in a matter of months.

Marvin Fox was a very large, imposing man, with a deep and sonorous voice which he could project in an auditorium filled with one thousand students, using no microphone. He had an infectious laugh and an extraordinary wit. He was more than a teacher—he was constantly involved in solving problems, which he did with consummate skill. He found jobs for students and supported them in obtaining tenure. He raised money for countless needy scholars, and helped them publish their books. He was an advocate for academic freedom and freedom to speak out for professors and students. He mediated disputes, and promoted academic harmony. He lived as an observant Jew among colleagues and friends who had never known an observant Jew and gained their respect. He knew well some of the greatest scholars of his day. He saw the creation of the State of Israel and had the great satisfaction of teaching there. He was the father of three dearly loved children, of whom, together with their spouses, he was inordinately proud. And he lived to see and know his eleven grandchildren, who were perhaps, the greatest joy of his life.

Shortly before he became ill with his last illness, he told me, one day, "I have lived the most richly rewarding life any man could have hoped for. How many of us can say that all the dreams of their youth have come true? I can—and I have been truly blessed."

His life was a blessing for us, as is his memory.

June T. Fox, PhD
Chicago, Illinois
March, 2001

BIBLIOGRAPHY OF MARVIN FOX

1. "Three Approaches to the Jewish Problem," *Antioch* Review, 6(l), Spring, 1946, pp. 54-68.

2. "Towards a Life of Joy: A Theological Critique," *Menorah Journal*, 36(2), Spring, 1948, pp. 248-25 1.

3. "On Calling Women to the Reading of the Torah," *The Reconstructionist*, 13(19), January, 1948. An exchange of letters with Robert Gordis. For Gordis' reply see *idem.*, 14(7), May, 1948.

4. *Kant's Fundamental Principles of the Metaphsic of Morals*, edited with an introduction, (Liberal Arts Press, 1949). Reprinted in numerous editions by the original publisher, then acquired by Bobbs-Merrill, and most recently by Macmillan.

5. Review of Chaim Weizmann, *Trial and Error*, *Heritage*, Spring, 1949, pp. 16-18.

6. Review of Morris R. Cohen, *Reason and Law, Illinois Law Review*, 45(2), May, 1950, pp. 305 -307.

7. *Moral Fact and Moral Theory: A Study of Some Methodological Problems in Contemporary Ethics*, Unpublished doctoral dissertation, University of Chicago, 1950.

8. Review of John A. Nicholson, *Philosophy of Religion, Philosophy and Phenomenological Research*, 11 (3), March, 195 1.

9. Review of Maxwell Silver, *The Way to God, Philosophy and Phenomenological Research*, 11 (4), June, 195 1.

10. "On the Diversity of Methods in Dewey's Ethical Theory," *Philosophy and Phenomenological Research*, 12(l), September, 1951.

11. Review of Abraham Joshua Heschel, *Man is Not Alone*, *Commentary*, 12(2), August, 1951, pp. 193-195.

12. "Kierkegaard and Rabbinic Judaism," *Judaism*, 2(2), April, 1953, pp. 160-169.

13. "Day Schools and the American Educational Pattern," *The Jewish Parent*, September, 1953.

14. Review of J. Guttmann, *Maimonides' Guide of the Perplexed*, *Judaism*, 2(4), October, 1953, pp. 363-367.

15. "Moral Facts and Moral Theory," *Perspectives*, (Ohio State University Press, 1953), pp. II I- 127.

16. Review of Martin Buber, *At the Turning*, *New Mexico Quarterly*, 24(2), Summer, 1954., pp. 217-220.

17. "What Can the Modern Jew Believe?," Alfred Jospe, ed., *Judaism for the Modern Age*, (B'nai B'rith Hillel Foundations, 1955).

18. "Our Missing Intellectuals: Another View," *National Jewish Monthly*, December, 1954, pp. 10-13.

19. Review of Abraham Cronbach, *Judaism for Today*, *Judaism*, 4(l), Winter, 1955, pp. 82-84.

20. "Amicus Jacobus, sed Magis Arnica Veritas," *Conservative Judaism*, 10(3), Spring, 1956, pp. 9-17.

21. "The Trials of Socrates: An Analysis of the First Tetralogy," *Archiv fuer Philosophie*, 6(3/4), 1956, pp. 226-261.

22. "What's Wrong — and Right — with Deweyism," *The Jewish Parent*, December, 1956.

23. Review of Abraham Joshua Heschel, *God in Search of Man: A Philosophy of Judaism, Judaism*, 6(1), Winter, 1957, pp. 77-81.

24. "Can Modern Man Believe in God," Alfred Jospe, ed., *The Jewish Heritage and the Jewish Student*, (New York, 1959), pp. 40-50.

25. "Who is Competent to Teach Religion," *Religious Education*, 54(2), March-April, 1959, pp. 112-114.

26. "Torah Jews in the Making," *The Jewish Parent*, April, 1960, pp. 4-5, 22.

27. "Heschel, Intuition, and the Halakhah," *Tradition*, 3(1), Fall, 1960, pp. 5-15.

28. "Tillich's Ontology and God," *Anglican Theological Review*, 43(3), July, 1961, pp. 260-267.

29. "Ve-al ha-Medinot Bo Ye'amer," *Panim el Panim*, No. 124-125, September 10, 1961, pp. 18-19. A symposium with Professor Salo Baron.

30. Review of Samuel Dresner, *The Zaddik, Conservative Judaism*, 15(4), Summer, 1961, pp. 39-42.

31. Review of Robert Gordis, *A Faith for Moderns*, *Commentary*, 32(4), October, 1961.

32. "Modern Faith," *Commentary*, 33(2), February, 1962. An exchange of letters with Robert Gordis.

33. Review of Jakob Petuchowski, *Ever Since Sinai, Judaism*, 10(4), Fall, 1961.

34. Review of Harry A. Wolfson, *Religious Philosophy: A Group of Essays*, *The Classical Journal*, 58(2), November, 1962.

35. "Einige Probleme in Buber's Moralphilosophie," Paul A. Schilpp and Maurice Friedman, eds., *Philosophen des 20. Jahrhunderts: Martin Buber,* (Kohlhammer, 1963), pp. 135-152. German translation of #47.

36. "Theistic Bases of Ethics," Robert Bartels, ed., *Ethics in Business*, (Ohio State University Press, 1963).

37. Review of Joseph Blau, *The Story of Jewish Philosophy*, and Gerald Abrahams, *The Jewish Mind*, *Commentary*, 35(1), January, 1963.

38. Review of Arthur A. Cohen, The Natural and the Super-Natural Jew, *Commentary*, 35(4), April, 1963.

39. Review of Ephraim Shmueli, *Bein Emunah Likfirah, Commentary* 36(2), August, 1963.

40. "Religion and Human Nature in the Philosophy of David Hume," William L. Reese and Eugene Freeman, eds., *Process and Divinily: Philosophical Essays Presented to Charles Hartshorne*, (Open Court, 1964), pp. 561-577.

41. "Character Training and Environmental Pressures," *The Jewish Parent*, October, 1964.

42. Review of W. Gunther Plaut, *The Rise of Reform Judaism*, *Commentary,* 37(6), June, 1964.

43. Review of Max Kadushin, *Worship and Ethics*, *Commentary*, 38(6), December, 1964.

44. Review of Israel Efros, *Ancient Jewish Philosophy*, *Commentary*, 40(1), July, 1965.

45. "Religion and the Public Schools — A Philosopher's Analysis," *Theory into Practice*, 4(1), February, 1965, pp. 40-44.

46. Review Essay on *Maimonides' Guide to the Perplexed*, Shlomo Pines, tr., with introductory essays by Leo Strauss and Shlomo Pines, *Journal of the History of Philosophy*, 3(2), October, 1965, pp. 265-274.

47. "Some Problems in Buber's Moral Philosophy," Paul A. Schilpp and Maurice Friedman, eds., *The Philosophy of Martin Buber*, (Open Court, 1966), pp. 151-170.

48. "The Case for the Jewish Day School," Judah Pilch and Meir BenHorin, eds., *Judaism and the Jewish School*, (New York, 1966), pp. 207213.

49. "The State of Jewish Belief: A Symposium," *Commentary*, 42(2), August, 1966, pp. 89-92.

50. "Heschel's Theology of Man," *Tradition*, 8(3), Fall, 1966, pp. 79-84.

51. "Jewish Education in a Pluralistic Community," *Proceedings of the Rabbinical Assembly of America*, 30, 1966, pp. 31-40, 47-51.

52. Review of Arnold Jacob Wolf, ed., *Rediscovering Judaism: Reflections on a New Theological Commentary*, 41(2), February, 1966.

53. "Sakkanah Lishelemutah shel ha-Yahadut," *Hadoar*, 47(38), October, 1967.

54. Chapter in *The State of Jewish Belief*, (Macmillan, 1967), pp. 59-69. Reprint of #49.

55. "Heschel, Intuition, and the Halakhah," Norman Lamm and Walter S. Wurzburger, eds., *A Treasury of Tradition*, (New York, 1967), pp. 426-435. Reprint of #27.

56. Review of *Harry Austryn Wolfson Jubilee Volumes*, *Judaism*, 16(4), Fall, 1967.

57. "Prolegomenon" to A. Cohen, *The Teachings of Maimonides*, (New York, 1968), pp. xv-xliv.

58. "The Meaning of Theology Today," *Bulletin of the Central Ohio Academy of Theology,* January, 1968.

59. Review Article on Sidney Hook, *Religion in a Free Society, The Journal of Value Inquiry*, 2(4), Winter, 1968, pp. 308-314.

60. "The Function of Religion," *Congress Bi-Weekly*, 36(3), February, 1969, pp. 56-63.

61. "La Teologia Dell'uomo Nel Pensiero di Abraham J. Heschel, " *La Rassegna Mensile di Israel*, 25(4), April, 1969. Italian translation of #50.

62. Review of Zvi Adar, *Humanistic Values in the Bible*, *Commentary* 47(l), January, 1969.

63. Review of Richard L. Rubenstein, *After Auschwitz* and *The Religious Imagination*, *Commentary*, 47(6), June, 1969.

64. "Religion and the Public Schools," Kaoru Jamamotie, ed., *Teaching*, (Houghton Mifflin, 1969), pp. 239-248. Reprint of #45.

65. "The 'Commentary' Problem," *Judaism*, 18(l), Winter, 1969, pp. 108-110.

66. Review of Nathan Rotenstreich, *Jewish Philosophy in Modern Times*, *Commentary*, 49(5), May, 1970.

67. "Naturalism, Rationalism and Jewish Faith," *Tradition*, 11(3), Fall, 1970, pp. 90-96.

68. "Day Schools and the American Educational Pattern," Joseph Kaminetsky, ed., *Hebrew Day School Education: An Overview*, (New York, 1970). Reprint of #13.

69. "Day Schools and the American Educational Pattern," Lloyd P. Gartner, ed., *Jewish Education in the United States*, (Teachers College, Columbia University Press, 1970), Classics in Education Series, No. 41. Reprint of #13.

70. "Continuity and Change in Jewish Theology," *Niv Hamidrashia*, Spring-Summer, 1971, pp. 15-23.

71. Review of Mendell Lewittes, *The Light of Redemption*, *The Jerusalem Post Magazine*, April 9, 1971.

72. "Moral Facts and Moral Theory," Julius Weinberg and Keith Yandell, eds., *Problems in Philosophical Inguiry*, (Holt Rinehart Winston, 1971), pp- 368-381. Reprint of# 15.

73. "Freedom and Freedom of Thought," *Encyclopaedia Judaica*, Vol. 7, 119-121.

74. "God, Conceptions of," *Encyclopaedia Judaica*, Vol. 7, 670-673.

75. "God in Medieval Jewish Philosophy," *Encyclopaedia Judaica*, Vol. 7, 658-661.

76. "God in Modern Jewish Philosophy," *Encyclopaedia Judaica*, Vol. 7, 662-664.

77. "God, Names of in Medieval Jewish Philosophy," *Encyclopaedia Judaica*, Vol. 7, 684-685.

78. "God, Names of in Modern Jewish Philosophy, *Encyclopaedia Judaica*, Vol. 7. 685.

79. "Maimonides and Aquinas on Natural Law," *Dine Israel: An Annual of Jewish Law, Tel-Aviv University*, Vol. 3, 1972, pp. 5-36.

80. "Kierkegaard and Rabbinic Judaism," Robert Gordis and Ruth B. Waxman, eds., *Faith and Reason*, (New York, 1972), pp. 115-124. Reprint of # 12.

81. "Tillich's Ontology and God," Keith Yandell, *God, Man and Religion*, (McGraw-Hill, 1972. Reprint of #28.

82. Review of Nathan Rotenstreich, *Tradition and Reality, Commentary*, 55(2), February, 1973.

83. "Philosophy and Contemporary Jewish Studies," *American Jewish Historical Quarterly*, 53(4), June, 1974, pp. 350-355.

84. "Berkovits on the Problem of Evil," *Tradition*, 14(3), Spring, 1974, pp. 116-124.

85. "God in Modern Jewish Philosophy," *Jewish Values*, (Keter, Jerusalem, 1974). Reprinted from #76.

86. "Conceptions of God," *Jewish Values*, (Keter, Jerusalem, 1974). Reprinted from #74.

87. "The Future of Hillel from the Perspective of the University," Alfred Jospe, ed., *The Test of Time*, (Washington, 1974).

88. "Philosophy and Contemporary Jewish Studies," Moshe Davis, ed., *Contemporary Jewish Civilization on the American Campus*, (Jerusalem, 1974). Reprinted from #83.

89. *Modern Jewish Ethics: Theory and Practice*, (Ohio State University Press, 1975). Edited with introduction.

90. "Judaism, Secularism and Textual Interpretation," M. Fox, ed., *Modern Jewish Ethics: Theology and Practice*, pp. 3-26.

91. "On the Rational Commandments in Saadia: A Re-examination," M. Fox, ed., *Modern Jewish Ethics: Theology and Practice*, pp. 174-187.

92. "Philosophy and Religious Values in Modern Jewish Thought," Jacob Katz, ed., *The Role of Religion in Modern Jewish History*, (AJS, 1975), pp. 69-86.

93. Review of *The Code of Maimonides: Book IV, The Book of Women*, *Journal of the American Academy of Religion.*, March, 1975.

94. "Maimonides and Aquinas on Natural Law," Jacob I. Dienstag, ed., *Studies in Maimonides and St. Thomas Aquinas*, (New York, 1975), pp. 75-106. Reprint of #79.

95. "Law and Ethics in Modern Jewish Philosophy: The Case of Moses Mendelssohn," *Proceedings of the American Academy for Jewish Research*, Vol 43, 1976, pp. 1- 13.

96. "Translating Jewish Thought into Curriculum," Seymour Fox and Geraldine Rosenfeld, eds., *From the Scholar to the Classroom*, (Jewish Theological Seminary, 1977),pp. 59-85.

97. Discussion on the "Centrality of Israel in the World Jewish Community," Moshe Davis, ed., *World Jewry and the State of Israel*, (New York, 1977).

98. "On the Rational Commandments in Saadia's Philosophy," *Proceedings of the Sixth World Congress of Jewish Studies*, Vol. 3, (Jerusalem, 1977), pp. 34-43. Slight revision of #9 1.

99. "Ha-Tefillah be-Mishnato shel ha-Rambam," Gabriel Cohn, ed., *Ha-Tefillah Ha-Yehudit*, (Jerusalem, 1978). pp. 142-167.

100. Review of Louis Jacobs, *Theology in the Responsa*, *AJS Newsletter*, No. 22, March, 1978.

101. Review of Frank Talmage, *David Kimhi: The Man and His Commentaries*, *Speculum*, 53(3), July, 1978.

102. "The Doctrine of the Mean in Aristotle and Maimonides: A Comparative Study," S. Stern and R. Loewe, eds., *Studies in Jewish Intellectual and Religious Histoty. Presented to Alexander Altmann*, (Alabama, 1979), pp. 43-70.

103. Foreword to Abraham Chill, *The Minhagim*, (New York, 1979).

104. *The Philosophical Foundations of Jewish Ethics: Some Initial Reflections.* The Second Annual Rabbi Louis Feinberg Memorial Lecture in Judaic Studies at the University of Cincinnati, 1979, pp. 1-24.

105. "Reflections on the Foundations of Jewish Ethics and their Relation to Public Policy," Joseph L. Allen, ed., *The Society of Christian Ethics, 1980 Selected Papers*, (Dallas, 1980), pp. 23-62. An expansion of # 104.

106. Introduction to the *Collected Papers of Rabbi Harry Kaplan*, (Columbus, 1980).

107. Review of Jacob Neusner, *A History of the Mishnaic Law of Women*, 5 Vols., AJS Newsletter, No. 29, 198 1.

108. "Human Suffering and Religious Faith: A Jewish Response to the Holocaust," *Questions of Jewish Survival*, (University of Denver, 1980), pp. 8-22.

109. "The Role of Philosophy in Jewish Studies," Raphael Jospe and Samuel Z. Fishman, eds., *Go and Study: Essays and Studies in Honor of Alfred Jospe*, (Washington, D.C., 1980). pp. 125-142.

110. "Conservative Tendencies in the Halakhah, "*Judaism*, 29(l), Winter, 1980, pp. 12-18.

111. Review of Isadore Twersky, *Introduction to the Code of Maimonides*, *AJS Newsletter*, No. 31, 1982.

112. "The Moral Philosophy of MaHaRaL," Bernard Cooperman, ed., *Jewish Thought in the Sixteenth Century*, (Cambridge, 1983), pp. 167185.

113. Review of Michael Wyschogrod, *The Body of Faith: Judaism as Corporeal Election*, *The Journal of Religion*, 67(l), January, 1987.

114. "Change is not Modern in Jewish Law," *Sh'ma*, 13/257, September 16, 1983.

115. "Graduate Education in Jewish Philosophy," Jacob Neusner, ed., *New Humanities and Academic Disciplines: The Case of Jewish Studies*, (University of Wisconsin Press, 1984, pp. 121-134.

116. "Some Reflections on Jewish Studies in American Universities," *Judaism*, 35(2), Spring, 1986, pp. 140-146.

117. "The Holiness of the Holy Land," Jonathan Sacks, ed., *Tradition and Transition: Essays Presented to Chief Rabbi Sir Immanuel Jakobovits*, (London, 1986), pp. 155-170.

118. "The Jewish Educator: The Ideology of the Profession in Jewish Tradition and its Contemporary Meaning," Joseph Reimer, ed., *To Build a Profession: Careers in Jewish Education*, (Waltham, 1987).

119. "A New View of Maimonides' Method of Contradictions," Moshe Hallamish, ed., *Bar-Ilan: Annual of Bar-Ilan University Studies in Judaica and the Humanities: Moshe Schwarcz Memorial Volume*, 22-23, (Ramat-Gan, 1987), pp. 19-43.

120. "Law and Morality in the Thought of Maimonides," Nahum Rakover, ed., *Maimonides as Codifier of Jewish Law*, (Jerusalem, 1987), pp. 105-120.

121. "Maimonides on the Foundations of Morality," *Proceedings of the Institute for Distinguished Community Leaders*, (Brandeis University, 1987), pp. 15-19.

122. Foreword to Morris Weitz, *Theories of Concepts*, (London & New York, 1988) pp. vii-xi.

123. "The Doctrine of the Mean in Aristotle and Maimonides: A Comparative Study," Joseph A. Buijs, ed., *Maimonides: A Collection of Critical Essays*, (University of Notre Dame Press, 1988), pp. 234-263. Reprint of # 102.

124. "Nahmanides on the Status of Aggadot: Perspectives on the Disputation at Barcelona, 1263," *Journal of Jewish Studies*, 40(1), Spring, 1989, pp. 95-109.

125. "The Holiness of the Holy Land," Shubert Spero, ed., *Religious Zionism - After 40 Years of Statehood* (Jerusalem, 1989). Reprint of #117.

126. "The Unity and Structure of Rav Joseph B. Soloveitchik's Thought," *Tradition*, 24(2), Spring, 1989.

127. "What Do We Expect of 'Jewish Studies'," *Sh'ma*, 20/383, December 8, 1989, pp. 20a-22b.

128. *Interpreting Maimonides: Studies in Methodology, Metaphysics and Moral Philosophy*, (The University of Chicago Press, 1990), pp. xiii+ 360.

129. Short articles in "Hebrew Books from the Harvard College Library": "Religious Ethics"; "Kabbalah and Hasidism"; "Philosophy and Theology"; (NewYork, 1990).

130. Prefatory essay to, Binyamin Richler, *Hebrew Manuscripts: A Treasured Legacy*, (Ofeq Institute, Cleveland/Jerusalem, 1990), pp. 11a- 13b.

131. Review of Yirmiyahu Yovel, *Spinoza and Other Heretics*: Vol. 1, *The Marrano of Reason*; Vol. 2, *The Adventures of Immanence*, (PrincetonUniversity Press, 1989), *Moment Magazine*, Vol. 15, No.5, October, 1990, pp. 64-66.

132. Review of *Perspectives on Maimonides*, Joel Kraemer, ed., (Oxford University Press, 199 1), TLS (Times Literary Supplement) June 14, 199 1, No.4602,p.12.

133. "R. Isaac Arama's Philosophical Exegesis of the Golden Calf Episode," *Minhah le-Nahum:Biblical and other Studies Presented to Nahum M. Sarna in Honour of his 70th Birthdqy*, (Sheffield Academic Press, 1993), pp. 87-102.

134. "Jewishness and Judaism at Brandeis University," *Cross Currents*, Vol.43, No.4, Winter, 1993-94, pp.464-469.

135. "The Mishnah as a Source for Jewish Ethics," *Studies in Halakha and Jewish Thought, Presented to Rabbi Prof. Menachem Emanuel Rackman on his 80th Anniversary*, Moshe Beer, ed., (Bar-Ilan University Press, 1994), pp. 33-48.

136. "Rav Kook: Neither Philosopher nor Kabbalist," *Rabbi Abraham Isaac Kook and Jewish Spirituality*, David Shatz and Lawrence Kaplan, eds., (New York University Press, 1995), pp. 78-87.

137. Review of Lenn Evan Goodman, *On Justice: An Essay in Jewish Philosophy* (Yale University Press, 1991), *Studies in Contemporary Jewry*, (Oxford University Press), X, 1994, pp. 382-384.

138. Entries in *Harper's Dictionary of Religion* , (Publication date, 1994):

Short Entries: Blasphemy; Holy Spirit in Judaism; Merit, Doctrine of in Judaism; Mishneh Torah; Providence, in Judaism; Shalom, in Judaism; Skull cap; Ten Commandments, in Judaism; Tradition, Massoret; Yetzer ha-ra, ha-tov; Yiddish.

Medium Sized Entries: Chosen People; Halakhah; Kingdom of Heaven, in Judaism; Kosher, Kashrut; Resurrection.

Major Articles: God, in Judaism; Judaism, Ethics of, Orthodox Judaism; Responsa;

139. "Holocaust Challenges to Religious Faith: Hersh Rasseyner and Yossel Rakover," the keynote lecture at the international conference on "Yiddish Literature of the Holocaust: Literary, Philosophical and Historical Implications" sponsored by Bar-Ilan University of Israel and Florida International University, October 29 & 30, 1990. To appear in the volume containing the Rakover story, with studies by Emmanuel Levinas, Fox, and one other. (KTAV Publishing House)

140. "Teaching the Philosophy of Maimonides: Materials, Problems, Goals, Strategies." Presented at the July, 1991 meeting of the International Center for the University Teaching of Jewish Civilization in Jerusalem. Published in a volume of papers on the teaching of Jewish Philosophy.

141. Review of Raymond Weiss, *Maimonides' Ethics: The Encounter of Philosophic and Religious Morality* (U. of Chicago Press, 1991), to appear in *International Studies in Philosophy*.

142. Review of Menachem Kellner, *Maimonides on Judaism and the Jewish People* (SUNY Press, 1991), to appear in *Jewish Quarterly Review*.

143. "Theodicy and Anti-theodicy in Biblical and Rabbinic Literature," a volume on theodicy edited by Dan Cohn-Sherbok for Mellen Press, 1994.

144. "The Rav as Maspid." In special issue of *Tradition* in memory of Rabbi Joseph. B. Soloveitchik, (Deals with the philosophy underlying his major published eulogies.)

145. "Torah U'Madda in the Middle Ages: The Case of Nahmanides," in a Festschrift in honor of Norman Lamm on his 70th birthday.

146. Paper on the philosophical chapters of Steven Katz, *The Holocaust and Historical Context*, (Oxford University Press). First given at a Symposium at the 1994 meeting of the Association for Jewish Studies, and then published.

147. "Power and Democracy in the Jewish Tradition," in memorial volume for Albert Elazar, edited by Daniel Elazar.

148. "A History of the Doctrine of the Mean in Early Greek Thought: From Homer Through Plato," in a festschrift for Professor William A. Johnson of Brandeis University.

1

THE TRIALS OF SOCRATES:

An Interpretation of the First Tetralogy

Relatively little is known to us of the reasons which were offered in defense of the ancient arrangement of Plato's dialogues into nine tetralogies. We do know, however, that modern Plato scholarship has tended to discredit the famous scheme of Thrasyllus the grammarian for a variety of reasons. A typical view of one school of interpretation is that each of the dialogues "must be regarded as a separate artistic unit." It follows from this that "no arrangement or grouping of Plato's works is satisfactory if it tends to obscure the independence of each individual work of Plato as a separate artistic whole."[1] Other well-known objections to the old tetralogies come from those students of Plato who have made the dating of the dialogues their main concern. Through the use of stylometry and other philological devices they have replaced the groupings of Thrasyllus with quite different orderings of the dialogues based on the supposed date of their composition. There are still other objections to the tetralogies familiar to most students of Plato.

In this essay I shall try to defend the first tetralogy, without any claim whatsoever concerning the other eight. Thrasyllus' reasons for making a single group out of the *Euthyphro, Apology, Crito* and *Phaedo* are unknown to us. I think it can be shown, however, that there are compelling reasons for us to accept the validity and importance of his arrangement. The usual tendency is to join these dialogues together because their narrative portion forms a fairly continuous story concerning the last episodes in the life of Socrates. My contention is that this obvious external connection between the dialogues should be seen as an invitation to the reader to look for deeper and more significant connections. And if we accept the invitation and make the search then we shall surely find that far more than a continuous story binds together the dialogues of Socrates' trial and death. There are, as a matter of fact, profoundly important and illuminating philosophical and literary connections between these four dialogues which must be grasped if each of the dialogues is to be seen in its proper perspective and interpreted correctly.

Before considering the detailed analysis and argument which follow it might be well to note that a *prima facie* case can easily be made for the view that the dialogues of Socrates' trial and death do belong together and must be studied as a unit. No matter when he may have written each of the dialogues Plato was surely aware that they tell a continuous story. He could hardly have failed to realize that most of his readers would tend to group them together as a matter of course. (Even Cooper groups them together in the very volume in which he denies that there are any significant connections between them.) In the light of this is it unreasonable to suppose that Plato deliberately wrote them as an artistic and philosophic unit and that he intended for them to be read together? Surely the fact that they may have appeared at widely separate times is not significant contrary evidence. The history of literature contains many instances in which succeeding volumes of the same book were published many years apart. There is no good reason to deny such a possibility in Plato's works.

The main point of this essay is that the *Apology, Crito, and Phaedo* may be fruitfully understood as three versions of the trial of Socrates. In the Apology Socrates appears before a court most of whose members suffer from a double defect. They are personally hostile to Socrates and are philosophically incompetent. In the Crito Socrates appears before a court, i.e. Crito, which has only one of these limitations. Crito is personally devoted to Socrates and appreciative of him. However, he is almost completely without philosophical understanding or capacity. In the *Phaedo* Socrates appears before a court which has neither of the defects of the Athenians who tried him formally. Simmias and Cebes are personally friendly to Socrates and they possess great philosophical insight and ability. There are, consequently, three levels to the trial of Socrates, or three separate trials. The first, before the Athenian masses, is at the lowest level of philosophical earnestness; the second, before Crito, is at a considerably higher level; while the last trial, that of the *Phaedo,* is philosophically the most intense. There is another and even more important dimension of the trials in each of the three dialogues, namely the trials of Socrates before himself. I shall try to show subsequently that this second level occurs in each of the dialogues, and shall explain how it relates to the first. For the present it is perhaps sufficient to mention that the seriousness and intensity of Socrates' private trial before himself is, in each case, a reflection of the intensity and quality of the public trial which is going on simultaneously. The highest and most demanding of the trials of Socrates is his final trial before himself in the *Phaedo*. For a man who is morally sensitive and intellectually responsible there is surely no more challenging and difficult occasion than that in which he passes judgment on himself and on the quality of his whole life as he faces his last moments on earth.

There is still a third dimension in each of the dialogues which takes the form of a third trial. In each case, the court which is trying Socrates is itself also on trial. We are told this explicitly in the *Apology*, and it is equally the case, though not as explicitly in the other two dialogues. We can summarize, then, by saying that each of the dialogues contains three trials, that of Socrates before his accusers, that of Socrates before himself, and that of the accusers and the court before the bar of justice and truth. Furthermore, these trials progress from a very low moral and philosophical level to a very high pitch of moral and philosophical intensity. Finally, we shall show that the *Euthyphro,* in addition to its intrinsic significance as the exposition of certain Platonic doctrines, is in our special context particularly important as a foil or background in terms of which we can get a clearer understanding of the inner significance of these trials.

There is a significant sense in which every Platonic dialogue involves a trial, namely insofar as each dialogue is a test of the participants in the conversation. They test each other and are all on trial before reason. However, it is my contention that the dialogues of the first tetralogy are trials in more than just this minimal sense. For an adequate understanding of these dialogues I believe that we must consider them as particular kinds of trials, with special interrelationships. It is as such special trials that I propose to examine them in this essay.

Finally, it should be noted that our explication proceeds from a conception of the dialogues as philosophic-artistic inventions rather than as historical documents. A voluminous literature has been produced which deals with such problems as the historicity of the *Apology* or the Phaedo. Interesting and valuable as these studies are in their own right they are irrelevant for our purposes. The Socrates whom we admire and the Athenians whom we condemn, as well as all the other participants in the dialogues, are the creations of Plato's artistic and philosophic genius. Whatever may have been the historical facts our conception of these characters and our judgment of them in the context of the present discussion is drawn exclusively from these and other dialogues of Plato.

II

The initial phase of our analysis will concern itself with the first dimension of each of the trials, namely the trial of Socrates before a court. From this point of view the *Apology* is a trial only in the minimal formal sense that Socrates appears before a legally constituted court to face certain charges. But it is not a trial in any proper sense, since, as we have already mentioned, his judges are unqualified to pass judgment on him. They suffer from the combination of personal antipathy and intellectual incompetence.

That this is Plato's view of the Athenian courts can be verified from many sources in the *Dialogues*. For example, in the *Gorgias* he makes Socrates use repeatedly the phrase "lawcourts and other mobs,"[2] which suggests the low esteem in which he held them. Socrates asserts that in such a court a philosopher would appear ridiculous since he would make the mistake of trying to convince the court of the truth by employing rational arguments and demonstrations, whereas in dealing with an undisciplined and unthinking mob only strong emotional appeals are likely to be successful. The man who wants to be acquitted must cater to the prejudices of the court, must tell them what they want to hear, must move them to pity and sympathy. This conception of the courts is common in Plato,[3] and it is evident enough why he believes that a philosopher could never take such a court seriously or expect that these courts could take him seriously. Socrates says that, "all those who have passed their days in the pursuit of philosophy are ridiculously at fault when they have to appear and speak in court."[4] The Athenian court, as Plato pictures it, is not a place where truth is victorious. Clever argument and skillful rhetoric serve a defendant far better than the dispassionate honesty of the philosopher.

There is striking internal evidence in the text of the *Apology* which supports the contention that from Socrates' point of view this is not a real trial at all. Most impressive is the fact that not once does Socrates address the court in the usual form, ὦ ἄνδρες δικασταί. He never calls them judges. He merely refers to them as ἄνδρες Ἀθηναῖοι, men of Athens. That this form of address is deliberate on his part is made clear beyond any doubt

One. The Trials of Socrates

when he speaks at the end to those who voted for his acquittal. This group, by its favorable vote, demonstrated its lack of prejudice and its approval of the philosophic life to which Socrates was dedicated. When he turns to them at the end of the Apology Socrates says, "O my judges - for you I may truly call judges."[5] Here we see how clearly Socrates has indicated that the majority of the court must not be taken seriously. His deliberate refusal to address them in the usual way (i.e. as "judges") is even more instructive when we realize that, in spite of his protests to the contrary, Socrates was thoroughly familiar with court procedures and with the usual form which the defendant's plea took. A number of scholars have pointed out, for example, that the opening of his speech follows in every detail the characteristic pattern for such speeches.[6] Even if (as some suggest) he intended this as a parody it still shows that Socrates knew the usual forms, and knew that the court was addressed (at least occasionally) as ἄνδρες δικασταί. In refusing to dignify them by the title "judges" Socrates expresses his evaluation of the court, and, thus, of the trial. For him this is not a real trial at all. On the other hand, his accuser, Meletus, who accepts the authority of the court, does refer to the court as οἱ δικασταί.[7]

We can now understand much more readily some otherwise puzzling aspects of the *Apology*. First, there is the problem posed by the frequently arrogant and overly assured manner in which Socrates addresses the court. The contrast (which we shall show later) with his humility, open-mindedness, and even uncertainty in the *Phaedo* is very strong. The difference in tone is determined by the differences in the kind of people he is conversing with. Socrates normally adjusts the level of his discourse to the level of the people whom he is addressing. He never "talks down" to a serious and thoughtful man, neither does he "talks up" to boors and dolts. Where a serious philosophic argument is required he is ready to attempt it. But one doesn't address an ignorant and prejudiced mob with the cautious circumspection of the philosopher. Here Socrates quite properly throws philosophic caution to the winds and makes those positive affirmations of his own worth which alone may impress the mob. That he cannot convince them of his innocence he knows in advance. In fact he quite deliberately makes reference to past events which he knows will hurt his case.[8] He antagonizes the judges by poking fun at the usual trial procedures, announcing his refusal to degrade himself by following them,[9] and then proposes a counter-penalty which is a direct insult to the court.[10]

We can understand all this readily if we remember that from Socrates' point of view these are not *really* judges and this is not *really* a trial. Consequently, he makes no serious attempts to defend himself against the official charges. This would have been futile, as he well knew, unless he would be willing to compromise his principles and to conduct himself in the groveling and fawning way which might have saved his life. But to do this would have meant the real defeat of Socrates. Instead we see how Socrates is victorious, precisely because he makes no effort to defend himself at the level which the court would accept, but rather devotes himself to a defense of the philosophic life and of moral integrity. Before such an audience, however, the best defense is not a closely reasoned argument, and the worst possible defense would be the philosopher's usual readiness to reveal his doubts or uncertainties. Socrates' greatest tribute to the philosophic life in this company of irrational men is the pride, the assurance, the great inner strength which he exhibits, pursuing his own way in open defiance of the Athenians and with complete contempt for their power to kill him. If this impressive display did not sway the mass of the Athenians who were at the trial, it certainly must have been a source of enlightenment and encouragement to that smaller group of men whose minds were still receptive to the claims of philosophy.

Socrates' closing speech in the *Apology,* addressed to the "true judges" who voted to acquit him, is markedly different in tone from his earlier speeches. Here there is none of the seeming arrogance, none of the overbearing taunting self-assurance which he had exhibited up to that point. The shift in tone is understandable, since he is talking to people whom he respects and who respect him. However, the speech still fits into the general setting of the *Apology,* since it is not, strictly speaking, a philosophic discourse, but rather a testament of faith and an exhortation to his hearers. Socrates explains why he feels sure that his death will be a good thing and pleads with them to "regard death hopefully."[11] How very different this is from the carefully reasoned way in which he seeks to show in the *Phaedo* tlat death is the true fulfillment of the philosopher's quest. In the *Apology,* even his address to his friends, can only be a plea, not a philosophic defense. This is determined by the court setting, and by the fact that he has to make a speech to a crowd rather than have a discussion with a few. For the dialectical method, which, in Plato's view, is the only proper philosophic method, depends on a dialogical situation. Where there is no real dialogue there can be no real philosophic inquiry. The circumstances of the Apology,

One. The Trials of Socrates 7

as we have shown, require of Socrates a defense of philosophy against the charges of ignorant and prejudiced men. Because this is not a real trial either of Socrates or of philosophy, it does not require and does not lend itself to a genuinely philosophical defense.

III

The Crito comes closer to being a real trial of Socrates, though it does not fully merit this designation either. Crito is superior to the Athenian court in the fact that he is a devoted friend and a loyal supporter of Socrates. The hostility of the court is in sharp contrast to Crito's appreciation of Socrates. It is, furthermore, an indication of Crito's own worth that he has the good judgment to have chosen a man like Socrates as a friend, and that he is ready to put himself and his fortune at Socrates' disposal. For these reasons Crito is a more understanding judge of Socrates than the Athenian mob could be, and Socrates, therefore, faces Crito's charges in a more nearly philosophical manner than that with which he faced the charges in the court.

However, in spite of his devotion to Socrates, Crito is still not an adequate judge, because he is not intellectually competent. Plato goes out of his way to make this quite clear in a number of places. Most important, perhaps, is the fact that Crito, as Socrates mentions in the *Phaedo*,[12] had offered to provide bail to the court as a surety that Socrates would not escape. Yet, he fails to see the moral objections to his then having arranged for Socrates' escape. Judging Crito as generously as Plato intends that we should, it is clear, at the very least, that he has no understanding of moral obligation. Crito's philosophic naiveté is equally evident when he explicitly says to Socrates that "it is necessary to care for the opinion of the public, for this very trouble we are in now shows that the public is able to accomplish not by any means the least, but almost the greatest of evils."[13] If Crito can still believe this after all of the time he has spent with Socrates, and after having heard Socrates' speech to the Athenian court, then he has not even minimal philosophic understanding. This is further borne out a little later in his conversation with Socrates when he expresses, among other things, his shame at the way in which the trial itself was carried on."[14] With all his love for Socrates he still has not understood what Socrates intended in his speech to the court.

To see fully this intellectual defect of Crito, as well as the strength of his personal devotion to Socrates, we must turn to the *Phaedo*. For we might, perhaps, find other ways of explaining away what seem to be his intellectual limitations in the *Crito* if we did not have the very clear picture of the man which Plato draws for us in *the Phaedo*. It could be argued, for example, that Crito understood Socrates' philosophic position thoroughly, but that he was moved by his deep friendship to make one last effort to save Socrates' life. Seen in this way his plea to Socrates would be understood as the desperate act of a dear friend, rather than as an indication of Crito's simple-mindedness. An examination of the Phaedo makes it impossible to support such an interpretation of Crito, but establishes, instead, in a precise and unambiguous way Crito's lack of philosophic understanding.

Our first introduction to Crito[15] in the *Phaedo* sets the tone for our understanding of him. He enters what is already a serious conversation to request Socrates, on behalf of the prison attendant, not to talk so much. Excessive talking will make it harder for the poison to work, and this may mean that Socrates will have to suffer the unpleasantness of taking several doses of the poison. Though Crito is not speaking for himself, only for the attendant, we still learn much about him from this conversation. He is anxious about Socrates' bodily comfort, and can think only in these terms. He cannot understand that Socrates is sincere in his disdain for the body and in his emphasis on the primary value of the soul. I believe that Plato deliberately introduces us to Crito in this way in order to give us a clear picture of him as a devoted but unphilosophic friend of Socrates. Looking back at the *Crito* we can now see how significant it is that he is pictured in exactly the same way in his first appearance in that dialogue. That his initial concern is for Socrates' bodily comfort is made evident by the fact that he sits by silently while Socrates is sleeping, marvels at the serene sleep of the condemned man, and refrains from waking him because he wants him to "pass the time as pleasantly as possible."[16] This is consistently the way in which Plato characterizes Crito in each of his appearances in the *Phaedo* as well. He is the warm friend whose main concern is with the body of Socrates, not with his soul. What better way could there be for Plato to present Crito as an essentially unphilosophic man? He takes no active part in the long philosophical discussions which occupy Socrates' last hours. However, he reappears at the end in his characteristic role when Socrates indicates that he is ready to bathe and then to take the poison. Crito's friendship is shown in the fact that it is he who asks Socrates, "Do you

One. The Trials of Socrates

wish to leave any directions with us about your children or anything else - anything we can do to serve you?"[17] But it is also Crito who goes on to ask, "How shall we bury you?", a question which could not have been raised by anyone who had even a slight understanding of the preceding discussion. Crito's question is so inappropriate that Socrates feels compelled to remark that though he has spoken at great length about the soul as distinct from the body and more valuable than the body, Crito has not grasped the point at all.

A little later Crito again shows his failure to understand when he pleads with Socrates to delay taking the poison until the last possible moment. This also calls forth a rather sharp response from Socrates, since no one who understood his views could have made such an irrelevant plea.[18] Finally, with a master's touch Plato has Crito close Socrates' eyes and mouth after he is dead.[19] In this way Crito is unmistakably identified as the loving friend of Socrates, a friend who cherished Socrates' body but lacked the intellect to appreciate the philosopher's spirit.

Socrates discussion with Crito takes the general form of a trial. In urging Socrates to escape from prison Crito makes a number of charges against him. He introduces the charges with the claim that if Socrates refuses to escape be will be a wrongdoer or a doer of evil, his act will be οὐδε δικαιοί.[20] This is approximately the same term used in introducing the formal charges against Socrates in the Apology, where the phrase is Σωκράτη ἀδικεῖν, "Socrates is a wrong doer."[21] In both cases this general charge is followed by a number of specific charges. This similarity of form ought to be enough to show us that in the *Crito* we also have Socrates on trial, but this time he stands in judgment before his friend Crito, rather than before the Athenian mob. The atmosphere of a trial is further provided in the *Crito* by Socrates' explicit statement of his readiness to defend himself. He says to Crito, "Then we agree that the question is whether it is right for me to try to escape from here without the permission of the Athenians, or not right (πότερον δίκαιον...ἢ οὐ δίκαιον)."[22]

That this trial is on a higher philosophic level than the trial in the *Apology* is made evident in a number of ways. In the first place, Crito respects Socrates and takes him seriously, while the Athenian court did not. Secondly with prodding from Socrates, Crito affirms the principle that we ought never do wrong, and that we must not even repay evil with evil.[23] This is an admission that Socrates could never have gotten from the mob. Even though Crito lacks any philosophic understanding of this principle, he is, nevertheless, a man with what we might call loosely "fundamental moral decency". He wants to do what is right though he is not always intelligent enough to know what is right. He appreciates moral integrity and even reveres it, while the Athenians, as their actions show, have only contempt for such uprightness.

Because of these differences Socrates makes some attempt, however, restricted, to discuss seriously with Crito the reasons for his refusal to escape, and thus to answer Crito's charges. In contrast, he refuses to take seriously the charge of Meletus. As he himself says, after a brief cross examination of Meletus, "Well then, men of Athens, that I am not a wrongdoer according to Meletus' indictment, seems to me not to need much of a defense, but what has been said is enough."[24] His address to the court, as a result, makes no attempt to refute Meletus directly, for in his examination of Meletus, (and it is clearly an examination of Meletus, not a discussion with him), he has shown the man to be a fool. All that remains for Socrates is to try to explain and defend himself against the "old accusations" which have prejudiced the Athenians. And, as we have already shown, in the court of Athens this was best done not by philosophic argument, but by the moving personal example of a Socrates who remained true to his principles and who had no fear of any punishment that lesser men might impose on him.

He does not dismiss Crito's charges so casually. In a mood quite different from that of the *Apology* Socrates accepts the earnestness of Crito's charges and makes a sincere effort to answer them. For it is not a hostile mob, or a few strongly prejudiced individuals who accuse him, but a very good and very simple man. Charges from such a source need to be answered properly. A proper answer, however, is not one which takes account only of the seriousness of the accusations. To be satisfactory an answer has to adjust itself to the level of both the accusations and the accuser. And in this case both are extremely simple. Crito has a very uncomplicated mind, and his indictment of Socrates reflects his complete lack of subtlety and intellectual penetration. Unlike the vague generalized charges in the *Apology* Crito's charges have the merit of being very direct and specific. But this is also their chief defect. They are much too restricted in scope, as is Crito himself, to merit a truly philosophic answer. Crito raises no questions of an ultimate sort. He is only concerned with the grounds for one particular moral decision. This is why Socrates treats the whole matter as a question of black or white. He talks as if there is one, and only one, unambiguously correct decision.

One. The Trials of Socrates

First, he gets Crito to agree to his major premise (that one must never do wrong) without any hesitation or equivocation. No really excellent philosophic mind would have assented as readily as Crito did even to a principle which he had undoubtedly heard countless times before. In contrast Simmias and Cebes in the *Phaedo* continue to question even those principles and doctrines which by their own admission they have believed, and which they have just again reaffirmed to be sound and reliable. This is a measure of the difference in intellectual ability between these young men and the aged Crito. Because of this difference Socrates (as we shall soon see) speaks with much tentativeness and hesitation in the *Phaedo*. Knowing the complexity of the charges against him and the deep insight of his accusers he proceeds with great caution, and does not claim absolute certainly.

But this is not the appropriate way to answer the simple Crito, any more than it would have been the appropriate way in the court. Crito can respond to moral instruction, but not to the complexities of a philosophical debate. Socrates recognizes this and answers his friend's charges in a clear, direct, and unambiguous way. It would be hard to deny that Socrates could have found flaws in his own argument. This would certainly not have been difficult for a man who was so marvelously skilled at finding the flaws in others' arguments. If Socrates does not do this in the *Crito*, if having considered the main counter-arguments, he still talks with complete assurance about the correctness of his own position; it is not due to intellectual dishonesty. It is, rather, Socrates' sensitive understanding that this is not the appropriate mode of discourse for a conversation with Crito. If this point seems doubtful now it should certainly be strengthened by our discussion of the parallel question in the *Phaedo*. As we turn to an examination of this last version of the trial of Socrates we shall see how ready Socrates is to admit his uncertainties when he is talking to men who are likely to be helped rather than injured by such admissions.

IV

The *Phaedo* is commonly thought of as a dialogue about immortality or the nature of the soul. Most of the discussion is, of course, taken up with these topics, but to understand the dialogue properly we must pay attention to the framework in which the discussion occurs. For the *Phaedo,* like the *Apology* and *Crito,* is explicitly conceived as a trial of Socrates, a trial, which is more satisfactory and more significant than the others. And it is as a trial (though, perhaps, not only as a trial), compared and contrasted with the earlier trials, that the dialogue should be studied.

Cebes and Simmias level a serious charge against Socrates. They argue that it is wrong for Socrates to welcome death. He ought to be troubled, they think, at the prospect of leaving this world, where he is in the service of the wise and just gods, to go to an unknown destiny and to unknown rulers. There is here the suggestion that his cheerfulness in the face of death, i.e. at leaving the governance of the gods, may, perhaps give some justification to the Athenians' charge that Socrates is an atheist. We can also see how these accusations are related to those which Crito had made. Crito had accused Socrates of being too unwilling to leave the Athenian prison. Cebes and Simmias accuse him of being overly willing to leave his bodily prison. As Simmias summarizes the charges he says to Socrates, "You are too ready to leave us, and too ready to leave the gods whom you acknowledge to be our good masters." The trial setting is established immediately by Socrates when he "And so you think that I ought to answer your indictment replies, as if I were in a court." He adds that he will "try to make a more convincing defense than I did before the judges."[26] This trial setting is carried out and emphasized in a number of places in the dialogue. Not only the preliminary conversation, but the whole discussion which follows is to be considered as Socrates' defense. To begin the conversation, Socrates gives a general statement of his position which concludes in this way: "And therefore I maintain that I am right Simmias and Cebes ... if then I succeed in convincing you by my defense better than I did the Athenian judges, it will be well."[27] The long dialogue which follows is Socrates defense of his position, the defense through which he seeks to be acquitted by his accusers who are also his judges.

That this trial stands on the highest philosophical level of the three is certainly evident. In the first place the judges are of a very high caliber, men who appreciate Socrates, who are devoted to him, and who are, at the same time, highly intelligent. Their personal friendship for Socrates is shown, above all else, by the fact that they are present during his last hours. Surely, no strangers would have been with him on such an occasion. Moreover, as we mentioned earlier, Simmias and Cebes had come to Athens bringing money with which they hoped to arrange for Socrates' escape. It seems reasonable to suppose that only friends would have done that. Yet, if the trial is to be fair and honest, precautions must be taken against the favoritism which intimate friends might show. It may be for this reason

One. The Trials of Socrates 13

that Plato makes Simmias and Cebes carry the burden of the argument against Socrates. For though they are friends of Socrates, we are informed that they are foreigners.[28] Their ties to Socrates are not as close as those of the Athenians. They have spent less time with him, have seen him less frequently, and it may, therefore, be hoped that they are more likely to be rigorous in their questioning and in their judgment.

Their great philosophic competence contrasts strikingly with the moral and intellectual irresponsibility of the Athenian court and with the simple-mindedness of Crito. Their questioning is sharp and penetrating; their attempted refutations of Socrates are deft and skillful; and their tenaciousness is exemplary. Only excellent philosophic minds could have carried on the high level of philosophic discussion which we have before us in the Phaedo. Very early in the dialogue Socrates shows his pleasure at Cebes' earnestness and depth. Speaking in praise of Cebes Socrates says, "Here ...is a man who is always enquiring, and is not so easily convinced by the first thing which he hears."[29] Cebes intellectual superiority as compared with Crito comes to mind at once. Crito is very readily convinced by the first thing he hears from Socrates. And even if he is not convinced, he lacks the intellectual ability to challenge Socrates successfully or to argue with him effectively. This is why *The Crito* is a trial at a much lower level. Socrates' victory there comes much too easily and with relatively casual analysis of the most basic questions. When, however, he stands in judgment before Simmias and Cebes he is dealing with men who require far more of him. They will not be convinced by positive and dogmatic assertions, nor will they allow Socrates to avoid the fundamental problems, no matter how perplexing they are. These are judges who probe each issue to its depths, who demand persuasive evidence, and who are not dazzled by apparently brilliant arguments. To meet their challenge Socrates is required to use his best powers, which means to think and to talk at his highest level. For these reasons they constitute a court worthy of Socrates, and they provide him with a trial which is fit for a philosopher.

The greater seriousness of the trial in the *Phaedo* is also reflected in the kind of accusations which are made against Socrates. In the *Apology and Crito* Socrates has to answer very simple charges. The indictments in the *Apology* are very vague and very general. It requires little skill for Socrates to meet them. His difficulties in the *Apology* are with the court. He knows how to meet their accusations, but their prejudice is so strong that their minds are closed to anything that Socrates might say in his own defense. Crito's charges suffer from the fact that they are much too detailed and specific. He raises issues which, as we have already shown, are so restricted in scope that they do not require Socrates to respond at a very profound level. In each case the charges mirror the men who made them. The Athenians, like their accusations, are confused and irrational. Crito, like his accusations, is naive and simple.

Similarly, the indictment of Simmias and Cebes is as profound and as subtle as we would properly expect. While the charges seem simple enough in their initial formulation, the further discussion brings out their depth and comprehensiveness. For these men are not merely repeating vague rumors and ancient prejudices, nor are they primarily moved by their anxiety as devoted friends who are trying to save the life of Socrates. What they are demanding is a justification of Socrates' entire life, a defense of those things which Socrates has held to be supremely valuable and, hence, of his highest commitments. At the very beginning of the dialogue Plato gives us the clue which should help us see the inner meaning of the charges. In the prologue to Phaedo's narration, while he is still addressing Echecrates Phaedo tells him that "philosophy was the theme of which we spoke."[30] It is as if Plato wants to protect his readers, and Phaedo his hearers, against a common mistake. The dialogue seems to have immortality as its main theme. Hasty readers and casual listeners might readily come to this conclusion. However, Plato cautions us (through Phaedo's comment) not to take the appearance for the reality. The real theme of the discussion is philosophy. The particular subjects which are taken up are ancillary to this central theme. Because philosophy is the main concern and the main activity of Socrates it is, in a way, the broader theme of each of his conversations, not only of this last one. However, here, in the last hours of his life he is being asked directly to defend philosophy. This is the deeper demand made of him by Simmias and Cebes—the demand that he justify his conception of the philosophic life and his commitment to that life. Such a demand is especially appropriate just prior to his death, since Socrates has argued that the philosopher is always pursuing death. If this is true (and it becomes clear later that it should not be taken literally), then Socrates, the philosopher, is now at the high point of his philosophic career. He is about to find his philosophic fulfillment in death. What time could be more appropriate to examine with him the grounds of his belief in philosophy? Carried out under the skillful questioning of friendly, but tough-minded men, such an examination of Socrates is the highest, the most earnest, and the most significant of his trials before others.

The manner in which Socrates deals with these difficult questions is also illuminating. In the *Phaedo* we find none of the seeming arrogance and smugness which Socrates exhibited in the *Apology,* nor do we find the complete assurance with which he answered Crito. Instead, his defense is always humble and always tentative. He is not before a mob whom he hopes to move to an appreciation of the philosophic life by emotional and rhetorical devices. Neither is he before an anxious and simple friend who seeks to be convinced in absolute terms that Socrates has made the right decision. In the *Phaedo* he is conversing with young philosophers who appreciate the complexity of their own questions. Only a fool would try to give final and absolute answers to such profound and searching questions. And Socrates was surely no fool. To Simmias and Cebes he can afford to reveal his uncertainties, while at the same time showing the grounds of his conviction. The questions they ask merit philosophic answers and require philosophic caution.

Comment on the philosophic depth of the *Phaedo* is hardly necessary. It is evident to any reader that the discussion in the *Phaedo* is carried on in a profounder and more earnest way than in the *Apology or Crito.* What is not ordinarily noticed is that Plato goes to great lengths to impress on his readers the fact that claims to certainty are studiously avoided by Socrates and his friends. But it is this very cautious and tentative attitude, so frequently overlooked by students of the *Phaedo,* that we shall find to be most instructive.

It would be well, perhaps, to cite some of the key passages in which his attitude of cautious restraint is expressed before we comment on their significance. Early in the discussion Socrates admits that his own views on the main question then before the group are gotten "only from hearsay."[31] A little farther on the strongest comment he makes about his doctrine is that "perhaps ... it is not unreasonable."[32] Later, when he expresses his strong conviction that the philosopher is the man who "employs pure, absolute reason in his attempt to search out the pure, absolute essence of things," Socrates asks, "Is not this the man, if anyone, to attain the knowledge of reality?" Even about this, which is so basic in his philosophic thinking, he does not claim certainty. Throughout the discussion there is present this atmosphere of questioning and of searching, rather than an air of dogmatic assurance.

The impact of this cautious attitude is strengthened when we find that it is the way in which the most important problems in the dialogue are consistently approached. Concerning his belief that the soul is immortal, Socrates proposes that they should inquire into the matter only "to see whether it is *probable* or not.[34] When he finishes the first major portion of his defense Socrates, himself, tells the others that, "There are still many subjects for doubt and many points open to attack, if anyone cares to discuss the matter thoroughly."[35] Throughout the following discussion he continues to refrain from claims to complete certainty. At the end of the formal argument, which has been very long and very arduous, Socrates does claim that he has arrived at a certain proof of his main contentions.[36] However, he goes on at once to caution Simmias not to stop inquiring. Socrates tells the young man that the fundamental assumptions on which his proof of immortality depends "ought to be more carefully examined, even though they seem to you to be certain." Then he adds, "And if you analyse them completely, you will, I think, follow and agree with the argument, so far as it is possible for man to do so."[37] Jowett shows the hesitation of Socrates even more forcefully. In his translation the last clause reads: "with a sort of hesitating confidence in human reason." Even when we *think* we have achieved certainty, Socrates is saying, we still must continue our inquiry, for human reason is never absolutely reliable when it confronts such ultimately difficult questions.

It should be made clear that neither Socrates, nor the other persons in the dialogue, underestimate the importance of certainty. Whereever certainty is possible one must settle for nothing less. A philosopher should never accept merely probable judgments about matters that can be known with demonstrable certainty. About this all the main participants in the *Phaedo* are in agreement. (This is, after all, why Socrates sees dialectic as a δεύτερος πλοῦς, a second best method.) But they also believe that it is equally the task of the philosopher to recognize when certainty is not possible and to have the courage to decide the issue in terms of the strongest probabilities. A true philosopher will take a stand on important questions, even though there is no certainty possible. He will not be deterred by the risk of being wrong. This way of the philosopher is magnificently summarized by Simmias with the apparent approval of Socrates and the others. He says:

> I think, Socrates, as perhaps you do yourself, that it is either impossible or very difficult to acquire clear knowledge about these matters in this life. And yet he is a weakling who does not test in every way what is said about them and persevere until he is worn out by

One. The Trials of Socrates

studying them on every side. For he must do one of two things; either he must learn or discover the truth about these matters, or if that is impossible, he must take whatever human doctrine is best and hardest to disprove and, embarking upon it as upon a raft, sail upon it through life in the midst of dangers, unless he can sail upon some stronger vessel, some divine revelation, and make his voyage more safely and securely.[38]

The tentativeness with which Socrates speaks in the *Phaedo*, his caution against even his own claims to certainty, and his readiness, nevertheless, to make a decision in terms of the strongest probabilities, all these are a true measure of the philosophic maturity of this trial as contrasted with the earlier ones.

The argument that it is the philosopher's right, and even his obligation, to struggle with those difficult questions whose answers can never be certain is the core of Socrates' defense of himself, and, therefore, of philosophy. For Socrates knew what many of us have not yet learned after more than two millennia of philosophic inquiry, that the most important questions can rarely be answered with certainty. Yet these are the very questions which concern us most profoundly as men, and, thus, the questions which we can least afford to leave unanswered. To give up the search, to lose faith in the continuing value and importance of philosophic inquiry is a major calamity. It is the danger against which Socrates wants most to protect us, for as he says, "no worse evil can happen to a man than to hate argument."[39] The passage in the *Phaedo* from 89 A to 91 C expands this thought. It is, I think, a major error to treat (as some commentators do) this passage which contains Socrates' cautions against the dangers of misology as a mere interlude.[40] My own conception of the dialogue as the third version of Socrates' trial gives us strong reason for believing that this passage is central to the whole discussion.[41] In this passage Socrates exposes the inner significance of the charges of Simmias and Cebes, and it is here also that he formulates his main defense. Without the cautions against misology the rest of the dialogue loses its direction, and Socrates' defense is unconvincing.

The indictment involves more than the simple claim that Socrates is much too ready to leave this world which, he admits, is governed by the good gods. What is important about the charge is the perplexity of Simmias and Cebes over the fact that Socrates should give up so readily the certainties of this life for the uncertainties of the next. Their arguments seem to have shown remarkably well that Socrates cannot help but be somewhat uncertain about his destiny after death. What Socrates has to convince them of is that there are times when thoughtful and honest men must exchange their trivial certainties for great, though uncertain, possibilities. The true philosopher, who is in Socrates' view the best of men, puts his faith in inquiry itself, in the dialectical process. This means that he may never gain certainty about some matters, but will not, on this account, be prevented from taking a stand on important issues, though he can only rely on probabilities, on what seem the best of the available arguments. Socrates' only certainty is that we must not give up our faith in the philosophic quest.

Misology is the worst evil that can befall a man because the misologist is the opposite of the philosopher. Wisdom, which the philosopher seeks, is the very best for man. If we can ever get wisdom it will only be through inquiry. The misologist, hating and rejecting inquiry, has given up the only road to wisdom. Since this means that he has abandoned the pursuit of man's highest aims, this is, obviously, the worst possible calamity. Exactly such a danger hangs over the head of the man who demands certainty always. First, he will be like Crito, accepting every argument indiscriminately. He dares not allow himself to see how rarely any argument about an important matter ends in certainty. Or perhaps he is not intelligent enough to see the limitations of most arguments. The usual result is that he soon finds that his cherished certainties collapse, that he has often been misled into belief, and he ends up hating and distrusting all inquiry. This is what has happened to the Athenians. They have become irrational men who no longer respect the quest for wisdom. Their hatred of argument is as great, as is their hatred of Socrates, the man who never stops arguing and inquiring. Their deepest resentment against Socrates stems from the fact that he so frequently attacked their unquestioned certainties as they were embodied in the most respected authorities in Athens. Instead of being stimulated by his attacks to continue the inquiry, the Athenians' and their leaders reacted by giving up all inquiry. Reason is considered by them to be utterly' unreliable, because so much about which they had once been completely convinced, on apparently solid, if not rational, grounds, turned out to be very doubtful under Socrates' criticisms. So many men whom they trusted implicitly were exposed by Socrates as shallow and ignorant.

Here, then, are the dangers—that represented by Crito who believes arguments too readily, and that represented by the Athenian court whose members distrust all rational argument. Men like Crito are always in peril of being easily misled and, when they discover their plight, they are likely to become misologists, just as the Athenians did. What Socrates has to show is that the best way is the middle way, that of continuing inquiry without stop, neither hoping for cheaply won certainties, nor hating inquiry because it rarely justifies such certainties. He has to defend his whole life, which has been devoted to the quest for truth, even while in his last moments on earth he still cannot claim to know the truth finally. Though Socrates has always spoken of the soul as more important than the body, and for this reason speaks of the philosopher as the man who is always pursuing death, i.e. the final separation of soul from body, he has not been able to establish this doctrine on absolutely unquestionable grounds. What if there is no soul apart from the body? What if it is the body which gives life to the soul? This is what Simmias and Cebes demand to know. They ask for Socrates' evidence, for the ground of his belief. But Socrates has to acknowledge, even at the very end, that his own certainties are still open to doubt and must be questioned by others. How, then, does he justify his life and his death? On what basis has he made his decision to die if he has not proved demonstrably that his views are correct?

His defense consists only in part of the formal arguments which he offers. It is true that he makes out a strong case, though not an absolute one, for his position. On the basis of his arguments there appear to be good reasons for believing in the superiority of the soul to the body. There is also considerable support given to the belief in the priority and independence of the soul. The evidence, however, is only strongly probable, not completely certain. Socrates' arguments depend on premises which need not be granted. This is why he still cautions the young men, even at the end of the discussion, that they must continue to examine the fundamental assumptions on which his proofs are based. This cannot be his complete defense, since Simmias and Cebes are asking why he is willing to settle for uncertainties, and how he can allow himself to make a decision in so grave a matter on the basis of only probable evidence.

Socrates' main defense is not in the substance of the arguments, but in the fact that he does continue to argue and inquire. It is especially impressive that he should persist in inquiry about such a subject at such a time. Every sensitive reader is deeply moved by the picture of the aged Socrates arguing the question of immortality until just a few moments before his death. Even more moving is Socrates' demand that no criticisms of his belief be withheld from him out of false sentimentality. This is his strongest defense. His own absolute commitment to philosophic inquiry as the highest human activity is his ultimate justification. In effect, he is saying to his friendly accusers that no man is obligated to achieve certainty, but every man is obligated to pursue it as long as he is on earth. The man who reaches conclusions about important matters without critical reflection is stupid or wicked or weak. So long as we have inquired into a question to the best of our ability we are justified in accepting provisionally the most persuasive conclusion, that we can arrive at. It is only provisional, however. We must continue to search if we are to hold our position in an intellectually and morally responsible way. However, when a man comes to the end of his life, or when he has to choose between ending life honorably or living on dishonorably, then he has to make a final and irrevocable commitment. There is very little time left for the continuation of the inquiry. The decision must be made now. The thoughtless unreflective man really cannot make a decision, and if he does can give no justification for it. The philosopher, who has made his decision after a lifetime of the most careful analysis of the main questions, has the only justification that a man can hope for. He can assert that he is deciding on the basis of the very best that his understanding teaches him. No more can be asked of any man. Socrates does not know for certain that the soul is to be valued above the body, or that the soul is immortal. But it is unquestionably the case that he has reached his conclusions about these matters only after the most thorough study. Down to the last moments of his life he continues his search for a final answer. This search alone justifies Socrates, for it is positive assurance that he has made up his mind in the only responsible way open to him. He is understandably concerned, above all else, to protect his friends from the dangers of misology. They must continue to have faith in philosophic inquiry as the highest human activity. If they do, then Socrates will be justified in their eyes, even though his arguments for the immortality of the soul lack certainty. Moreover, so long as they seek knowledge, the way to the good life will continue to be open to them, as well. If, however, they yield to the dangers of misology then, like the Athenians, they will condemn Socrates and will, themselves, also be lost. The judgment of Socrates' whole life, not only of his death, hangs in the balance. For his readiness to die appears to him to be the appropriate conclusion of the way in which he has lived. In life, as well as in death, he has valued the soul above the body. The true end of the soul being wisdom, inquiry, which would lead to wisdom, has been his main activity. That same inquiry causes him now to meet death hopefully and cheerfully. Condemn and hate inquiry, and you must condemn and hate Socrates. Respect inquiry as man's only hope, and you will respect both the life and the death of Socrates.

One. The Trials of Socrates

One of Socrates' greatest concerns, therefore, is with the effect which the argument is having on Phaedo and the other silent members of the group, and on each person who will hear repeated the conversations of his last hours. If they become misologists, then, like the Athenians they will condemn Socrates for misleading them. He sees how readily Phaedo and the others are distressed by the varying fortunes of the argument, just when they were most convinced that Socrates had made his case irrefutable Simmias and Cebes offered what seemed like crushing objections. As Phaedo tells his own hearers:

> Now all of us, as we remarked to one another afterwards, were very uncomfortable when we heard what they said; for we had been thoroughly convinced by the previous argument, and now they seemed to be throwing us again into confusion and distrust, not only in respect to the past discussion but also with regard to any future one. They made us fear that our judgment was worthless or that no certainty could be attained in these matters.

To which Echecrates, (a later hearer, like each of us, of Socrates' last conversation) replies:

> By the gods, Phaedo, I sympathise with you; for I myself after listening to you am inclined to ask myself: "What argument shall we believe henceforth? For the argument of Socrates was perfectly convincing, and now it has fallen into discredit."[42]

Socrates addresses his plea against misology to Phaedo, and through him to all men, urging that he retain his faith in the search for knowledge. He even has to caution Simmias and Cebes, though the dangers are far smaller for them, since they have shown their unswerving devotion to inquiry. He pleads with them to drive on as hard as they can, seeking the truth even if it should be an unpleasant truth. If they yield too readily there is great danger. For as Socrates says, "I may ... in my eagerness deceive myself and you alike and go away, like a bee, leaving my sting sticking in you."[43] The true function of Socrates is to be the gadfly who spurs men on to inquiry, rather than the bee whose sting poisons them and causes them to stagnate. If he succeeds as a gadfly, then his own defense is assured, for all his judges will see in their own experience the worth of Socrates' way of life and his consistency in accepting death. But if his arguments have the effect of the poisonous bee, if their sting destroys men's faith in the philosopher's quest, then both Socrates and the arguments are condemned.

We can now understand the results of the three trials. The Athenians condemned Socrates, but were utterly unfit to judge him. The Socrates whom they condemned was Socrates the citizens who was a threat to their security. He had tried to teach them that "the unexamined life was not worth living," and they never forgave him for having taken away their false, but comfortable, certainties. They hated human reason because it was less than perfect, and they hated Socrates, who forced them to see that the assurance of their self-proclaimed "experts" was never very reliable. In sum, they could not forgive the man who taught them that wisdom begins in the awareness of our own ignorance, and that curing our ignorance is an arduous and unending labor. Their course of action was predetermined, as Socrates knew.[44] Having had their faith in reason destroyed they had to destroy Socrates, the unpleasant reminder of their own folly.

Crito, on the other hand, acquitted Socrates completely, but this acquittal was won much too easily to be very significant. There was no struggle, no effort, no real defense—just Socrates' statement of his position and Crito's unquestioning acceptance of it. At most we can say that Crito approved of his friend Socrates and loved him as a friend. This was a great personal testimony, but it was not a serious trial of a mature man facing serious charges.

In the *Phaedo* we reached the climax of the trials. Here it was neither Socrates the citizen, nor Socrates the friend, but Socrates the philosopher who was on trial. The Athenians condemned him; Crito acquitted him; but the court in the *Phaedo* justified him. They justified him, even while they continued to question the certainty of his proofs. In fact, this is the very justification, namely that they never gave up their faith in the importance and reliability of philosophic inquiry. So long as they continued to trust inquiry they would necessarily approve of Socrates whose decisions were always based on inquiry. Simmias and Cebes showed their dedication to the continuing search for truth by the courage with which they pressed Socrates to defend his belief in immortality almost down to the moment of his death. Here normal human sentiment and the tender concerns of anxious friends yielded to the endless search for truth. This was the way in which they rendered their verdict, by following in Socrates' own path.

Even the lesser people in the group, who are represented by Phaedo, were led to appreciate and to follow the way of Socrates. They were almost driven to despair by the twists and turns of the argument. It seemed to them as if there was no point in trying to inquire into such difficult questions. They failed to see that thoughtful argument could ever justify serious decisions. At the moment when they were most threatened by the danger of misology they were saved. It was the example of Socrates which saved them, even more than the strength of his defense against the criticisms of Simmias and Cebes. Socrates' important concern was that they should not lose faith in rational inquiry, and he protected them against this danger. As Phaedo tells us:

> Echecrates, I have often wondered at Socrates, but never did I admire him more than then. That he had an answer ready was perhaps to be expected; but what astonished me more about him was, first, the pleasant, gentle, and respectful manner in which he listened to the young men's criticisms, secondly, his quick sense of the effect their words had upon us, and lastly, the skill with which he cured us and, as it were, recalled us from our flight and defeat and made us face about and follow him and join in his examination of the argument.[45]

Thus we see that even Phaedo and the others were saved from misology. They did return to the argument, which means that they, too, justified Socrates by imitating him. Their renewed faith in rational inquiry also restored their faith in Socrates' right to his decision.

It was, thus, in his last hours that Socrates had his genuine trial, the trial of Socrates the philosopher and of the philosophic life to which he had dedicated himself. This was the only one of the trials worthy of Socrates, for it was the only one in which the judges were competent and the charges profoundly searching. It was only natural that this should have been the trial that evoked the most earnest and the most completely philosophic defense. The success of the defense was guaranteed when the judges themselves followed Socrates' example and accepted his way as their own.

V

Having examined carefully the trials of Socrates we can now understand more readily the trials of his accusers and judges. Whenever a man is on trial his judges and accusers are also on trial. The way in which the proceedings are conducted and the quality of the final judgment is a test of the prosecutors and judges. If the trial proceedings are careful, and searching, and fair, if the final judgment is wise and just, then the court has shown itself to be worthy of its charge. If, on the other hand, the proceedings are careless or prejudiced, or the decision foolish and unjust, then the court is condemned by its own actions. What is true of every trial was magnificently exemplified in the trials of Socrates. As he stood before his judges, they, too, were being judged. Plato first brings this to our attention in the *Apology* when Socrates says to the Athenians, "I am now making my defense not for my own sake, as one might imagine, but more for yours, that you may not by condemning me err in your treatment of the gift the God gave you."[46] Socrates knew that the Athenians were also on trial, and that he alone had the possibility of saving them.

However, this possibility was very slim indeed, and Socrates, though he made an earnest effort, failed in his attempted defense. The Athenians presented an especially difficult problem, since they had to be protected from their own worst inclinations. If their prejudice and irrationality would control the trial and determine the verdict, then they would certainly fail their test. It was this danger which Socrates, serving as their defender, sought to overcome, but the task was almost hopeless. For the Athenians to have been justified it would not have been enough for them to acquit Socrates. They would have had to acquit him for the right reasons. Socrates could almost certainly have won acquittal had he followed the usual pattern of defense. Flattery of the court, emotional appeals for sympathy, and similar devices which had served other defendants so well would undoubtedly have helped Socrates' case. We know that he refused to employ such tactics for his own sake, since this would have been a denial of the principles which he had always taught. It is equally clear that he had to avoid such tactics for the sake of the Athenians as well. Socrates' employment of the usual strategies of defense might have caused the Athenians to acquit him, but the acquittal would be for the wrong reasons and, thus, would be a condemnation of the court.

Only an acquittal of Socrates which was motivated by justice and truth would be, at the same time, an acquittal of the Athenians. This defines for us the near impossibility of Socrates' task, for he had to try to make essentially irrational men think and act rationally. They had not only to acquit him, but had to do so out of an appreciation and approval of the worth of his life and a recognition of his true service to Athens. This meant that a mob which was suspicious and hostile to Socrates because he was a philosopher, would have to reverse itself completely and become a patron of philosophy. How could Socrates possibly work such a miracle?

One. The Trials of Socrates

There was no hope that he could achieve this goal through reasoned argument, since his hearers were irrational men. The only way open to Socrates, as we have seen, was to exhibit the inner strength and nobility of character which he had achieved through the pursuit of philosophy. He had some hope that this might impress the court, that they would be moved by his display of courage and integrity to respect the life of philosophy which could produce courageous men like Socrates. This was the only way he could defend them. Certainly Socrates had some success. The large vote in his favor gives evidence that his speech must have exercised strong influence on a large number of the judges. However, he did not influence enough of them to save his life, and thus, to save the Athenians. The final vote, which condemned Socrates to death, also condemned the Athenians as violent passionate men, who decided even the gravest questions by prejudice rather than by reason, who valued flattery far more than they valued truth.

This is the very point which Socrates makes in his closing comments to the court. He points out that he has been convicted not because he deserved conviction, nor even because he lacked the skill at words with which he might have moved the court. He has rather been convicted, he says, by a lack of "impudence and of shamelessness, and of willingness to say to you such things as you would have liked best to hear."[47] As a result his accusers and judges are also convicted.[48] But they are convicted by the highest and most exacting court. They are convicted, as Socrates tells them, by truth, for having been guilty of "villainy and wrong."[49] Thus, Socrates who is formally condemned is in reality acquitted by a higher tribunal, while his judges, who are also on trial, are convicted before that same tribunal.

In the *Crito* we find a similar situation. When he accuses Socrates, Crito also puts himself on trial. Truth and justice stand ready to judge him as they judged the Athenians. The issue is exactly the same. Will Crito reach his verdict and act on it through passion, or will he yield to the demands of reason? The Athenians were challenged to overcome their hatred of Socrates in order to make a just decision. Crito is challenged to overcome his love of Socrates, as well as his love of himself, in order to render a just decision. It is as hard, perhaps even harder, for Crito to yield the life of Socrates whom he loves, as it was for the Athenians to spare the life of Socrates whom they hated. But to be fully justified a man must not only do what is right. He must do it, as we have said, for the right reasons. For the Athenians this meant that they had not only to acquit Socrates, but to acquit him because they recognized his worth as a philosopher. They failed on both scores. Crito, similarly, has not only to accept Socrates' decision to remain in prison, but be must do so because he understands that this is what justice requires. Crito is only partially successful, and, hence, only partially acquitted.

He passed the first part of the test admirably. Having come to the prison in the hope of saving Socrates' life, it, no doubt, pained him deeply to concur in Socrates' refusal to escape. In accepting Socrates' decision Crito rose above his love of Socrates and recognized the higher claim of justice. He also had to rise above self-love, and this in two regards. His desire to save Socrates' life was motivated partly by a fear that he would miss his friend intensely, and partly by a fear that he would suffer personal disgrace since it might seem that he had made no effort to save Socrates. Yet strong as these forces were Crito was able to suppress them, to replace self-love and love of Socrates with justice, and, thus, to render an honest verdict. Much as it pained him to admit it, Crito did grant that Socrates was doing right by remaining in prison. This part of his trial he completed successfully. He passed his test before the bar of truth, and was shown thereby to be far superior to the Athenian court. However, he failed on a second count. Though he made the right decision, it does not seem that he made it for the right reasons. Crito gave no evidence that he really had considered Socrates' arguments. As we pointed out earlier, he did not struggle with or against them in order to put them to the test. His acquittal of Socrates was not the result of a genuine understanding and appreciation of Socrates' position. It was, rather, the helpless yielding of a mediocre mind to the great force of Socrates' dialectical skill. For this reason Crito's acquittal was only partial. He overcame his passion, but did not replace it with a judgment of reason. In this respect Crito fell short of the mark, and was consequently convicted. We can realize the extent of Crito's failure when we compare his trial with that of Simmias and Cebes.

It is evident that the trial in which Socrates is most successful is also the trial in which the judges are most successful. Simmias and Cebes have to be judged on grounds similar to those on which the Athenians and Crito were judged. They, too, are in a situation where reason and passion are in conflict. Their trial is a test of their devotion to and belief in philosophy. This is crucially important, since it is only if they are true philosophers that they will be fit judges of Socrates. A double demand is made of them. The first is that they must be capable of carrying on a discussion of abstract and complex philosophic questions at a time of great emotional stress. The second, and even more difficult, is that they should voice honestly their doubts about immortality in the hours just before Socrates' death. Only genuine philosophers would have the capacity to suppress, in the interests of truth, the inclination to say whatever they think a dying man might want to hear. In this regard the trials have gone full circle. Socrates had to try to protect the Athenians from yielding to the desire to have him say only that they wanted to hear. Now he has to protect Simmias and Cebes from yielding to the desire to say only what they think Socrates might want to hear. It is as much their trial as his, for they must demonstrate that their commitment to philosophy is genuine by remaining philosophers even under these very trying conditions.

In spite of their occasional hesitations the two young judges acquit themselves completely. Not only do they turn the last hours of Socrates' life into an earnest and searching philosophic discussion, they center it on the topic which requires of them the greatest courage. It is true that they almost give up on one occasion. They hesitate to challenge Socrates though they are not convinced by his argument.[50] However, with only a little prodding from Socrates they return to the battle, and expose brilliantly the defects which they have found in Socrates' defense of immortality. From this point on no quarter is given in the discussion. They do not yield again to their emotions, but place instead the demands of philosophic inquiry above all else. In so doing they pass their own test, for they prove that, in contrast with the Athenians, truth is their greatest concern. Moreover, they are men, in contrast with Crito, who do not merely respect justice and truth. They are also determined to understand, and they have the intellectual drive and ability to achieve such understanding. These qualities which bring about the acquittal of Simmias and Cebes in their own trial, are the very considerations which qualify them to judge Socrates and which make their verdict significant.

VI

The third trial in each of the dialogues is Socrates' trial before himself. Each case is concerned with more than Socrates' defense before his judges. He is his own most severe judge and makes the most earnest demands of himself. At each trial he stands in judgment before his own principles and ideals, and each of the trials puts to the test Socrates' devotion to those principles. These are the most important of the trials, at least for his own inner life. There would be little value in being acquitted by his judges, were he to remain condemned in his own eyes and by his own understanding of justice and truth. Some men might be untroubled by such a possibility. But for Socrates, who teaches that the unexamined life is not worth living, the process of self-criticism is unavoidable. He is always being judged by his own conception of the good life, and his highest concern is to live in consonance with his own ideal.

That this is the guiding principle by which Socrates lives is made evident in a moving passage in the *Apology*. Socrates proclaims that he is on trial before the court of his own moral ideals in these words: "For thus it is, men of Athens, in truth; wherever a man stations himself, thinking it is best to be there, or is stationed by his commander, there he must, as it seems to me, remain and run his risks, considering neither death nor any other thing more than disgrace." Above all else a man must be true to himself and true to his obligations (which is what is implied by "his commander") no matter what the cost. He must only consider disgrace, but surely not the disgrace which he may be subject to in the opinions of wicked or foolish men. Socrates has made it eminently clear that this does not concern him. The only real disgrace is that which comes from violating true principles, i.e. from doing evil. In this regard Socrates, the philosopher, is his own best judge. He can accept death if need be. He can be calm in the face of the contempt and hostility of the Athenian mob. But, as long as he remains a philosopher, he cannot live with himself if he is faithless to his own beliefs and commitments. Nor may he change his principles to suit his circumstances. Whatever the situation in which he finds himself he must "remain and run his risks", i.e. he must be true to himself at all costs.

This is the setting for each of Socrates' trials before himself. In each case there are temptations, or, at least, potential temptations which could lead him to do what he knows he should not. In each case it would be possible for him to find some justification for taking the easy way, justification which would probably be convincing to the other people present. But Socrates knows that, whatever others might say in his defense, he would be defenseless before himself if he yielded to these temptations.

The potential temptations in the *Apology* are very apparent. It might readily seem like a minor offense if a man were to speak less than the whole truth in order to save his own life. What ordinary man would not sympathize with a defendant who flattered his judges a bit or played on their sympathies, especially when his life was at stake? This was the common practice in the Athenian courts, as in our own, and men were not condemned for it. If Socrates had done such things it probably would not have caused any unfavorable reaction. He knows, however, that his obligation is to his own principles and to his mission as a philosopher. While no one else might judge him harshly for following the set pattern for defendants, he would have to judge himself, and the judgment would necessarily be adverse.

We know, of course, that Socrates passes the test, that he does not yield to the temptations, that they do not even become temptations for him, and that he is, therefore, justified in his own eyes. In this first trial, however, this is not very difficult for him to do. On the one side the public situation is one which would tend to call forth heroism even from lesser men. In the face of a severe public attack on all that his life has accomplished it is not surprising that Socrates should be ready to choose death rather than submission. Weaker and more foolish men have often risen to the challenge of such public martyrdom. For Socrates this could hardly have been difficult. On the other hand, it would have been difficult for Socrates to find any convincing reasons to justify his yielding to the mob. It is hard to imagine what he might have said in his own defense had he chosen to speak falsehood rather than truth, or to cater to the irrationality of these irrational men rather than to remain true to reason. Thus, there was no way that Socrates could have justified himself in his own eyes if he had not remained true to himself. This was a situation, therefore in which it was relatively easy for him to be strong, and in which almost no excuse could have been found for his doing anything else. Other men might not see this, but Socrates certainly did. He passes the test, and is acquitted in this first trial before himself. However, it is a rather easy trial which makes only the smallest demands on him.

Socrates' trial before himself in the *Crito* makes much greater demands on him. Here, too, be faces a temptation, namely the temptation to save his life by escaping. He need fear no public disgrace, since the ease with which Crito arranged for the escape suggests that this was a common course for political prisoners. Neither need Socrates fear disgrace before his friends. As Crito tells him,[52] many of them, even foreigners among them, are prepared to help finance the escape and to arrange the details. In addition Crito offers a number of very plausible positive reasons for believing that Socrates is obligated to escape. All of this puts Socrates on trial before himself. He can yield easily enough to the importunities of his friends and, in doing so, will seem to be responsible and prudent rather than evil. The great question is whether he can justify his escape in his own eyes and by his own principles.

Socrates points out to Crito that his only concern is with justice, not with the opinions of men. "The question is whether it is right for me to try to escape from here without the permission of the Athenians, or not right."[53] No other considerations are relevant to Socrates' decision. Now he has to argue the case before himself, and only incidentally before Crito. His trial is now set, for the issue is whether he can argue before himself honestly and with loyalty to the principles of justice. Crito and his other friends are tempting him and may well strengthen his natural inclination to save his life. But Socrates shows that he values the salvation of his soul far more than the preservation of his body, that he prefers to die as a just man rather than to live as an unjust man.

The argument of the laws with Socrates is in reality his argument with himself. He makes this quite clear since he speaks for the laws. Moreover, at the very end of the conversation Socrates tells Crito, "this is what I seem to hear... and this sound of these words re-echoes within me and prevents my hearing any other words."[54] This trial before himself is a more earnest and difficult one than he faced in the *Apology*. There he had no arguments which could justify his yielding to the temptations, and he was in a public situation which encouraged heroics. In the *Crito* he stands before a single man who is an intimate friend. In these circumstances it is far more difficult to be a hero. In addition, he now has some excellent arguments to justify his yielding to the temptation to escape. Crito had offered a number of seemingly good reasons why Socrates should escape. He spoke of Socrates' obligations to himself, to his family, and to his friends. Since Socrates is far more intelligent than Crito he adds a better and more convincing reason. As he suggests, the best answer to the accusation of the laws, i.e. to this own accusation of himself in the justice, is that, "The state wronged me and did not judge the case rightly." This seems like an almost irrefutable argument. It certainly would have convinced Crito. But Socrates is on trial before himself, and has, therefore, to convince himself and this he cannot do. The address of the laws, which is an almost unbroken soliloquy, is a great tribute to Socrates' intellectual honesty and moral integrity. Instead of twisting the argument even slightly in favor of saving his life, Socrates is rigorously honest and acutely perceptive of the real issues. The argument is even more impressive when we realize that this man is talking to himself, and that his life is at stake. In the course of the soliloquy he answers each point that Crito made, and, what is more important, also answers himself. As he expounds the issues to himself it becomes clear that he cannot justify his escape. As unpleasant as this conclusion may be Socrates draws it without hesitation. In so doing he is successful in this second trial before himself, a trial far more demanding than that in the *Apology*.

In the *Phaedo* we have found the most intense and most rigorous of the earlier trials we have discussed. This is also the case with regard to Socrates' trial before himself. In the *Phaedo* his trial reaches its highest level, requiring most of Socrates and, thus, exhibiting to us his most impressive qualities. As in the other trials Socrates is here also subject to a temptation, namely the temptation to avoid in his last hours discussion of so delicate a question as immortality. But as we have seen the topic of the discussion is not only immortality but the philosophic life, i.e. his own life, and it is this even more difficult matter which Socrates has to defend. Had he wanted to avoid this troubling topic he could certainly have done so without any embarrassment. It would have been easy from the very first to direct the conversation elsewhere, aid even after it was under way he had several opportunities to end the discussion gracefully. He could have done this without any fear of being condemned by his friends, especially since they were themselves hesitant about pursuing the discussion.

But Socrates is also on trial before himself and his own principles. If his lifelong pursuit of philosophy has been sincere, if he has been honest in his insistence that the unexamined life is not worth living, then he must prove this to himself by continuing to philosophize to the end. For he has to satisfy his own standards which are the standards of the philosophic life, and not merely the views of other men. As he himself tells us, an unphilosophic man argues "to convince his hearers that what he says is true. I am rather seeking to convince myself; to convince my hearers is a secondary matter with me."[56] This is the most earnest trial of Socrates, a trial in which he has to defend himself before himself, a trial in which he has the last opportunity to convince himself, and only incidentally others, that the philosophic life is the best life for man. To succeed in this trial he needs to do two things. First he must make the most convincing possible argument in behalf of the immortality of the soul, and hence of the superiority of the soul to the body and of wisdom to sensual pleasure. Secondly, since the argument itself is insufficient he must bolster his position by continuing to trust in argument and inquiry. That is to say, he defends himself both by the content of his arguments and by the fact that he is arguing. It is this latter fact which does most to defend Socrates in his own eyes as in the eyes of his judges. For by continuing to inquire at such a time he establishes the very point which is in question, mainly that the soul is superior to the body and that inquiry alone makes life fit for man. In this way alone can Socrates be acquitted, namely, if he remains true to himself. While recognizing the risks to which inquiry exposes him he, nevertheless, pursues it fearlessly, for he knows that only so long as he continues to philosophize can both his life and his death be justified.

This third trial before himself is by far the most earnest for several reasons. In the *Apology* there were no serious arguments offered against his position. In the Crito some arguments were offered by Crito, but the most telling argument, as we saw, had to be supplied by Socrates himself. This meant that he had control over the argument and how far it would go. In the *Phaedo* it is no longer Socrates who formulates the main objections, but two skilled and tenacious young philosophers. To convince himself he must face their objections, not merely his own. Moreover, in the *Apology and Crito* he is risking only his physical life. Nothing more seems to Socrates to be in danger, and he does not value his life very highly. But the situation in the *Phaedo* is one in which Socrates has to risk his soul, which he believes to be the most valuable of his possessions. If he avoids the argument, then be has already condemned himself by showing that he does not believe in philosophy, which means that the soul is not superior to the body. If he pursues the argument only part way, he will still not satisfy his own standards. Only by a full and frank analysis of his most cherished beliefs can he justify those very beliefs, and thus his entire life, in his own eyes. As we know, Socrates meets the challenge admirably. He overcomes any temptation he might feet to be comfortable but unthinking in his last moments on earth by avoiding the discussion. Instead he debates the issues vigorously, and in so doing convinces himself again that philosophy is man's noblest activity and sole salvation. Thus does Socrates succeed in his last trial before himself.

This admitted attempt on Socrates' part to convince himself contains a lesson which is deeply rooted in Plato's teaching. He holds that ultimately each man must find his own understanding of the truth and must find it within himself. Others may stimulate and direct us, but only we can convince ourselves. Perhaps this is suggested by the doctrine of reminiscence, with its implication that each man has within himself potentially as much truth as he can know. A "midwife" may help him give birth to this truth or a "gadfly" may direct his attention to it, but no man can supply truth to another nor bring about conviction in another. Socrates says

One. The Trials of Socrates 33

this to his young friends in the *Phaedo* when they express their concern that once he is gone there will be no one left to teach them. He reminds them that there are other good and wise men to whom they can turn. Then he concludes, "And you must seek by yourselves too; for you will not find others better able to make the search."[57] This is exactly what Socrates has done, and what each man must do if he is devoted to truth. He must search diligently and seek, above all else, to convince himself.

The last moment of Socrates' life offers the most eloquent testimony that he did convince himself. His famous and puzzling last words have been interpreted in various ways. The whole scheme of our analysis supports the claims of one of these interpretations; namely, that when Socrates says, "I owe a cock to Asclepius", he is assuring his friends that he believes that he is now finally healed of the impurities of the body and is about to achieve his fulfillment as a philosopher. These last words show that Socrates did succeed in convincing himself of the supreme value of the philosophic life, and that he was, therefore, successful in this as in his other trials.

VII

The purpose of this essay as it was set down at the beginning was to examine the interconnections between the dialogues in the first tetralogy. I have tried to show, at length, how the *Apology, Crito* and Phaedo are interrelated. However, no mention has been made yet of the way in which the *Euthyphro* fits into the group. There is a tendency, even among those commentators who admit that there are some interconnections between the other three dialogues, to discuss the *Euthyphro* as having no proper place in the grouping. Typical examples are Cooper and Burnet. Cooper's introduction to his edition of the four dialogues begins with these words: "The four dialogues here translated concern the trial and death of Socrates, and hence belong together, though *Euthyphro* is hard to place among them. The other three are ideally conjoined; somehow it is not ideally in close relation to anyone of them, nor to all three. It does not seem to have been written with them in mind, and may have been composed as an afterthought..."[58] Burnet puts the matter this way in his edition of the *Euthyphro, Apology,* and *Crito:* "Its [i.e. the *Euthyphro's]* position as the first dialogue of the first tetralogy is due solely to the consideration that, in the story of the trial and death of Socrates, it comes before the *Apology* just as the Crito comes after it."[59]

There is very good ground for quite a different view of the matter. Plato was surely aware that the dramatic setting of the *Euthyphro* on the steps of the court already provides an external connection with the other dialogues in the tetralogy. My contention is that this is sufficient indication that he wanted his readers to consider the *Euthyphro* as part of the group of dialogues concerned with Socrates' trials and death. If this contention is justified, then there must be a deeper connection than just temporal sequence between *the Euthyphro* and the *Apology, Crito, and Phaedo*. I suggest that *the Euthyphro* can be understood best (though not exclusively) as the foil or background for the other dialogues. Euthyphro is the opposite of Socrates, the philosopher, in every fundamental regard, and as we study his character we can understand and appreciate Socrates more fully. Since, according to our interpretation, the character of Socrates and of his commitment to the philosophic life are among the prime considerations in the dialogues we have been discussing, it is especially appropriate that they should be preceded by the *Euthyphro,* a dialogue which helps us understand Socrates, the philosopher, by characterizing sharply his complete opposite.

Superficially there may appear to be a similarity between Euthyphro and the Socrates of the Apology. Both claim to be assured of their own virtuousness and exhibit a certain smugness. However, from the point of view of our present understanding of the *Apology* the differences are striking and instructive. We know that Socrates' smugness and his claims to virtue are a pose which he assumes because the circumstances require it. This is 'his way of defending philosophy before the Athenians. But for Euthyphro the self-assurance is no pose at all. He really thinks he is as wise and as virtuous as he says. When Socrates challenges him, asking whether his knowledge of religion and morals is so exact that he can risk indicting his own father for murder, Euthyphro replies in terms which mark him as a self-satisfied fool. "The best of Euthyphro," he says, "and that which distinguishes him, Socrates, from other men, is his exact knowledge of all such matters. What should I be good for without it?"[60] We should note that Euthyphro has acted on the basis of his supposed certainties to the detriment of another man, and of all people, his father. Socrates, in contrast, was ready to pursue his own certainties only to his own possible detriment, but certainly not at the expense of other men.

However, we know that it is an error to speak of Socrates' certainties. For the apparent certainties of the *Apology and Crito* are shown in the *Phaedo* to be far from certain, and Socrates knows this better than anyone

One. The Trials of Socrates

else and admits it readily. This brings us to another illuminating contrast between Socrates and Euthyphro. Both claim to be wise men, even the wisest of men. Euthyphro makes the claim because he believes that he has exact knowledge of the most difficult matters. Socrates makes the claim because he believes that he is more deeply aware of his own ignorance than other men. This contrast is borne out by the fact that while Euthyphro persists in his claims to have certain knowledge, Socrates makes explicit his own uncertainties.

This brings us to a further opposition between these men. Euthyphro believes he has certain knowledge because he never examines his beliefs with care and never subjects them to analysis and criticism. Socrates denies that he has certain knowledge because he is continually scrutinizing and criticizing his convictions and is, therefore, sensitively aware of their limitations. When Euthyphro is pressed by Socrates to exhibit some of the knowledge which he claims to have he fails miserably. It is evident that he has not thought through the issues even on an elementary level, and that he has neither analytic skill nor intellectual honesty. Instead of facing Socrates' questions he objects with annoyance that Socrates is playing tricks on him.[61] This is the only explanation he can think of for his difficulties. It never even occurs to him that his understanding of the issues or his formulation of his position may be defective. But his certainty remains unaffected. Socrates, in the *Phaedo,* is brilliant in argument, searching in his self-criticism, deeply persuasive, and yet he avoids certainty so long as he can.

Only at the very last moments of his life does he allow himself to say that he is completely convinced that he is right, and then only because there is no more time left for inquiry. On the other hand, young Euthyphro, with most of his life ahead of him, is already suffering from intellectual mummification. He is sure of his answers, precisely because he has not and cannot ask himself questions. As a result, Euthyphro has no hesitation about imposing his certainties on others, while Socrates takes the greatest pains to urge other men to continue to question especially what he himself believes most firmly.

These differences are brought into sharpest focus by one other crucial fact. Because of his stupid certainly Euthyphro is ill at ease during inquiry and takes the first opportunity that he can to bring it to an end. The dialogue closes abruptly, long before the question under discussion has been resolved, because Euthyphro insists that he is in a hurry and has no time to talk. It is obvious, in the context, that this is just his excuse for running away from the discussion, when it begins to get uncomfortable. But Socrates was the man who pursued avidly the most uncomfortable of all discussions down to his last moments on earth. Not only did he pursue the discussion, but he stimulated it and would not allow others to stop. For Socrates places truth and the search for truth above all else, while Euthyphro gives supremacy to his own self-satisfied convictions irrespective of their truth, and, therefore, hates any search which throws doubt on his beliefs.

Through this very forceful contrast Plato tries to tell us what to look for in the *Apology, Crito, and Phaedo. The Euthyphro* is placed first in the tetralogy as a kind of guide or map. As we see clearly each of Euthyphro's characteristics we know what opposite qualities to look for in Socrates. And it is precisely these opposite qualities which are the important ones for our understanding of the other dialogues in the group. In seeing Euthyphro's certainties we should recognize the importance of Socrates' uncertainties. In seeing Euthyphro's fear and hatred of inquiry we should recognize the importance of Socrates' trust in and devotion to inquiry. In seeing Euthyphro's arrogance we should recognize the importance and the genuineness of Socrates' humility. Above all, in scorning Euthyphro the fool, we should also come to revere Socrates the philosopher.[62]

I have tried to show in this study that, contrary to many opinions, the dialogues of the first tetralogy are closely interrelated. Without denying the interest of each of the dialogues when taken independently, I have tried to give some grounds for the view that any proper interpretation requires that they be understood through the light shed by their literary and philosophic interconnections. Finally, I should point out that I have not intended or tried to give a complete interpretation of each of these dialogues, but only to show how essential it is for the achievement of such an interpretation that we study them as a unit.

Marvin Fox
Department of
Philosophy
Ohio State University
Columbus 10, Ohio

One. The Trials of Socrates 37

NOTES

[1] Lane Cooper, Plato - On *the Trial and Death of Socrates* (Ithaca, New York, 1941), p. 2.

[2] Cf. *Gorgias,* 454 B, 454 E, 455 A. Jowett renders this "courts of law and other assemblies"; Lamb in the Loeb edition translates it as "law-courts and any public gatherings." These terms are surely much too mild for ὄλλοζ unless we understand "assemblies", as the Liddell & Scott Lexicon suggests, "in a contemptuous sense." This correction of the usual translations first came to my attention in an excellent article by W. A. Oldfather, entitled "Socrates in Court", *Classical Weekly,* April 25, 1938. I am also indebted to this article for a number of illuminating references on the question of Socrates' attitude to the Athenian courts.

[3] E. g., *Gorgias,* 484 D-E, 486 A-C, 521 A -523 A; *Republic,* 517 A & D; *Theaetetus,* 172 C -175 D; *Laches.* 196 B.

[4] Theaetetus, 172 C.

[5] *Apology,* 40 A. The Loeb translation, less poetically but more precisely, renders this passage "and in calling you judges, I give you your right name." Cf. also *Apology* 41 A, where Socrates again distinguishes between those who "claim to be judges and those who are really judges" ἀπαλλαγείς τούτων τῶν φασκόντων δικαστῶν εἶναι. I have quoted throughout from the Loeb translation. On the few occasions where, for rhetorical convenience, I have quoted the Jowett translation this is indicated by (J) after the reference. In a few other cases, as is made clear in the text, I have adjusted the existing translations.

[6] Cf., Burnet, *Plato's Euthyphro, Apology, & Crito,* (Oxford, 1924), notes, pp. 66-67. Also the edition of the *Apology* by Riddell which Burnet cites.

[7] *Apology,* 24 E & 26 D.

[8] Cf., *Ibid,* 21 A. In pointing out that Chaerephon went into exile with the now ruling democratic party he underscores in their memories the fact that he remained in Athens. This is surely not calculated to win the sympathy of the court. A similar situation occurs at 30 C ff., where what he says is certain to irritate his hearers.

[9] 34 C-35 C.

[10] 36 B-E.

[11] 41 CD.

[12] 115 D.

[13] Crito, 44 D.

[14] Ibid., 45 E.

[15] 63 D- E.

[16] *Crito.* 43 B.

[17] *Phaedo,* 115 B.

[18] *Ibid.,* 116 E-117A.

[19] *Ibid.,* 118 A.

[20] *Crito,* 45 C.

21 *Apology*, 24 B.
22 *Crito*, 48 C.
23 *Ibid.*, 49 A-E.
24 *Apology*, 28 A.
25 *Phaedo*, 63 A, (J).
26 *Ibid.*, 63 B.
27 *Ibid.*, 69 E, (J). The fact that Socrates here refers to his Athenian "judges" in no way refutes our earlier thesis. In the *Apology* where he addressed them directly he refused to dignify them by the title "judges". Here, where he is merely referring to them, the title is no more than a convenient identification.
28 *Ibid.*, 59 C. Jowett's rendering of ξένοι as "strangers" is very misleading. They are not strangers in our ordinary sense at all. They are "foreigners," i.e. non-Athenians. However, they are received in Athens as friends and are given hospitality. It is completely clear that these are not strangers, i.e. men unknown to Socrates who are meeting him now for the first time.
29 *Ibid.*, 63 A, (J).
30 *Ibid.*, 59 A, (J).
31 *Ibid.*, 61 D.
32 *Ibid.*, 62 C.
33 *Ibid.*, 66 A. Underscore my own.
34 *Ibid.*, 70 B. Underscore my own.
35 *Ibid.*, 84 C.
36 *Ibid.*, 107 A.
37 *Ibid.*, 107 B. ἀκολουθήσετε τῷ λόγῳ καθ' ὅσον δυνατὸν μάλιστ' ἀνθρώπῳ ἐπακολουθῆσαι; literally, "you shall follow the λόγος far as that is within the capacity of man."
38 *Ibid.*, 85 CD.
39 *Ibid.*, 89 D.
40 For example, Burnet in his notes to his text of the *Phaedo* labels the passage: — "Protreptic Interlude (89a9-91c5). A Warning against μισολογία."
41 It may not be wholly irrelevant to note, incidentally that the passage is located at the approximate geographic center of the dialogue.
42 *Phaedo*, 88 CD.
43 *Ibid.*, 91 C.
44 Cf., *Apology*, 36 A, where Socrates tells them, "Your decision was not a surprise to me."
45 *Phaedo* 89 A.
46 *Apology*, 30 DE.
47 *Ibid.*, 38 D.
48 Since the court is prejudiced by the 11 old accusations", and since they have inclined to believe these accusations, the entire body of judges is, at the same time, a body of accusers. In the other trials the accusers, i.e., Crito, and Simmias and Cebes, are also the judges.

[49] *Ibid.*, 39 B
[50] *Cf., Phaedo*, 84 CD.
[51] *Apology*, 28 D.
[52] *Crito*, 45 B.
[53] *Ibid.*, 48 C.
[54] *Ibid.*, 54 D. Burnet, in his edition of the *Euthyphro, Apology, Crito*, p. 200, makes this same point, i.e. that the speech of the laws is really Socrates speaking to himself.
[55] *Ibid.*, 50 C
[56] *Phaedo*, 91 A, (J).
[57] *Ibid.*, 78A. The phrase, καί αὐτοὺς μετ' ἀλλήλων is rendered by Jowett and in the Loeb edition as "among, yourselves." Burnet in his edition of the *Phaedo*, Notes. p. 65, argues on philological grounds that this is an impossible translation. He suggests instead, "by yourselves," and the sense of the passage seems to bear him out.
[58] Cooper, *op. cit.*, p.1. Cooper takes the view that each dialogue is a separate unit. Nevertheless, he rants that there is some kind of relationship between he *Apology, Crito, and Phaedo*. To the *Euthyphro* he denies any relationship with the others.
[59] Burnet, *op. cit.*, Notes, p. 4.
[60] Euthyphro, 4 E-5 A, (J).
[61] Cf., *ibid.*, 11 B-D.
[62] There are still other elements in the *Euthyphro* which relate it to the other dialogues, e.g., the discussion of the meaning of piety as an introduction to the charge against Socrates of impiety. However, I have omitted these because they do not seem to me to be strictly necessary for our theme.

2

THE DOCTRINE OF THE MEAN IN ARISTOTLE AND MAIMONIDES: A COMPARATIVE STUDY

The scholarly literature dealing with the interpretation of the philosophy of Maimonides moves between two poles. There are those who insist that Maimonides was in all significant respects a true and faithful disciple of Aristotle, or of the Aristotelianism which he knew through the Arabic sources. At the other extreme there are those who argue that the Aristotelianism of Maimonides is only a surface appearance but that he is, in fact, not an Aristotelian at all in his actual philosophical and theological doctrines.

This difference of opinion is especially sharp in the discussions of Maimonides' ethics, particularly with respect to his doctrine of the mean. Many writers take the position that the Aristotelianism of Maimonides' doctrine of the mean is so obvious that it does not even require discussion or evidence. Writing about Shem Tov ben Joseph Palqera, Malter says that "the Aristotelian ethics of the golden mean found in Palqera a disciple scarcely less devoted than his master Maimonides."[1] Gorfinkle, in his edition of the *Eight Chapters of Maimonides* speaks of the chapter "in which the Aristotelian doctrine of the *Mean* ...is applied to Jewish ethics." He adds that "Although Maimonides follows Aristotle in defining virtue as a state intermediate between two extremes, ...he still remains on Jewish ground as there are biblical and talmudical passages expressing such a thought."[2] Harry S. Lewis speaks of "the famous attempt of Maimonides to equate Jewish ethics with the Aristotelian doctrine of the mean." He goes on to affirm that "Maimonides derived his doctrine of the Mean from Greek sources, but it was quite congenial to the native Hebraic spirit."[3] Rosin, in his basic study of the ethics of Maimonides, sees the doctrine of the mean as essentially Aristotelian in origin and character, despite some of Maimonides' deviations from the Aristotelian pattern. "*Handlungen, sagt M. in Übereinstimmung mit Aristoteles, sind gut, wenn sie angemessen sind indem sie in der Mitte zwischen zwei Extremen hegen...*"[4] Even those writers, like Rosin, who seek also in rabbinic literature for the sources of Maimonides' doctrine of the mean, take the position that these are supports which legitimate the Jewishness of the doctrine, but they do not claim that they are the actual sources from which Maimonides derived his position.

Opposed to these writers are those who deny that Maimonides' ethics are Aristotelian in any significant respect. A typical voice from the traditional camp, that of Rabbi Ya'akov Mosheh Harlap, affirms with the greatest passion that no non-Jewish source can make any contribution to Jewish doctrine. After having discussed at great length various aspects of Maimonides' doctrine of the mean, Harlap is concerned to protect his readers from the mistake of supposing that this doctrine has any non-Jewish origin. If it appears to be similar to the teachings of Aristotle, this is no more than an appearance, and we must understand it properly. Such a doctrine can enter Jewish teaching from the outside only if it is first thoroughly Judaized, only if, like the convert, it is reborn and acquires a new, specifically Jewish, nature. "Whatever is taught by others cannot be presented as Jewish teaching unless it has first undergone conversion *(geruth)*. Just as it is possible to convert souls, so is it possible to convert doctrines."[5] Harlap claims that this is what happened with Maimonides' doctrine of the mean. It may appear to be similar to Aristotle's doctrine, but after having been converted, it is a totally new and uniquely Jewish creation.

Coming to the materials from a different background and perspective, Hermann Cohen also argues fiercely against the Aristotelianism of Maimonides' ethics. Cohen holds that for purposes of tactical effectiveness Maimonides chose to give the appearance that he was agreeing with Aristotle since otherwise he would open himself to endless attack.[6] In fact, says Cohen, his doctrine is not Aristotelian at all. It is independent of Aristotle and not in agreement with him. If we were forced to affirm that Maimonides derived his ethics from Aristotle and was in agreement with him, "*so wäre die Ethik Maimunis nicht nur keine philosophische Ethik mit einem selbstständigen und einheitlichen Prinzip, sondern auch als religiöse Ethik wäre sie widerspruchsvoll in sich; auch als ein Anhang zum Moreh als eine Art von Homille, würde sie sich nicht anpassen; und selbst als ein Ghed in seinem System der Theologie wäre sie unorganisch und exoterisch.*"[7]

Cohen goes on later to delineate carefully and in detail the ways in which Maimonides' doctrine of the mean differs from that of Aristotle.[8]

Our aim in the present paper is to present a fresh investigation of the question. We shall focus our attention specifically on the doctrine of the mean as it is treated by Maimonides in his various works. It is one of our main contentions, however, that no responsible treatment can be offered of the relationships between Maimonides' and Aristotle's doctrines unless we are first clear about what it was that Aristotle actually taught. In our view, conventional representations of the doctrine of the mean in Aristotle fail to grasp the fundamental philosophical ground on which that doctrine rests. We shall, therefore, attempt in this study to set forth a careful interpretation of the Aristotelian position as the basis on which to make the comparison. Our interpretation of Maimonides will then be directed to the double task of understanding him in his own right and of seeing him in comparison to Aristotle.

I

Although the doctrine of the mean is among the most familiar and popular of Aristotle's teachings, it has been widely misunderstood and misrepresented. This failure to grasp the essential elements in Aristotle's doctrine is evident in the standard criticisms to which it has been subjected, as a brief survey will reveal.

Some writers have argued that the mean is no more than Aristotle's adaptation of the long established Greek folk rule, *meden agan*, nothing to excess. They deny that it is or is based on a philosophical principle but see instead in Aristotle's doctrine nothing but a restatement of the common sense of the ages. A related, but a more pointed and more serious charge, is that the Aristotelian mean is, in the last analysis, nothing more than an affirmation of the proprieties of social convention. Typical of this approach is the statement of Gomperz in which he charges that Aristotle's ethics rest on the view that "Current opinion, when purged or corroborated by the settlement of real or apparent contradictions, is identified with absolute truth so far as concerns questions relating to the conduct of life."[9] Hans Kelsen has expressed the criticism even more vigorously in charging that "Although the ethics of the *mesotes* doctrine pretends to establish in an authoritative way the moral value, it leaves the solution of its very problem to another authority... It is the authority of the positive morality and positive law; it is the established social order. By presupposing in its *mesotes* formula the established social order, the ethics of Aristotle justifies the positive morality and the positive law.... In this justification of the established social order lies the true function of the tautology which a critical analysis of the *mesotes* formula reveals."[10] This criticism gains support from Aristotle's admission that all judgment concerning the application of the doctrine of the mean to particular cases depends completely on the insight of the man of practical wisdom; but, the critics argue, that man has no standard to which he can appeal other than the accepted conventional attitudes and values of his society.

The absence of any objective standard appears to be underscored by the fact that the Aristotelian mean is not determined arithmetically and is thus not the same for all men. It is, rather, a rule which must be applied only with full cognizance of the particular circumstances and the characteristic peculiarities of the individual in question. It is *pros hemas*, determined in relation to the individual moral agent. This compounds the difficulty, since it would now appear that in the doctrine of the mean we have merely social convention adjusted to individual differences—a far cry indeed, so it seems, from a serious philosophical principle.

Perhaps the most contemptuous of all the criticisms was made by Kant, when he wrote:

> The proposition that one should never do too much or do too little says nothing for it is tautological. What is it to do too much? Answer: More than is good. What is it to do too little? Answer: To do less than is good. What is meant by I ought (to do something or forbear doing something)? Answer: It is not good (contrary to duty) to do more or less than is good. If this is the wisdom we are to seek by returning to the ancients (Aristotle) as being precisely those who were nearer to the source of wisdom, then we have chosen badly to turn to their oracle... For to be much too virtuous, i.e., to adhere too closely to one's duty, would be like making a circle much too round or a straight line much too straight. [11]

If these charges are justified, they are grave indeed, since they challenge what Aristotle himself claims explicitly. In his definition of moral virtue he includes the proviso that the choice in accordance with the mean is *horismene logo,* determined by a *logos,* that is by a rule or principle of reason.[12] It is clear that in his view what he is offering is a principle of reason, not just the arbitrariness of convention.

Yet the charges against him do not appear to be totally without foundation. Does he not himself inform us early in the *Nicomachaean Ethics* that the actions which are the subject matter of ethical reflection and choice "admit of much variety and fluctuation of opinion, so that they may be thought to exist only by convention (*nomos*), and not by nature (*physis*)?"[13] Does he not, near the end of the same book, express the view that, "what all think to be good, that, we assert, is good?"[14] Moreover, he regularly invokes common opinion about moral matters and the good life as if it were clearly worthy of being considered authoritative. In all this he seems to be admitting the very criticisms that are thought by many to be fatal to his position. What can we make out of the doctrine of the mean in the light of these critical attacks? In what follows I seek to answer that question by offering an interpretation of the doctrine of the mean which takes account of and copes with the difficulties that have been raised.

To grasp the doctrine correctly it is extremely useful to take full account of the medical model which Aristotle uses repeatedly, the recurring comparison that he draws between the process of attaining moral virtue and the work of the physician who brings his patients to a state of physical health. At almost every important point in his exposition of the way to moral virtue, Aristotle employs the practice of medicine as a paradigm which illuminates and clarifies his basic points. The subject has been treated carefully and convincingly by Jaeger, who concludes on the basis of his study of the *Nicomachaean Ethics* that the appeal to the medical pattern is so deep and pervasive that "in the light of it Aristotle tries to justify almost every step he takes in his ethical philosophy."[15]

The essential elements in that medical model are easy to discern. The practice of medicine has as its end the attainment of health for the patient. That end is given in and defined by the physical nature of the human patient. There is nothing arbitrary about what physical health is in general. It is the proper excellence of the body which is gained when the body is brought to its highest degree of natural perfection. Insofar as it concerns the treatment of bodies in general, the practice of medicine involves a knowledge of principles that are fixed because they are the principles of a type of being which exists by nature and has its own nature. Yet, these general principles alone are insufficient for the practice of medicine. The physician's art requires him to deal with particular cases, to make practical decisions, and to offer practical guidance for each individual case. His prescriptions can be approximately correct only, at best, never absolutely precise. Even when he knows what foods are healthful, he is ineffective unless he is able to prescribe for each particular case a diet which is adjusted to the special needs and specific circumstances of the patient before him. It is here that his special art comes into play, for anyone who is modestly educated might be expected to know general rules of health, but only the skilled physician can be relied upon to diagnose individual cases and to apply the general rules to the particular needs of each patient. In his medical practice the doctor must use the rule of the mean as Aristotle repeatedly notes. As the work *On Ancient Medicine* (sometimes attributed to Hippocrates) expresses it, in the treatment of human ailments "it is necessary to aim at some measure."[16]

If we follow Aristotle in thinking about ethics on the model of medical practice, then we can solve most of the problems which his critics raise concerning the doctrine of the mean. Like medicine, ethics rests on a natural base. If there were not this base in the nature of man, a nature which is fixed, there could be no talk of ethics as a practical *science*. It would be at best a fairly sophisticated art, but even as an art it could not proceed successfully if it had no fixed points of reference. Like medicine, ethics is concerned not with knowledge for its own sake but for the sake of action. This is what makes it *practical*. This practical element is carried out primarily with respect to particular men in particular circumstances, as is the case with medicine. To achieve this, the moral teacher (the *phronimos*) cannot rely only on his knowledge of the nature of man in general. He must have the capacity to deal with particular cases, and that is done finally through *aisthesis,* a kind of immediate perception of what is required in order to apply the general rules to the particular individual before him. In this situation he cannot expect to achieve demonstrative certainty. At best he can offer the kind of informed judgment which emerges from the total combination of his theoretical understanding, his practical experience, and the special intelligence of the practically wise man, which is a capacity to deliberate well about such moral issues. Finally, his judgment will depend, in some degree, on *nomos,* on the accepted patterns and attitudes of the society in which the individual lives. The doctor prescribes for his patient taking account both of his particular situation with respect to physical health and development and of his particular needs. Thus, when he prescribes for Milo, he must know not only that this patient has such and such specific complaints and that his physical condition is so and so, but also that he is a wrestler and wants to be restored to the state of health which is requisite for a successful wrestler. Similarly, the moral guide must know not only what the particular moral situation of his client is, but also what his place is in society and what the norms are of the society in which he must function. The norm of courage for a soldier at the battle front is likely to be different from that which is proper for a professional baby sitter.

Where the critics have gone wrong is in supposing that all Aristotle offers us is the social framework and the individual peculiarities of the moral agent. They have utterly ignored the crucial fact that his moral philosophy and his doctrine of the mean, in particular, are rooted in principles of nature. They have failed to see that Aristotle carefully introduces qualifications whenever he speaks of the conventional aspects of morality, The earliest passage in the *Nicomachaean Ethics* which deals with this topic is a case in point. Aristotle stresses that we must not expect in ethics the same kind of precision and the same degree of certainty that we expect in the demonstrative sciences. The subject matter of ethics and politics are *ta kala kai ta dikaia,* the fine or noble and the just, "but these conceptions involve much difference of opinion and uncertainty, so that they may be thought to exist only by convention and not by nature." [17] The stress is on the fact that "they may be *thought*" to be nothing more than convention, but those who think this are mistaken. For while they are, of course, in some measure dependent on convention, that is not the whole of the content or foundation of moral virtue. Let us, then, examine that natural foundation of moral virtue which has escaped the attention of Aristotle's critics.

Moral virtue, like any virtue *(arete),* is concerned with the proper excellence of its subject, in this case man, and this is determined by his proper end as it is given in nature. This is standard doctrine for Aristotle, to be found consistently in those of his works which deal with the question in any way at all. The principle is stated in *Metaphysics* v, 1021b 21ff., where he says that virtue *(arete,)* is a *telos,* the perfection of a thing by achieving its proper end. "And excellence is a completion *(telos);* for each thing is complete and every substance is complete *(teleion),* when in respect of the form of its proper excellence it lacks no natural part of its excellence." Note that the *arete,* the excellence of virtue, is natural, it is determined by the nature of the thing. The same point is made in *Physics* vii, 246a 10 247a 20. "Excellence *(arete,* i.e., virtue) is a kind of perfection *(teleion),* since a thing is said to be perfect *(teleion)* when it has acquired its proper excellence, for it is then in most complete conformity to its own nature.... Excellence and defect are in every case concerned with the influences whereby their possessor is, according to its natural constitution, liable to be modified.... The same is true of the moral habits *(tes psyches hexeon,* the states of the soul), for they, too, consist in conditions determined by certain relations, and the virtues are perfections of nature, the vices departures from it." These passages speak for themselves and merely reinforce what is stated in the *N.E.* on the same subject. The stress is on the nature of a thing, since for all things that exist by nature there can be no knowledge of their virtue except in terms of their nature.

That ethics is closely tied to nature is eminently clear, since man's virtue is determined by his nature, and this, in turn, requires a knowledge of psychology, the principles of the human soul. Aristotle sets out some of these principles in *N.E.* as a first step in defining human virtue. Lest there be any doubt that psychology is a subject matter that is natural, one need only turn to the opening of *De Anima,* where Aristotle says explicitly that the knowledge of the soul admittedly contributes greatly to the advance of truth in general and, above all, to our understanding of nature. The particular problems of ethics arise because of the complex nature of man. To the extent that man is truly rational, it is easy for Aristotle to specify what his proper end is. Here the nature of rationality itself determines the end, namely, the use of reason for the knowledge and contemplation of that which is highest and most perfect. The most virtuous life for man would be one in which he would engage most completely in that supreme contemplative activity which is philosophical wisdom.

However, man is not a purely and perfectly rational being. He is a rational animal, an animal that has the capacity for being rational. This animal aspect of his nature must be given its due but must not be allowed to control him, otherwise man will be only animal and not rational at all. The problem then is to determine what it would be like for man's animal nature to be subject, to the fullest possible degree, to the rule of reason, and to discover the practical means by which this end might be achieved. True virtue for man will be the fullest realization of his *telos,* his proper end as a rational being, a life in which not only his contemplative powers, but also his actions and passions are directed and controlled by reason. But what exactly does it mean to say that action and passion are controlled by reason? Aristotle's answer is that formally such a state can be defined as that in which action and passion are directed in accordance with the rule of the mean, and this is what we call moral virtue.

The crucial question is, then, why should we consider the rule of the mean to be a rule of reason? Aristotle's answer is that the mean is the way in which nature and art normally achieve their goals of proper excellence, the realization of the proper end of each thing which exists by nature or is the product of art. To the extent that moral virtue has its foundations in nature, reason requires that it accord with nature. Otherwise it will not be virtue, i.e., the proper excellence of man (in this case). If the end is to fulfill our proper nature as men, then virtue will consist in the fullest completion of that nature. If the nature of all things is to find their proper completion, *qua* natural, in the mean or the middle way, then this is also the way which reason requires us to choose in order to achieve moral virtue.

For it is a rule, according to Aristotle, that a rational being acts always with an end in view, and that he must choose the means which are requisite to that end.[18]

The principle that all things that exist by nature tend toward the mean, or middle way, in order to attain their proper perfection is common to various areas of Aristotle's thought and is by no means peculiar to his ethics only. The simplest version of this point may be found in his discussions of the anatomical structure of animals. Over and over again he stresses that the middle is the best. "Eyes may be large or small, or medium sized *(mesoi)*. The medium-sized are the best."[19] "Ears may be smooth, or hairy, or intermediate; the last are the best for hearing.... They may stand well out, or not stand out at all, or intermediately. The last are a sign of the finest disposition."[20] "Now the tongue can be broad, or narrow, or intermediate; and the last is the best and gives the clearest perception."[21] The principle that nature always seeks the middle way is set forth in more complex cases as well. For example, Aristotle holds that all motions of sensation begin and end in the heart. This is as it should properly be he says, since reason requires that, if possible, there should be only a single source, "and the best of places in accordance with nature is the middle." *(euphuestatos de ton topon ho mesos).*[22] In this passage we see clearly how Aristotle ties together the way of reason with the normal way of nature, which tends always toward the mean.

He further expands and generalizes this doctrine when he propounds the view that nature always aims at the mean, always strives to overcome excess of every sort by counterbalancing it in such way that the mean is achieved. That is why the brain, which is cold, is continuous with the spinal marrow, which is hot. "Nature is always contriving to set next to anything that is excessive a reinforcement of the opposite substance, so that the one may level out *(anisaze)* the excess of the other."[23] Moreover, whatever comes into existence does so by way of the mean. In the process of generation opposites meet and are balanced, and in that way form new creatures by way of the mean. "It is thus, then, that in the first place the 'elements' are transformed; and that out of the 'elements' there come to be flesh and bones and the like—the hot becoming cold and the cold becoming hot when they have been brought to the mean *(pros to meson)*.... Similarly, it is *qua* reduced to a mean condition that the dry and the moist produce flesh and bone and the remaining compounds."[24] This principle that nature always follows the middle way is explicitly viewed by Aristotle as a rule of reason. This might be expected in view of the relationship between *logos* and *ratio*, between reason and proportion or due measure. As Aristotle puts it, "Everything needs an opposite to counterbalance it so that it may hit at the mark of proper measure and the mean (*tou metriou kai tou mesou*). The mean, and not any of the extremes alone, has being (*ousia*) and reason (*logos*)."[25]

Since "art imitates nature," it is to be expected that the product of art will also conform with the rule of the mean. For art is defined by Aristotle as "concerned with making involving a true course of reasoning."[26] Consequently, it too must follow the rule of reason that all things achieve their proper realization when they have been formed in accordance with the right measure, that is, with the mean which stands at the proper point between excess and defect. The point is expressed charmingly by Aristotle in his discussion of the proper speed for narration in ceremonial oratory. "Nowadays it is said, absurdly enough, that the narration should be rapid. Remember what the man said to the baker who asked whether he was to make the cake hard or soft: 'What, can't you make it *right*?' Just so here. We are not to make long narrations, just as we are not to make long introductions or long arguments. Here, again, rightness does not consist either in rapidity or in conciseness, but in the happy mean."[27]

The principle is carried through consistently by Aristotle when he deals with what may be thought of as the highest products of art working in conjunction with nature, namely, virtuous men and good states. In his discussions of the various aspects of life in the city-state and of the constitution of such a state, he always considers the mean or the middle way to be the model which is most desirable. The structure and order of the state, which is, like the order of the life of the individual man, the combined work of art and nature, must be in accordance with the mean if it is to achieve its own proper perfection. Men would do well as individuals also to seek no more than moderate amounts of all desirable things. For since the mean is always best, "it is manifest that the middle amount of all of the good things of fortune is the best amount to possess. For this degree of wealth is the readiest to obey reason."[28]

We have now established clearly that Aristotle's doctrine of the mean is not peculiar to moral virtue. In his system of thought it is an overarching principle that encompasses the operations of the world of nature and the world of art. One cannot properly understand his treatment of moral virtue without seeing the mean in this wider context. Given this context, we can now turn to a specific examination of the way in which the doctrine of the mean is conceived by Aristotle as the pattern in accordance with which moral virtue is brought about. As a first step, we must note that he is quite explicit about the fact that there is a natural foundation for moral virtue. We indicated this earlier in a general way when we noted that our knowledge of the proper end of man depends on the science of psychology. In introducing the discussion of moral virtue, Aristotle makes the point that it exists neither fully by nature nor fully contrary to nature but is a combination of nature and art. Virtue arises in us through habit as its efficient cause. This process of deliberate habituation, however, could not occur at all unless there were a natural medium in which it took place and to which it was adapted. "The virtues therefore are engendered in us neither by nature nor yet in violation of nature; nature gives us the capacity to receive them, and this capacity is brought to its proper completion by habit."[29]

In a later discussion in *N.E.* he expands his treatment of this topic. There he makes it clear that while all virtue is the product of a certain deliberate effort on man's part, nevertheless it has its origin and base in what is natural. For there is that which Aristotle calls natural virtue, and it is this natural virtue which is the initial source of all true moral virtue. Natural virtue is our inborn capacity for those states of character which become, when properly developed, the moral virtues. Without this inborn capacity we could not become morally virtuous. For it is that aspect alone of our nature which makes moral virtue possible. Just as cleverness is the natural base which, when developed properly, becomes practical wisdom, so, says Aristotle, is "natural virtue *(hē physikē aretē,)* to true virtue (or virtue in the strict sense). It is generally agreed that the various kinds of character are present in man by nature, for we are just, and capable of temperance, and brave, or have the other virtues from the very moment of our birth. Nevertheless, we expect to find that true goodness is something different, and that the virtues in the true sense come to belong to us in another way."[30] There are, then, two types of virtue in us; natural virtue, which has a potentiality for development in a way which is appropriate to man, and true moral virtue, which is the actualization of that natural potentiality. The model for the development of that potentiality is the model which is followed by all natures seeking their own perfection, and that is, of course, the doctrine of the mean. Aristotle's insistence that moral virtue follows the rule of the mean is, thus, in no sense arbitrary. It is, following his own principles, a rule of reason. If the proper perfection of the moral part of our nature is specified by nature in accordance with its general rule that the middle is best and most complete, then reason requires that in seeking moral virtue we must employ as our guide and criterion that pattern which is the only appropriate instrument for attaining the end which we desire.

If this is so evident, how shall we understand all those criticisms which accuse Aristotle of offering us nothing more than a formalized approval of social convention The answer, I believe, lies in the fact that the critics have ignored the natural foundations of moral virtue, despite the trouble Aristotle took to make his position clear. They have been further misled by two other considerations to which we must now turn our attention. The first is that there is, of course, a social-conventional aspect to moral virtue, as we already noted earlier. About this there can be no issue or difference of opinion. What is at issue is the question of how we should understand this dimension of' moral virtue, what its nature is, what function it serves, and what weight we should put on it. Man is not an animal who ever achieves his goal of self-development in isolation or solitude. For Aristotle, man is a being whose development, whose excellence, whose true humanity, in fact, depends on society. By himself, detached from all social relations and structures, he is barely, if at all human. Man is by nature a political animal, a creature whose nature requires the association of community with other men of which the *polis* is a model. For this reason Aristotle considers the *polis,* or more widely the forms of human society, to exist by nature. Whatever the elements of human art that account for and cause the diversity of societies, society itself is natural, and only in society can man fulfill himself. Only in society, his natural setting, can he be humanly virtuous.

Aristotle is fully aware that, despite the natural basis on which human society rests, societies differ in their customs and value patterns. To the extent that there is such difference, moral virtue will always reflect the particular characteristics of the community in which a given man lives. Yet, this is not to say that moral virtue is only *nomos,* only convention and nothing more. Moral virtue is, rather, the result of the development of natural virtue toward its proper end in the context of a particular social setting. In fact, the existence of society is dependent on man's natural capacity for moral virtue. "For it is the special property of man, in distinction from the other animals, that he alone has the perception of good and bad and right and wrong and the other moral qualities, and it is partnership (community) in these things that makes a household and a city-state.[31] Without the natural capacity for morality there could be no human community at all. Given this capacity, there emerges a community in which moral virtue is possible for men. That virtue exhibits both the fixed elements which its nature determines and the varying elements which derive from the diverse characteristics of particular societies. When the man of practical wisdom deals with moral issues, he is guided by his knowledge of the natural character of moral virtue tempered by his knowledge of the standards of the society in which he lives. He is a model precisely because he has developed to its ideal level this combination of the natural and the socially conditioned. To understand Aristotle's conception of moral virtue one must give full weight both to the natural and the social elements. Those who say that morality is merely *nomos* are mistaken. Those who say that it is merely *physis* are equally mistaken.

The second factor which has led Aristotle's critics astray is the inescapable particularity of each moral situation. If the rule of the mean is to be applied to an individual with full cognizance of his own particular level of development and with equal cognizance of the circumstances in which he finds himself and of the special characteristics of his society, how can there be anything more than just individual and private judgments? To the extent to which this is a sound criticism it would appear to apply with equal force to any moral philosophy. The problem of moving from general moral principles to particular moral judgments is hardly peculiar to Aristotle. One need only think, as a classic example, of the agonies which interpreters of Kant suffer when they try to give an account of how he moves from the categorical imperative to particular moral judgments. The troubles that

Kant's famous four examples have caused the commentators are sufficient to make the case.

Yet it seems that Aristotle is not without resources for dealing even with this aggravating problem. To begin with, let us note that he is fully aware of the problem. In the first chapter of *Book* vi of the *N.E.* he explicitly expresses his dissatisfaction with a moral rule which is general, unless one can show how to go about making it applicable to particular cases. In many places in the *N.E.* he repeats the same point, that judgments about conduct always deal with particular cases, and that it is especially difficult to apply the rule of the mean in an exact way to particular cases. Having laid down some procedural cautions for anyone who is trying to hit the mark of the mean, Aristotle recognizes that even if they are heeded, they offer no guarantee of success. One should aim at the mean, guided by these rules, "But no doubt it is a difficult thing to do, and especially in particular cases; for instance, it is not easy to define in what manner and with what people and on what sort of grounds and how long one ought to be angry."[32]

The difficulty of applying the rule to particular cases results in judgments which can never claim to be absolute or exact. They are, at best, approximations, guidelines for conduct leading to proper self-development, never demonstrated certainties. The lack of precision is compounded by the dependence on social circumstances as well as individual particularities. It is this that caused Aristotle to remark early in the *N.E.* that one should expect in ethics no more precision than the subject matter is capable of yielding. He stresses at several points that inquiry in this field can only be carried out successfully if one recognizes as a condition of the inquiry that he can expect conclusions which are far from certain or precise. "This must be agreed upon beforehand (i.e., before beginning to inquire into moral philosophy), that the whole account of matters of conduct must be given in outline and not precisely ...matters concerned with conduct and questions of what is good for us have no fixity, any more than matters of health. The general account being of this nature, the account of particular cases is yet more lacking in exactness; for they do not fall under any art or set of rules, but the agents themselves must in each case consider what is appropriate to the occasion...."[33] Nowhere does Aristotle claim that he is offering us a system which will result in precise and absolutely fixed and reliable moral judgments. In fact, he says exactly the contrary over and over again, so that it is difficult to understand why his critics think that they have discovered some secret dark failure in his treatment of these matters. Even general moral rules cannot be laid down, he believes, with precision, much less so judgments in particular cases.

Such judgments rest, according to him, with perception. The term used consistently is *aisthesis,* which refers to a kind of immediate intuitive grasp of the particulars and a capacity to make a judgment concerning them. *Aisthesis* is the only way in which we know particulars. It is one of the essential components of practical wisdom, which unlike scientific knowledge is concerned with particular cases. "Practical wisdom is concerned with the ultimate particular, which is the object not of scientific knowledge but of perception *(aisthesis)* not the perception of qualities peculiar to one sense but a perception akin to that by which we perceive that the particular figure before us is a triangle."[34] Here again Aristotle claims no certainty. On the contrary, he is fully aware of the fact that what he offers is both less than exact and less than certain. The development of the capacity of moral perception depends upon maturity and experience. There is no other source. Practical wisdom, though an intellectual virtue, is that part of the intellect that deals with opinion, not demonstrated knowledge. Its subject matter is not fixed but varies with individual and social circumstance. Yet it is capable of making judgments and offering guidance, precisely because it brings together the range of knowledge, experience, and perception out of which alone any reasonably sound moral judgment might emerge.

The problem which men face in their effort to attain moral virtue can now be readily formulated. Like all things that exist by nature, man has a fixed nature. This confers upon him certain fixed ends, the realization of which constitute his proper excellence. Unlike man, other things that exist by nature are without any independent power of choice and are moved by their internal principle of development in the direction of their proper ends only. It is outside forces or internal defects that prevent their attaining their end. The healthy acorn will become a full-grown oak if nothing prevents it from the outside. Its nature, its internal principle of development, is fixed, and it can go only one way. Things are not nearly so simple for human beings. While they have a nature, they also have the capacity to choose their own actions. They can, by their choice, either advance or frustrate their development in accordance with their nature. If man had no fixed natural disposition toward moral virtue, such virtue would not be possible for him at all. If he had only a fixed natural disposition, moral virtue would be unnecessary; for he would achieve his end automatically. However, he is in the middle. He has a nature, but he must choose to bring it to its full actuality. He must develop his own character in accordance with his true nature, if he chooses to be a man in the full and proper meaning of the term. It is at this point that he must cope with the problem of knowing exactly what kind of action to choose. Nature specifies his end in a general way. It also specifies the criterion of virtuous character in a general way, namely, by the rule of the mean. However, this is insufficient as a guide to action in particular cases, and all action is particular. The components of the social framework, individual differences, and the special circumstances must all play a role in the decision. Here no precise rule can be specified. One can only appeal, within the context of a rule of reason determined by nature, to the perception and judgment of the man of practical wisdom.

Does it follow from all this that the doctrine of the mean is, as the critics claim, no more than an appeal to social convention, or that it is utterly useless as a guide to moral action, or that it is merely an empty tautology? I believe that we have shown otherwise. The doctrine of the mean is not a matter of social convention. It is a rational rule, which derives from nature and shows us the general way to actualize a deeply fixed principle of nature. It is not a fixed or precise rule, because it involves varying social circumstances and deals with a diversity of individuals, each of whom must be considered in the context of his special personal and social conditions. Even this is not arbitrary, however, since man is by nature a social animal, and action is by nature always particular.

Perhaps the matter can be made clear and the argument persuasive by returning to the medical model. The work of the physician, seeking the physical health of his patient, deals to a large extent with what is natural. No one wants to deny the natural aspect of the body and of bodily health. However, this is only part of the story. Health has to be achieved for each individual patient in the light of his special circumstances and conditions, and in the light of his particular constitution and its special possibilities. No diagnosis is foolproof. It can only claim to be probable, and it is never absolutely exact and absolutely certain. Similarly, no prescription is ever absolutely precise, nor is its anticipated effectiveness more than probable. All this is the case, just because medicine must take account of the particular. As Aristotle never tires of saying, a proper diet for Milo may be all wrong for the local chess champion. Despite its inexactness and uncertainty, we do not ordinarily condemn all medical practice as pointless. On the contrary, we see in it the very best we can achieve, considering the built-in limitations of the subject matter. Even if we doubt the soundness of a particular doctor's diagnosis, or if we fail to be helped by his prescriptions, we do not conclude that the practice of medicine is a fraud. We do know what good health is, and we do recognize that, with limitations, there are men of special knowledge and experience who can help us achieve that desirable goal. Similarly, Aristotle argues, we do know what a virtuous character is, for that is specified by our nature. Physicians of the soul may be harder to find than physicians of the body. It may also be more difficult for the former to lay out and justify their general principles and their rules of practice, to say nothing of their judgments in individual cases. It is our contention, nevertheless, that we have explained why Aristotle believes that this difficult task is not impossible and that his critics have misunderstood him.

II

As we reflect on the relationship of Maimonides' doctrine of the mean to Aristotle's, we are confronted by puzzles which demand resolution. Of all the areas concerning which Maimonides wrote, the ordering of human behavior should have presented him with the fewest problems. As an expositor of Jewish tradition and as a master of the law, he had a complete system of behavioral rules and norms ready-made for him in the *halakhah*. It would seem, then, that there should have been no need to seek beyond the *halakhah* itself for the principles and the specific patterns of virtue and the good life, all the more since Maimonides himself denied that there is any independent rational ground for morality. He rejected all claims that there is a natural moral law, holding rather that morality derives either from social convention or divine command. It is obvious that for Judaism the latter source only can be decisive. Why, then, was it necessary for Maimonides to appeal to the doctrine of the mean at all? The elaborate and detailed principles and directions for the life of the Jew which he codified in his *Mishneh Torah* would seem to be sufficient to answer every need for guidance toward the virtuous life.

Furthermore, with respect to this subject matter in particular, an appeal to non-Jewish sources would seem to be singularly inappropriate. It might be argued plausibly that to the extent that his Jewish theology required principles of natural science or metaphysics as a foundation, these might appropriately have been drawn from non-Jewish sources, since the biblical and rabbinic literatures are relatively poor in these areas. This is surely not the case with regard to the area of human conduct. How strange, then, that in a treatise devoted to setting forth the principles and the end of the good life, Maimonides begins by telling us explicitly that he drew his materials from non-Jewish as well as Jewish sources. In his Foreword to *Shemonah Peraqim* he makes a special point of denying that the work contains any original ideas. All that is of consequence in the treatise has been gleaned, says Maimonides, "from the words of the wise occurring in the *Midrashim,* in the Talmud, and in other of their works, as well as from the words of the philosophers, ancient and recent, and also from the works of various authors." He immediately goes on to justify this procedure by invoking the principle that "one should accept the truth from whatever source it proceeds."[36]

The force of this open appeal to non-Jewish sources is even greater when we remember that these statements are contained in the introduction to at commentary on *'Avoth,* a treatise that takes great pains to establish its legitimacy (in its opening words) by associating itself with the tradition whose source is in the Torah which "Moses received at Sinai."[37] Our analysis of Maimonides' version of the doctrine of the mean will seek to resolve some of these puzzles. Our primary concern is to understand the doctrine precisely, to see it in relationship to the Aristotelian doctrine, and to determine how it fits into the Jewish tradition.

With respect to the general nature of ethical inquiry, Maimonides holds views which are similar to those of Aristotle. Like Aristotle, he makes clear at the very outset that he is concerned above all with the truly good life for man and that his interest in individual actions and states of character is primarily because they are instrumental to the realization of the ultimate good. In his foreword to *Shemonah Peraqim* he makes a point of explaining that the treatise on which he is commenting contains a rule of life which "leads to great perfection and true happiness." In fact, one who puts into practice the teachings of *'Avoth* can hope to be led even to prophecy. This ultimate human felicity comes to one who attains the knowledge of God "as far as it is possible for man to know Him" and the truly good life is that in which all of man's effort, thought and activity are directed toward the realization of that goal.[38] The same ideal is developed in *H. De'oth,* iii, and of course it constitutes a central theme which reaches its climax in the final chapters of the *Guide of the Perplexed.*

Maimonides also follows Aristotle in his view that the ultimate aim, the contemplative life, presupposes the achievement of moral virtue.

Man is so constituted that he can only devote himself to the highest intellectual activity if he has first achieved that personal and social discipline which is included under the heading of moral virtue. The crucial question then emerges, namely, what specifically is the character and shape of the morally virtuous life. Here, too, in his initial approach Maimonides remains faithful to the Aristotelian pattern. His primary concern, like that of Aristotle, is with states of character, not with individual acts. Thus, in *Shemonah Peraqim* he introduces his discussion of the rule of the mean by distinguishing between good acts and good states of character. "Good deeds are such as are equibalanced, maintaining the mean between two equally bad extremes.... Virtues are psychic conditions and dispositions *(tekhunoth nafshiyyoth we-qinyanim)* which are midway between two reprehensible extremes...."[39] The very title of the section of the *Mishneh Torah* which deals with the mean is *Deᶜoth,* and it is beyond any question that the term is used to refer to states of character. This is obvious enough from the way the term is used in its context and is confirmed in a passage in which Maimonides explicitly distinguishes *deᶜoth,* as states of character, from particular actions. In *H. Teshuvah,* vii, 3, Maimonides tells us that just as one must repent for those sins which involve a particular action, such as robbery or theft, so is one obligated "to search out his evil *deᶜoth* and repent of them, i.e., from such states as anger, etc."

Aristotle had already defined virtue as a state of character, or, according to another translation, "a settled disposition of the mind" which observes the mean.[40] Maimonides follows him here, as he does with respect to his view that our actions follow from the fixed states of our character, so that what must concern us most is the development of the appropriate states of character, since that is the best assurance that our acts will also be virtuous. Finally, in what appears to be a thoroughly Aristotelian fashion, Maimonides also defines the good character as one which is determined by the mean and avoids the extremes. Given these general similarities, we must now ask just exactly what the main elements are of Maimonides' doctrine of the mean and how they compare with Aristotle's views as we set them forth above.

The most fundamental distinction of all is in the ground on which the mean rests. It is striking that both in *Shemonah Peraqim* and in the *Mishneh Torah* Maimonides introduces the rule of the mean without any discussion as to its origins or justification. He treats it rather as an established truth to which one need only refer but which does not require any evidence to support it. In both works he proceeds as if it were an established fact that good deeds and good states of character follow the mean between extremes. In the *Mishneh Torah* he opens the discussion with some empirical observations about the diversity of states of character that are to be found among men and then informs us that "the two extremes which are at the farthest distance from each other with respect to each state of character are not the good way ...while the right way is the middle way."[41] Not only does he offer no defense of this claim, but he goes on to say that because it is the case that the mean is the right way, "therefore the early sages *(hakhamim ha-rishonim)* commanded that man should always make an estimate of his various states of character and direct them toward the middle way." If we accept the view of most commentators, that the reference is to the sages of Israel, a view which seems plausible enough in this context, then we have the remarkable situation that Maimonides appears to be telling us that the principle that the middle way is good is known as an independent truth and that because it is known to be true the Jewish religious authorities accepted it as their rule of conduct and character development. So far he would seem to be doing exactly what he says in his introduction to *Shemonah Peraqim,* namely, relying on established knowledge without regard to its source.

There is evidence to support the view that Maimonides was convinced that the rule of the mean was a well-established basic principle of explanation in the sciences and in philosophy. In the *Guide of the Perplexed he* was explicit about this point. In thoroughly Aristotelian fashion, he strongly supports the view that the order of nature is such that all things achieve their proper excellence when they reach the mean which suffers from neither excess nor deficiency. The highest praise that he can pay to the divine creation of the world is that it has been formed in accordance with the mean, from which it follows that in the created world there can be no change in the fixed order of nature. "The thing that is changed, is changed because of a deficiency in it that should be made good or because of some excess that is not needed and should be got rid of. Now the works of the Deity are most perfect, and with regard to them there is no possibility of an excess or a deficiency. Accordingly, they are of necessity permanently established as they are, for there is no possibility of something calling for a change in them.... *'The Rock, his work is perfect'* ...means that all his works ...are most perfect, that no deficiency at all is commingled with them, that there is no superfluity in them and nothing that is not needed."[42]

Viewing the doctrine of the mean as a scientific principle, Maimonides treats it as fully established and needing no further evidence. He is explicit about the general rule that whatever is scientifically known, whatever is demonstrated, must command our assent. For such matters we do not need to look for confirmation in the official Jewish literature, nor should we be uneasy if on such matters the views of the sages of Israel are contradicted by our contemporary knowledge. Here the sages spoke not with the authority of the prophetic tradition but only as students of physics or metaphysics who were bound by the limits of their own knowledge and the general state of knowledge at their time." It seems clear enough that this is one of the points that Maimonides had in mind when he informed his readers in the foreword to *Shemonah Peraqim* that he would seek the truth from whatever source it could be found. Even with respect to the standards and rules of virtuous behavior, good character, and the good life for the faithful Jew, we need certain general principles of explanation, a general theoretical framework, in order to give a philosophical account of the subject. We also need a sound psychology on which to base our understanding of human character and its development. Without these theoretical foundations, our account of moral virtue, even of specifically Jewish moral virtue, will be incomplete and will lack an essential dimension. Moreover, no practical guidance toward the achievement of good character and the performance of good acts is possible, unless we first have sound theoretical understanding of human nature and of the nature of the good in general. These are universal truths, in no way peculiar to the Jewish religious community, and for them we may, nay we must turn to the most reliable scientific authority that we can find. This is the point of Maimonides' elaborate announcement that he seeks guidance wherever he can find it.

So far we might say without hesitation that Maimonides has followed Aristotle or the Aristotelian tradition faithfully. However, when we move away from the general theoretical foundations to his specific way of understanding and applying the doctrine of the mean the differences emerge sharply and clearly. Perhaps the most significant single difference is that while Aristotle construes moral virtue as a case of art imitating nature, Maimonides has as his standard the imitation of God. The first of the eleven *miswoth* set forth in *H. De͑oth* is *le-hiddaimoth bi-derakhaw,* and it is to this commandment of *imitatio Dei* that the first five of the seven chapters of *H. De͑oth* are devoted. The imitation of nature was for Aristotle nothing more than a general indication that the good life for man, like the pattern of all natural excellence, should be one of perfect measure. Nature does not itself give us specific norms or standards of behavior, nor does it tell us what a virtuous character is, apart from its general principle that the middle way is the best. Thus, given the imitation of nature as the only ideal, Aristotle has no choice but to fill out the specific details of the good life for man by appealing to the norms of society and to the judgment of the man of practical wisdom. Nature gives us only the form, i.e., the mean but not the content. It does not, and cannot teach us what the rule of the mean is in concrete cases of human action or human character development.

In striking contrast, Maimonides works here fully inside the Jewish tradition. He readily adopts the outer form of the mean as his theoretical base and principle of explanation, but the specific contents of the good life are defined not by way of nature but by way of the imitation of God. Now, viewed as metaphysically ultimate, Maimonides' God is not truly knowable, except by way of negative attributes; however, Maimonides does permit us knowledge of God through the attributes of action. We can know Him indirectly through his works in the world, and in this way we can speak meaningfully of *imitatio Dei* as the human ideal. This is why Maimonides is so careful to formulate the commandment as *le-hiddamoth bi-derakhaw*, since strictly speaking we can imitate his ways only, but not his nature. The God who is represented as Creator, who continues in some manner to make his presence felt in history as well as in nature, is a being whom man can meaningfully hold before himself as an ideal to follow.

As in the case of Aristotle's prescription for the imitation of nature, the general rule is insufficient as a guide to man. It must be made specific and concrete. For Maimonides this is achieved simply enough. The commandments of the Torah are, in fact, according to his view, the specification of ideal behavior in accordance with the rule of the mean, and this is what is meant when we are told to imitate the ways of God. The structure of his argument is clear and unambiguous, though it has often been ignored or misunderstood. First he gives us the theoretical principle which is generally known and acknowledged. Good action and good states of character are those which follow the middle way. So far we are in accord with all men who follow the way of scientific knowledge. Next we face the question of what it means specifically to act in accordance with the mean, and here Maimonides answers, unlike Aristotle (for whom such an answer would have been meaningless), that we should imitate God. Finally, he faces the question of what divine behavior is like, so that we can have a concrete model for imitation; and he answers that it is the rule of the Torah that is the divine paradigm and therefore also the concretization of the middle way. Maimonides is absolutely consistent in his adherence to this principle that the rule of the Torah is in actual fact the rule of the mean, that is, whatever the Torah commands is the middle way. There is no external standard which measures the commandments in order to determine whether they accord with the mean. This is impossible, precisely because the only standard we have is that given by the commandments. In *Shemonah Peraqim* he writes that "The Law did not lay down its prohibitions, or enjoin its commandments, except for just this purpose, namely, that by its disciplinary effects we may persistently maintain the proper distance from either extreme.[44] He goes on to stress that since "*the Law of the Lord is perfect*", (*Ps.* 19:9) it is its injunctions and prohibitions alone that give us the proper standard. To impose upon ourselves ascetic practices or disciplines of self-denial that go beyond what the Torah commands is vice and not virtue.

The same principle is set forth in *H. De^coth*[45] and receives full expression in the *Guide,* where he argues that the Mosaic Law is absolutely perfect, the ideal and exact embodiment of true measure, the middle way in all regards. Thus, every law which deviates from it suffers from the fact that it moves away from the mean toward one of the extremes. "For when a thing is as perfect as it is possible to be within its species, it is impossible that within that species there should be found another thing that does not fall short of that perfection either because of excess or deficiency.... Things are similar with regard to this Law, as is clear from its equibalance. For it says: '*Just statutes and judgments*' (*Deut.* 4:8); now you know that the meaning of 'just' is equibalanced. For these are manners of worship in which there is no burden and excess ...nor a deficiency.... When we shall speak in this treatise about the reasons accounting for the commandments, their equibalance and wisdom will be made clear to you insofar as this is necessary. For this reason it is said with reference to them: '*The Law of the Lord is perfect*'."[46] For the Aristotelian reliance on *nomos* as interpreted and applied by the *phronimos,* Maimonides has substituted the law of the Torah. The divine origin of this Law guarantees its perfection as a standard of behavior. All others fall short. Only the Torah "is called by us divine Law, whereas the other political regimens—such as the *nomoi* of the Greeks and the ravings of the Sabians and of others are due, as I have explained several times, to the action of groups of rulers who were not prophets."[47] The Torah alone, according to Maimonides, can give us the true standard of the mean.

There is, however, more to be considered. We recall that the main interest in ethics is the development of virtuous states of character, not merely the performance of virtuous actions. The latter are derived from the former and are significant especially as outer evidences of a stable moral character. The passages we cited make the Torah the standard of the mean in action, but it is obvious that Maimonides must also provide for the Torah as the standard of the mean with respect to states of character. This is, in fact, precisely what he does in *H. De͑oth*. The ideal of *imitatio Dei* is concerned primarily with states of character, and these are dispositions which are described as generally in accordance with the middle way. "We are commanded to follow these middle ways which are the paths that are good and right, as is written, *'And you shall walk in His ways.'* (*Deut.* 28:9). Thus have they taught with respect to this *miswah:* Just as He is called *hannun* (gracious), so shall you be *hannun;* just as He is called *rahum* (merciful), so shall you be *rahum*."[48]

In the case of states of character Maimonides does not simply make a rule that the Torah standard specifies the mean in every case, but rather that whatever standard the Torah sets is the standard that we are obligated to use as our norm, even in those cases where it clearly deviates from the mean toward one of the extremes. Thus, in the very discussion in which he takes the mean as the ideal Torah model of virtuous states of character, Maimonides proceeds to rule that "there are certain states of character with respect to which it is forbidden for a man to pursue the middle way."[49] Pride and anger are dispositions which should be avoided completely, as we have been specifically commanded. Aristotle also spoke of actions and passions for which the mean is an inappropriate rule. They are those, as he puts it, whose very names imply evil.[50] The problems which this passage has posed for the commentators are familiar, and this is not the place to review them. What is significant for our purposes is the fact that here again Maimonides has a different ground on which he rests his cases of deviation from the mean. Not the name itself, or some other self-evident ground, but the commandments of the Torah determine which are the cases in which we are required to abandon the mean. We know that there can be no proper moderation with respect to pride and anger, simply because we are so taught by various biblical verses and the explicit rulings of the rabbis.

With this background we can also appreciate the difference between the medical analogy which is used by Maimonides and that of Aristotle. On the surface both seem very similar, yet the foundations on which they

Two. The Doctrine of the Mean in Aristotle and Maimonides...

rest differ very significantly. In his various ethical writings Maimonides, like Aristotle, recommends that those who are in need of moral guidance seek out physicians of the soul. Moral decay is viewed by him as a sickness of the soul, and those who treat it do so on the analogy of the therapy of the physicians of the sick body. So far all is similar to Aristotle. Yet here, too, we find very important differences that result from the basically distinct foundations on which the doctrine of the mean rests in each case.[51]

Both Aristotle and Maimonides require the physician of the soul to be one who knows how to take account of individual circumstances and to advise in accordance with those circumstances. Both require their physicians of the soul to have a sound understanding of human psychology, otherwise they will be incompetent to give guidance. Both agree on the practical rule that the morally sick soul is to be treated by being directed toward the extreme opposite of his present state; and both agree that the aim should be to arrive at a stable state of character determined by the mean. Both consider the true physician of the soul to be a wise man. For Aristotle, he is the *phronimos,* the man of practical wisdom, and for Maimonides he is the *hakham,* the model Jewish scholar-teacher-man of piety. He advises that the proper way for sick souls to be healed is to "go to the *hakhamim,* who are the healers of souls, and they will cure the illness by teaching them to achieve the proper states of character, thereby bringing them back to the virtuous way."[52] Despite all these similarities, the differences are of crucial importance. While Aristotle's *phronimos* has only shifting conventional standards to guide him, Maimonides' *hakham has* the fixed discipline of the Torah as his standard. Of course, he must take account of the special condition of each individual and must tailor his particular advice to fit the special needs and circumstances in which he finds himself. Nevertheless, he is bound not by a conventional *nomos* but by a fixed law, by commandments, and by principles which are held to be divine and thus unchanging. The divine-human ideal is set, and to be virtuous a man must direct himself to that ideal. Maimonides is fully aware of the variations and diversity of human temperament and of social conditions. Nevertheless, his physician of the soul carries out his function by adhering rigorously to the fixed Law. He only varies his advice for each individual in order to move that individual closer to the one common ideal. Aristotle's mean, even when viewed as a principle of nature, always reflects something of the attitudes and values of the particular society in which it is invoked as the principle of moral virtue. Maimonides' mean permits no such variation, because it is controlled by the ideal of *imitatio Dei*, and this, in turn, is concretized and fixed in the commandments and principles of the Torah. It is revealing that this point, which is evident enough in the earlier works, comes out with striking force and clarity in the *Guide*. Here, where he deals with the law as a primary force for the ordering of society, Maimonides shows openly his deviation from the Aristotelian norm. He first argues that men differ from each other in their temperaments and moral habits far more than any other living creatures, yet man, being by nature a political animal, must live in society. He then goes on: "Now as the nature of the human species requires that there be those differences among the individuals belonging to it and as in addition society is a necessity for this nature, it is by no means possible that this society should be perfected except and this is necessarily so through a ruler who gauges the actions of the individuals, perfecting that which is deficient and reducing that which is excessive, and who prescribes actions and moral habits that all of them must always practice in the same way, so that the natural diversity is hidden through the multiple points of conventional accord and so that the community becomes well ordered."[53] With this background he subsequently goes on to distinguish the application of the Law from the model of medical treatment, The Law is, he says, a divine thing, a perfect ideal which is not necessarily actualized in the life of each individual. He argues, therefore, against Aristotle, that "in view of this consideration, it also will not be possible that the laws be dependent on changes in the circumstances of the individuals and of the times, *as in the case with regard to medical treatment*, which is particularized for every individual in conformity with his present temperament. On the contrary, governance of the Law ought to be absolute and universal, including everyone, even if it is suitable only for certain individuals and not suitable for others; for if it were to be made to fit individuals, the whole world would be corrupted 'and you would make out of it something that varies' (*we-nathatta devarekha le-shi-urin*)."[54]

With all the seeming similarities between Aristotle's and Maimonides' doctrine of the mean, and with the especially striking similarity between the medical analogies of both thinkers, there is at the core a most fundamental difference. On these matters, Maimonides is finally controlled by the Jewish tradition, rather than by the principles of Greek philosophy. *Nomos* has about it an inescapable element of changing convention, while Torah has an equally inescapable element of fixity and permanence. For this reason Maimonides holds that a Jewish thinker may freely adopt general theoretical structures and principles of explanation which come to him from the world of Greek thought, if he finds them to be scientifically sound and useful in setting the foundations for his own doctrine. If, however, he is to remain loyal to his religious community, then he cannot substitute for the permanence of the Law and its divine-human ideal the shifting conventions of any society. (This is certainly true for Jewish thinkers of the Middle Ages, although it might well be challenged by our contemporaries.) Whatever the extent of Maimonides' possible deviation from orthodox Jewish theological norms, when he dealt with the world of practice, with the ordering of individual human life, and with the life of society, he was consistently faithful to Jewish law. At this point he is no longer an Aristotelian, but a Jew who stands fully inside the tradition.

The depth of this difference between Maimonides and Aristotle is underscored by the fact that even with respect to their understanding of psychology and the nature of man they diverge very significantly. For Aristotle, those faculties of the soul which man shares with other animals are essentially the same in man as in animals. Speaking of the nutritive faculty, Aristotle says that "The excellence of this faculty ...appears to be common to all animate things and not peculiar to man." For this reason he concludes that in his discussion he "may omit from consideration the nutritive part of the soul, since it exhibits no specifically human excellence."[55] Maimonides categorically opposes this view. In his discussion of the faculties of the soul he makes a special point of emphasizing the fact that the human faculties, even when they carry the same name and exercise the same functions as the parallel animal faculties, are absolutely distinct and essentially different. As he puts it, "Our words concern themselves only with the human soul; for the nutritive faculty by which man is nourished is not the same, for instance, as that of the ass or the horse.... Although we apply the same term *nutrition* to all of them indiscriminately, nevertheless, its signification is by no means the same. In the same way, the term *sensation* is used homonymously for man and beast.... Mark this point well, for it is very important, as many so-called philosophers have fallen into error regarding it...."[56] Little attention has been paid to this passage, but it seems to be of great importance. Maimonides is here saying explicitly that the standard psychology deriving from Aristotle (with whatever variations) is in error on a basic point. Man is not simply an animal, in all respects, with the addition of the faculty of reason. Man is absolutely distinct from animals, even with regard to those faculties that constitute what we usually call his animal nature. It is not our task here to take up the historical question of which "so-called philosophers" he had in mind.[57] We may wonder whether it was possible that Maimonides, with all his regard for Aristotle, should have included him among the "so-called philosophers."[58] However troubling it may be for Maimonides to have included Aristotle in this unflattering category of thinkers, it is certainly clear that he contradicts his great Greek predecessor directly and rejects his views. In the last analysis, it could not be otherwise; for if man is conceived as created in the image of God, he can no longer be understood as one more animal living in the order of nature. This affects the moral ideal and the medical analogy directly. In all respects man is now viewed as different from animals, and his ideal end, i.e., *imitatio Dei,* encompasses not only his reason, but all of his peculiarly human faculties. With such an understanding of man, the physician of the soul must be controlled by the divine norms. He is not training man on the analogy of training a dog or a horse. He is rather directing a human soul, in its totality, toward the divine ideal.

As a result of this difference we can understand why it is that Maimonides is so ready to deviate from the ideal of the middle way, while Aristotle holds to it firmly. Both acknowledge that moral virtue is only a propaedeutic to intellectual virtue and thus to the life of ultimate felicity. For Aristotle, however, the life of moral virtue, as he describes it in the *Nicomachaean Ethics,* is, with minor exceptions, a life in accordance with the mean. Maimonides, on the other hand, regularly invokes the rule of the mean but just as regularly deviates from it. In the foreword to his *Shemonah Peraqim* he reminds us that the treatise to which this is a commentary is concerned with *hasiduth,* with the life of special saintliness, and that such saintliness "paves the way to prophecy." If, therefore, one practices the teachings of *'Avoth,* one may hope to acquire prophecy. In short, the ultimate felicity is open to all who practice saintliness, and this is the subject under discussion in the treatise before us. Now saintliness is not simply a life in accordance with the mean but rather a deviation towards one of the extremes. Maimonides both recommends and defends this deviation at various points in those of his writings that deal with the good life in general and even in those that deal specifically with the mean. What is especially significant, however, is the fact that he sets forth an ideal which is, in principle, no longer in any way similar to the balanced life of the Aristotelian middle way. In *Shemonah Peraqim, in H. De^coth,* and in the *Guide* he repeats essentially the same line, namely, that all of a man's thought and activity, all of his striving, and all of his concern must be directed exclusively to the one single goal of the knowledge of God and fellowship with Him. It is especially revealing that Maimonides sets out this ideal immediately after having discussed the doctrine of the mean, as if to make clear that the mean is not the true ideal at all. He considers it man's proper duty to devote himself to one single goal only, namely, "the attainment of the knowledge of God as far as it is possible for man to know Him. Consequently one must so adjust all his actions, his whole conduct, and even his very words, that they lead to this goal.... So, his only design in eating, drinking, cohabiting, sleeping, waking, moving about, and resting should be ... all to the end that man may reach the highest goal in his endeavors."[59]

It may well be that, as some scholars hold, Maimonides is here betraying Neo-Platonic influences on his thought. Our interest is not in tracing out the possible sources and lines of influence but in recognizing how far Maimonides has moved from the Aristotelian line. He has, in effect, rejected the mean as a guiding principle and criterion of the good life and has substituted for it a single controlling ideal; the good is that which leads to true knowledge and continuing contemplation of the divine being. Though Aristotle agrees, he does not counsel, as does Maimonides, that in ordering his life man should have this one concern only, that every activity, every choice, every state of character should be such as will move him effectively toward the ideal end. Maimonides holds that the mean may be a good general rule for this purpose, but it is not in and of itself the controlling consideration. In both *Shemonah Peraqim and H. De^{c}oth,* Maimonides cites in this connection the rule of the sages, "Let all your deeds be done for the sake of God," and the verse which teaches, "*In all thy ways know Him."* This, rather than the mean, is decisive. Unlike Aristotle, Maimonides wants this extreme to be the practical rule for all men.

We can now see that the extreme opinions on both sides of the question with which we have been dealing are equally mistaken. There are both Aristotelian and non-Aristotelian aspects to Maimonides' treatment of the doctrine of the mean. It is impossible to support the view that there is nothing whatsoever of Aristotle in him, since it is clear that the general form of his doctrine of the mean and much of his psychology are Aristotelian. It is just as impossible to defend the view that there is in Maimonides' version nothing more than a repetition of the Aristotelian teachings. As we have seen, there are deep and important differences. As heir, interpreter, and creative contributor to two traditions, Maimonides could not have been a pure Aristotelian in these matters. If Greek philosophy lived in him, and it did, the Jewish tradition and its Law never departed from the center of his concerns. In dealing with the nature of man, the ideal of human existence and the practical patterns by which human life should be ordered, Maimonides learned much from Aristotle but even more from the Torah.

NOTES

[1] Henry Malter, "Shem Tob ben Joseph Palquera," *JQR,* N.S., 1 (1910 11), p. 160. See his extended footnote on pp. 160 161. See also Henry Malter, *Saadia Gaon: His Life and Works,* (New York, 1926), p. 257.

[2] Joseph I. Gorfinkle (ed.), *The Eight Chapters of Maimonides on Ethics* (New York, 1966, Reprint of 1912 edition), p. 54.

[3] Harry S. Lewis, "The 'Golden Mean' in Judaism," *Jewish Studies in Memory of Israel Abrahams,* (New York, 1927), p. 283.

[4] David Rosin, *Die Ethik des Maimonides,* (Breslau, 1876), p. 79. Throughout the book, and particularly in his discussion of the mean, Rosin repeatedly cites the Aristotelian sources of Maimonides' doctrines. For similar views with respect to the mean see M. Wolff, *Musa Maimunis Acht Capitel,* (Leiden, 1903) pp. xiiif.

[5] Yaʿakov Mosheh Harlap, *Mey Marom: Mi-Saiviv li-Shemonah Peraqim le-ha-Rambam,* (Jerusalem, 5705), pp. 85-86. An even stronger statement is made by Shem Tov ben Abraham ibn Ga'on in his *Migdal ʿOz.* Commenting on the passage in *H. Dëoth,* i, 4, in which Maimonides attributes the doctrine of the mean to the *hakhamim ha-rishonim* (presumably, though not necessarily the earher rabbinic authorities), the *Migdal ʿOz* makes the following observation: "All the moralists (*hakhmey ha-Musar*) have taught this principle, which they stole from the teachings of our sages (*genuvah hi 'ittam me-asher dareshu z"l*). Additional sources which make similar extreme attempts to find the doctrine of the mean in Jewish literature are cited in S. Rawidowicz, *"Sefer ha-Petihah le-Mishneh Torah",* in his *ʿIyyunim be-mahasheveth yisra'el,* p. 429, n. II 3. (Reprinted from *Metsudah,* 7 (1954). See also M. D. Rabinowitch (ed.), *Shemonah Peraqim le-ha-rambam* (Jerusalem, 1968), pp. 20-21, n. 9, and especially the quotation there from Holzberg.

[6] Hermann Cohen, "Charakteristik der Ethik Maimunis," *Moses ben Maimon,* i, (Leipzig, 1908), p. 109. This important study by Cohen (reprinted in his *Jüdishe Shriften,* iii) has as one of its main purposes the development of evidence that Maimonides was not an Aristotelian. In striking contrast is the view of Husik, who asserts without any qualification that in his ethics "Maimonides is an Aristotelian, and he endeavors to harmonize the intellectualism and theorism of the Stagirite with the diametrically opposed ethics and religion of the Hebrew Bible. And he is apparently unaware of the yawning gulf extending between them.... It is so absolutely clear and evident that one wonders how so clear-sighted a thinker like Maimonides could have been misled by the authority of Aristotle and the intellectual atmosphere of the days to imagine otherwise." Isaac Husik, *A History of Mediaeval Jewish Philosophy,* (Philadelphia, 1944), p. 300.

[7] Cohen, *op. cit.,* p. 85.

[8] *Ibid.,* especially pp. 113-115.

[9] Theodor Gomperz, *Greek Thinkers,* (London, 1929), iv, p. 274,

[10] "Aristotle's Doctrine of Justice," Walsh and Shapiro, *Aristotle's Ethics,* (Belmont, California, 1967), p. 109.

[11] *Metaphysical Principles of Virtue,* (Indianapolis, 1968), p. 95, n. 10.

[12] *Nicomachaean Ethics* (hereafter N.E.), 1107a 1.

[13] *N.E.,* 1094b 15 17.

[14] *N.E.,* 1173a 1f.

[15] Werner Jaeger, "Aristotle's Use of Medicine as a Model of Method in his Ethics," *Journal of Hellenic Studies,* 77 (1952), p. 57.

[16] *De Vet. Med.* ix.
[17] *N.E.*, 1094a 16.
[18] Cf., *N.E.* vi, 1139a 32f.
[19] *Historia Animalium* i, 492a 7f.
[20] *Ibid.*, 492a 33f.
[21] *Ibid.*, 492b 31f.
[22] *Part. Animalium*, iii, 666a 15.
[23] *Ibid.* ii, 652a 31f.
[24] *De Gen. et Corr. ii*, 334b 25 30.
[25] *Part. Animalium*, ii, 652b 17 20.
[26] *N. E.*, vi, 1140a 20.
[27] *Rhet.* iii, 1416b 30ff.
[28] *Pol.* iv, 1295b 3-7.
[29] *N.E.* ii, 1103a 24.
[30] *N.E.* vi, 1144b 1f.
[31] *Pol.* i, 1253a 16-19.
[32] *N.E.* ii, 1109b 13f.
[33] *N.E. i* i, 1104a 1f.
[34] *N.E.* vi, 1142a 25f.
[35] For an extended discussion of this point see, M. Fox, "Maimonides and Aquinas on Natural Law," *Diney, Yisra'el*, iii, 1972; Reprinted in J. 1. Dienstag (ed.), *Maimonides and Aquinas*, (New York, 1975).
[36] Joseph I. Gorfinkle (ed.), *The Eight Chapters (see supra*, p. 118, n. 2), pp. 35-36.
[37] For the attitudes of traditional commentators who see this first mishnah as an attempt to underscore the independence of Jewish ethics from all external sources, see the comments of Bertinoro and *Tosefoth Yom Tov, ad loc.*
[38] *Shemonah Peraqim*, v.
[39] *Ibid.*, iv, Gorfinkle, pp. 54 55.
[40] *N.E.*, ii, 6, 1106b 36f.
[41] *H. De'oth*, i, 3, 4.
[42] *Guide of the Perplexed*, II, 28; ed. Pines, pp. 335-336.
[43] For explicit comments on this point see *Guide*, II, 8 and III, 14; *Letter on Astrology*, ed. A. Marx, *HUCA* iii (1926), p. 356 and *Qobes teshuvoth ha-rambam* (Leipzig, 1859), ii, f. 26a.
[44] Gorfinkle, p. 64.
[45] iii, 1.
[46] *Guide*, II, 39, ed. Pines, p. 380.
[47] *Ibid.*, p. 381.
[48] *H. De'oth* i, 5, 6. (From the manuscripts it seems clear that the end of i, 5, as we have cited it here from the printed versions, should really be the beginning of i, 6).
[49] *Ibid.*, ii, 3.
[50] *N.E.*, ii, 6, 1107a 9f.
[51] The main sources for the moral-medical analogy in Maimonides are: *Shemonah Peraqim*, i, ed. Gorfinkle, p. 38, iii, iv, Gorfinkle, pp. 62f.; *H. De'oth*, especially ii; *Guide*, III, 34.
[52] *H. De'oth, ii*, 1.
[53] *Guide* II, 40; ed. Pines, p. 382.
[54] *Guide* III, 34; ed. Pines, pp. 534 535 (my italics).
[55] *N.E.*, i, 13,1102b 2-12.

[56] *Shemonah Peraqim,* i; ed. Gorfinkle, pp. 39 40.
[57] An inadequate comment on this question is made by D. Rosin in *Die Ethik des Maimonides,* (Breslau, 1876), p. 48, n. 1.
[58] The usual printed Hebrew texts read *harbeh min ha-Pilosofim,* but there is no doubt, as is evident from the Arabic text, that the reading should be *mithpalsefim.* On this point, see the editions of Gorfinkle and Kafih.
[59] *Shemonah Peraqim,* v, ed. Gorfinkle, p. 69ff; for almost identical language see *H. Deʿoth* iii, 2, 3; the very same idea is set forth elaborately in the *Guide,* III, 51.

3

A HISTORY OF THE DOCTRINE OF THE MEAN IN EARLY GREEK THOUGHT: FROM HOMER THROUGH PLATO

Aristotle's doctrine that virtue lies in a mean between the extreme vices of excess and defect dominated western moral philosophy for many centuries. Even during the middle ages such eminent philosophers as Maimonides and Aquinas accepted the doctrine and gave it a place of central importance in the systematic structure of their own ethical theories.[1] Yet this same doctrine has been subjected to sharp and bitter criticisms by equally eminent philosophers. Perhaps the most famous attack was made by Kant who believed that he had shown conclusively the uselessness of Aristotle's doctrine of the mean. Kant argued that the doctrine is a tautology. It leads, in his opinion, to the absurd conclusion that we ought not be too virtuous, which makes as much sense as saying that a circle should not be too round or a straight line too straight.[2] More recently Edward Von Hartmann attacked the doctrine, saying that it barely scratches the outer surface of morality and that it results in an "apotheosis of mediocrity." He adds, with irritation, that "It is difficult to grasp how a Greek thinker with the acumen and farsightedness of an Aristotle could have allowed his ethical theory ... to be limited by such a trivially restricted horizon."[3] This claim that the Aristotelian mean makes virtue identical with mediocrity is a common complaint among Aristotle's critics.

Other writers have accused Aristotle of arguing in a circle or merely propounding as the most basic moral rule the principle that we should always be bound by moral convention. The doctrine of the mean is held by them to be an empty formal principle which depends always on social convention for its identification of the middle way and the extremes. One must know the extremes to determine the mean and the mean to determine the extremes.

"In order to determine that an action is a virtue or a vice one must already have developed fixed moral principles. This involves us in a circle."[4] The fixed moral principles are not themselves derived from the mean, but serve instead to establish the mean. The only source for these principles is, according to this interpretation of Aristotle, the prudent man, the man of practical wisdom, and he turns out to be the man who has achieved a mastery of the conventional rules, values and expectations of his society. Aristotle, on this view, fails to show that the prudent man employs any principle other than moral convention. Should there be moral differences among societies Aristotle has given us no way to resolve them, nor is it ever possible on his grounds to show that given social conventions are in moral error. Such is the direction of a second major line of criticism of Aristotle's doctrine of the mean.[5] The net effect of these criticisms is to deny both Aristotle's claim that ethical decision consists in choosing the middle way between the extremes of excess and defect, and his belief that this is a rational doctrine.

The present study intends to set the foundations for a full argument that will try to show that these criticisms rest on a misunderstanding of Aristotle. (This argument is made in the materials cited above in endnote 1.) The doctrine of the mean was not Aristotle's invention. It had a long history in pre-Aristotelian Greek thought. To understand its specific Aristotelian form we must set the doctrine in the context of its historical sources and development. Moreover, we must recognize that it is not only an important principle in Aristotle's moral philosophy, but that he makes significant use of it in a number of other branches of his system. It seems clear that unless we grasp the nature and function of the mean in the rest of Aristotle's philosophy we shall not be able to come to terms with it in his ethics. A full understanding of the doctrine of the mean in Aristotle depends on a grasp of how this doctrine developed in earlier Greek thought. Aristotle did not emerge from a vacuum. He was the product of the long and rich history of Greek culture. Without that history as background we have only a bland and incomplete account of the way in which his teaching on this subject developed, and an inadequate basis for interpreting it. Our task in this study is to fill in that history by examining the ways in which the doctrine of the mean was understood and taught in the literature and philosophy of early Greece, beginning with Homer and culminating in Plato.

II

Classical scholars have regularly noted that Greek thought "is dominated everywhere by the omnipresent idea of the 'mean' (τὸ μέτρον),"and that Aristotle, in developing this doctrine, "reflects the general mind of Greece."[6] Aristotle's *Nicomachean Ethics* is seen by many as a culmination of Greek ethical thought, a work which has absorbed the results of centuries of Greek moral reflection and experience. Gomperz, for example, speaks of "that law of moderation which played so eminent a part in the popular naturalistic morality of the Greeks."[8] In fact, Aristotle is thought to be the Greek moral philosopher, *par excellence*, because he grasped more clearly than any of his predecessors the central importance of the doctrine of the mean.[9]

The sources of the doctrine are diverse. Some scholars lay the primary stress on the principle of the mean in Greek medicine. Bodily health was thought to depend on the achievement of a proper balance, measure, and harmony. Disease is understood as a disturbance of this harmony, an upsetting of the mean. Jaeger holds that "The ethics of measure or μέτρον rests on a transference into the mental sphere of contemporary mathematical views in medicine. The Aristotelian mean (μεσότης) is a conscious return to this point of departure, and carries the analogy through still more strictly."[10] Others see the main source in the folk-wisdom which arose out of efforts to till the soil successfully. Hesiod's advice to farmers is "observe thou measure: due measure is ever best."[11] This, and similar bits of folk-wisdom are thought to express the view that in dealing with nature the farmer must avoid extremes and aim for the mean. His work must not begin too early or too late; he must not sow too much or too little; in short, he should follow the mean if he is to be successful. From the limited sphere of agriculture the doctrine of the mean was then expanded to encompass all of man's life.[12]

Still another view connects the origins of the doctrine of the mean with Greek theology. One of the cardinal sins in early Greek thought was hybris, the state of excessive pride and self-assertion in which a man seemed to assert his superiority even to the gods. Such pride could easily arouse the wrath of the gods. A man who is too successful or too strong incurs divine resentment because he seems to have risen to a semi-divine status. The gods will destroy a man who has unrestrained confidence in the continuance of his own good fortune. To avoid divine retribution man needs to pursue a kind of moderation which testifies to his lack of hybris. Following the mean both in thought and action seemed to the Greeks a properly virtuous way of life, since this way, above all, was beloved to the gods.[13]

We shall attempt shortly to set forth detailed evidence of the extent to which the doctrine of the mean dominated pre-Aristotelian Greek ethical thought. It is important first, however, to understand that though Aristotle was a product of a long line of development he did not merely reproduce or summarize the thought of his predecessors. In fact, in his own version of the doctrine of the mean he barely mentions his predecessors. This is a point of some importance, since Aristotle normally introduces a topic by examining the opinions of earlier Greek philosophers. Though this is not the place for a full interpretation of this point I believe it is significant enough to require some preliminary attention. Basically, Aristotle is anxious to distinguish himself and his doctrine from the earlier Greek tradition. His achievement lies in the fact that while recognizing the validity of the well-established views concerning the mean, he was able to transform them from popular slogans into a philosophical principle. Aristotle was not merely a popular moralist who set forth the accumulated folk-wisdom and the cherished convictions of his people. He was a philosopher who frequently began with established views, but never ended with a mere repetition of those views.[14]

In the very earliest Greek writers the terms μέτρον and μεσότης do not occur in their later technical sense, i.e., referring to the mean as the morally right way. However, in Homer we find a stress on the importance of moderation and the mean though he employs other terms. Sometimes it takes the form of practical advice not too drink too much (i.e., beyond the right measure) or not to sleep too much. In the *Odyssey* Homer has Menelaus censure a man "who loves overmuch or hates overmuch; better is due measure in all things."[15] In a later passage Homer warns against the dangers of too much wine, drunk in large gulps and without moderation.[16] We noted earlier that Hesiod counsels that in his actions one should observe the proper measure, μέτρα φυλάσσεσθαι. Since he is advising farmers it seems likely that this is no more a technical usage than Homer's. Both seem to be saying that to get along in the world a man needs to be moderate and to do what is fitting in a way that is fitting. But from this early folk-wisdom there begins to develop a noticeable pattern in classical Greek literature. First, certain general slogans became widely accepted. The most prominent of these is, perhaps, μηδὲν ἄγαν, "nothing to excess." This is frequently paralleled with the warning that the gods resent man's overbearing pride, that hybris brings about man's destruction. As Solon puts it in his plea for moderation, τίκει γὰρ κόρος ὕρριν, "Excess produces hybris, " the insolent pride which arouses the wrath of the gods.[17]

In the writings of Theognis we find for the first time an explicitly formulated view which can be seriously considered as a direct forerunner of Aristotle's doctrine of the mean. To be sure, Theognis also exhibits the general approval of moderation which we noted in his predecessors. Like them he urges moderation in material possessions; [18] he also warns of the dangers of immoderate drinking.[19] At a second level we find in Theognis, as in most ancient Greek writers, the advice that nothing should be done to excess, μηδὲν ἄγαν.[20] Theognis, however, goes beyond this kind of generality. First, there are passages in which he explicitly ties together the good man and the man who achieves an appropriate measure in all things. "The good know how to keep due measure in every matter." οἱ δὸ ἀγαθοὶ πάντων μέτρον ἴσασιν ἔχειν. "Of the men of our time the Sun can see none that is altogether good and observes due measure (ἀγαθὸν καὶ μέτριον)."[21] But he goes farther in the direction which can be seen, in retrospect, to be leading to Aristotle. In Theognis we find one of the earliest instances of the use of the μέσον in an ethical sense. Initially it occurs in conjunction with μηδὲν ἄγαν, and seems to be a consequence of it. If one is to avoid excess, then he should pursue the middle way—not, as some might think, the opposite extreme. This can be seen in his advice to Cyrnus, when thy fellow townsmen are confounded, Cyrnus, be not thou too much vexed (μηδὲν ἄγαν) at aught they do, but walk the road, like me, in the middle (μέσην δὸ ἔρχευ τὴν)."[22] Somewhat later he expresses the same idea, but he does not tie the mean to μηδὲν ἄγαν. He simply urges Cyrnus, "Walk gently, as I, in the midst of the way (ἥ σ υ χ ο ς ὥ σ π ε ρ ἐ γ ὼ μ έ σ σ η ν ὁ δ ὸ ν ἔ ρ χ ε ο ποσσίν)."[23] Finally, Theognis explicitly makes the connection between "nothing to excess," the mean, and virtue in a kind of foreshadowing of the subsequent development of Greek ethics which culminated in Aristotle. "Be not over-eager in any matter (μηηὲν ἄγαν σπεύδειν)—the middleway is best in all things (πάντων μέσὸ ἄριστα)— and thus shalt thou have virtue, Cyrnus (καὶ οὕτως, Κυρνὸ, ἔξειςἄριστα)."[24] Here we see how he moves from a folk-saying to the explicit formulation of the moral claim of the mean (μεσὸ ἄριστα) and then views the mean as the way to virtue (ἄρετη). So far as I can discover this is the earliest instance in Greek literature where these connections are made explicitly and in the terminology subsequently adopted and formalized by Plato and Aristotle. That Aristotle knew the writings of Theognis is evident from the fact that he quotes him on a number of occasions. More significant is the fact that every single quotation from Theognis that Aristotle cites occurs either in the *Nicomachean Ethics* or the *Eudemian Ethics* and always in connection with a moral question.[25] Aristotle cites none of the passages in which Theognis propounds the doctrine of the mean as the way to virtue. However, it seems undeniable that he must have known these passages and that they constitute one important element in the complex of factors which influenced the development of his moral philosophy. Though there is a long way from the relatively unphilosophical moralizing of the early poet to the philosophical subtlety and sophistication of Aristotle, I shall try to show later that much that is obscure in the latter's doctrine of the mean can be understood if we set it in the historical line of development from which that doctrine emerged.

Some additional evidence for the early sources of influence on Aristotle's ethics can be found in a fragment of Phocylides, who was a contemporary of Theognis. In this fragment he gives unambiguous testimony to the desirability of the middle way. Πολλὰ μέσοισιν · μέσος θέλφ ἕν πόλει εἶναι. "Many things are best in the mean; I desire to be of a middle condition in my city."[26] This statement is quoted by Aristotle in his *Politics,* 1295b28, and it seems clear that he sees it as an instructive non-technical statement of his own doctrine.

In the next generation of poets and thinkers of ancient Greece we find the doctrine of the mean becoming more explicit. They tend to resort less to such general slogans as μηδὲν ἄγαν and concentrate instead on more specific moral advice. Thus, Pindar repeats the warnings of his predecessors concerning the danger of excessive prosperity. Tantalus, though loved by the gods aroused their wrath and "got himself an overpowering curse."[27] Moreover, such punishment is deserved, according to Pindar, since a man ought never allow himself to go beyond what is proper and fitting. Like the Aristotelian mean, the good way, says Pindar, has to be appropriate to the particular individual and the particular circumstances. Ixion, for example, was guilty of inexcusable hybris when he allowed himself to fall in love with Hera, "The allotted partner of the wedded joys of Zeus." Such insolence brings doom to a man, since he has forgotten that "it is ever right to mark the measure of all things by one's own station (χρὴ δὲ αὐτὸν αἰεὶ πάντος ὁρᾶν μέτρον)."[28] However, it is not only hybris that Pindar sees as morally unacceptable. He takes another step toward the later doctrine of the mean when he shows the danger, as well, of excessive humility. For, he says, "among mortals, one is cast down from his blessings by empty-headed conceit, whereas, another, underrating his strength too far, hath been thwarted from winning the honours within his reach, by an uncourageous spirit that draggeth him back by the hand."[29] Neither hybris, nor self-deprecation is appropriate, says Pindar. In making our way in the world, when we search for gain, i.e. for our own best advantage, "it is right to pursue the due measure (χρὴ μέτρον θηρευέμεν)"[30] and this always includes a proper estimate of oneself, one's station and one's capacities. This proper estimate of oneself and acceptance of one's appropriate place is one form of the mean as Pindar views it. For, he says, "I am eager only for that which is within in my powers. For of all the orders in the State, I find that the middle rank (τὰ μέσα) flourisheth with a more enduring prosperity... "[31] When he speaks in praise of Lampon, who pursues the mean in his heart and holds to the mean in action,[32] Pindar is lauding the same qualities. Lampon is a good man, because his thoughts, feeling and self-awareness, as well as his actions, follow the rule of due measure. In Archilocus, a contemporary of Pindar, we find the same belief that excess and defect are harmful to a man. He counsels, for example, that a man should not rejoice excessively in victory, nor lament excessively in defeat, but should strive instead for that middle way which is appropriate to his human condition.[33]

In the great Greek dramatists of the fifth century, Aeschylus, Sophocles, and Euripides, we find further substantial evidence of the pervasiveness of the doctrine of the mean in pre-Aristotelian Greek thought. The theme of the danger of hybris and its evil consequences is common in Aeschylus. "For presumptuous pride (ὕβρις), when it has burgeoned, bears as its fruit a crop of calamity, whence it reaps a plenteous harvest of tears."[34] Similarly, we find general counsel to avoid the extremes. Thus, Athena urges that citizens should avoid both anarchy and tyranny, since both extremes threaten the welfare of the state.[35] And the chorus in Agamemnon proclaims that, "glory in excess is fraught with peril."[36] Finally, we find all these themes coming together and explicitly connected with the μέσον, the fullest and least ambiguous idea of the mean. In the *Eumenides* the chorus, at almost the exact center of the play, says, "approve thou not a life ungoverned nor one subjected to a tyrant's sway. To moderation (παντὶ μέσῳ) in every form God giveth the victory... arrogance (ὕβρις) is in very sooth the child of impiety."[37] The extremes are to be avoided; the danger of hybris is ever-present; the one safe and desirable path open to a man is the mean. God is the forerunner of nature, who, like nature in later Greek thought, sets the framework in which human activity must be pursued. We can see here that the ancient folk-attitudes persist, but that they seem to be leading more and more toward a sophisticated version of the doctrine of the mean.

In Sophocles, as well, we find the general expression of the fact that the gods disapprove of excessive pride and applaud moderation. This is coupled with the dangers to human affairs that go with such unrestrained pride.[38] Even the desire for life itself should be restrained and moderate. As in all things, one should not want too much life, certainly not more than is fitting. A man is a fool if he "craves excess of days," because such craving means that the has "let go his hold of moderation (τοῦ μετρίου παρείς)."[39]

The principle of the mean is a basic and recurrent theme in the works of Euripides which is applied to a variety of circumstances and situations. In its most general expression it takes the form of metaphors which employ none of the technical terms later associated with the doctrine. So, for example, Menelaus urges Orestes to think of himself as a ship which makes no progress if its sails are completely slack, but which suffers the danger of keeling over if its sails are too taut. Just as the ship's captain must adjust the sails to exactly the right point between the extremes of slackness and tautness, so must a man order his actions and passions in accordance with the rule of the mean.[40] Part of this same general insistence on moderation is the familiar caution against overpraise and its corollary, excessive pride. Euripides follows the tradition of his predecessors in his belief that excessive praise may arouse the anger of the gods, especially if it leads to unrestrained self-esteem. "Overpraise is odious,"[41] says Iolaus, and Clytemnestra repeats the same thought.[42] Both of them point out that a good man finds excessive praise intolerable. A man who is not offended by such excessive praise, shows that he is insolently proud, and the gods punish men for such "overweening arrogance."[43] The same rule of the mean is applied to many other specific areas of human experience. It is best neither to grieve too much nor to rejoice too much, for men who have learned to temper these emotions are able to live their lives "in cool judgment self-reliant."[44] Neither can excessive anger or fear be approved for they also injure a man.[45] The same is true of eating and drinking beyond the proper measure. Gluttony and drunkenness are to be condemned.[46]

Three. A History of the Doctrine of the Mean in Early Greek Thought... 83

In many of the passages dealing with these topics Euripides uses the term μέτρον, one of the terms that subsequently became part of the technical language of the doctrine of the mean. We see it particularly when he speaks in praise of moderate material wealth. Too much gold is injurious, and too little makes life a burden. In facing trouble one might say, "gold overhears all this, and wealth is sweet." However, the poet argues, "Would I clutch lucre—groan under its load, with curses in mine ears? Nay, wealth for me in measure sorrowless (εἴη δὸ ἔμοιγε μέτρια μὴ λυπουμένῳ)."[47] Moderate wealth is not only most desirable for the individual; such moderation also makes a man the best kind of citizen. "For in a nation there be orders three: —The highest, useless rich, aye craving more; the lowest, poor, aye on starvation's brink, a dangerous folk, of envy overfull." Both classes threaten the well-being of the state. It is the middle-class, those of moderate material wealth on whom society depends. "Of the three the midmost saveth states (τριῶν δὲ μοιρῶν ἡ ὀν μέσῳ σῴζει πολείς)."[48]

Even love which is unrestrained is undesirable, according to Euripides. An old woman, Phaedra's nurse, expresses it well; claiming to speak out of the experience of a long life, she says that ties of love which are too intense consume and destroy men. "Much have I learned by living a long time. Mortals, I know, should join with each other in loving feelings that are not excessive (χρῆν γὰρ μετρίας εἰς ἀλλήλους φιλίας θνητοὺς ἀνακίρνασθαι)."[49] She concludes the passage asserting that μηδὲν ἄγαν is the true counsel of the wise, which applies not only to love, but to all things human. And it is precisely this conclusion that the poet expresses (this time through the nurse of Medea's children) when he pays tribute to the mean as the highest principle of human behavior. "Sweeter name than 'The Mean' shall ye say not, and to taste it is sweetness untold. But to men never weal above measure availed."[50] All the specific rules of conduct in accordance with the mean are drawn together in this general pronouncement.

What is true of the poets and the dramatists is equally true of historians, the physicians and orators. Hippocrates employs the rule of the mean as a basic principle in medical practice. Herodotus in various places speaks in praise of those true heroes who met even the most challenging circumstances without deviating from the rule of right measure. Isaeus, Aeschines, Isocrates—all praise the men of moderation. There is no reason to give extensive and detailed examples from these sources. What is significant for us is that in none of these pre-Aristotelian instances has the mean reached the status of a philosophical principle or a technical rule of reason. In the writings of these men one can see ancient folk-wisdom coming to an ever higher level of explicit self-consciousness, moving from a general slogan like μηδὲν ἄγαν to the detailed and sophisticated formulations in Euripides. However, at its best it is, in these writers, little more than folk-wisdom, a kind of rule of thumb for dealing with nature, man and oneself. This approach to the mean is pervaded by two anti-philosophical elements; one is a regular appeal to practicality and the other is the all-encompassing fear of the gods. The former tends to be tied to individual circumstances, rather than general principles, while the latter, though general, involves elements of caprice and arbitrariness. Both inhibit the development of a moral *philosophy* as against mere moralizing or practical counsel. Our understanding of Aristotle's doctrine of the mean will depend on seeing how he retains the folk-elements while transforming the mean into a basic principle of his philosophy. But before we can turn to Aristotle we must study the development of the doctrine in the pre-Socratic philosophers and in Plato.

IV

The principle of the mean may be thought to be operative in the doctrine of those early philosophers like Empedocles who see the world as resulting from a combination of extreme elements. However, this is far too vague and generalized to be considered a significant and relevant source for the understanding of the Aristotelian mean. There are two pre-Aristotelian philosophers (apart from Plato) in whom the doctrine seems to have reached a conscious and sophisticated form, namely, Heraclitus and Democritus. In Heraclitus the mean is primarily a principle of nature while in Democritus it assumes the form of an ethical principle. One of the most cryptic fragments of Heraclitus deals with this subject. It is cited by Aristotle, who understands it as referring to nature as a harmony constituted out of parts which are opposed and contradictory. "Junctions are: wholes and not wholes, that which agrees and that which differs, that which produces harmony and that which produces discord; from all you get one and from one you get all."[51] This seems to suggest that the world exists as a kind of mean harmonizing and uniting contradictory extremes. In a more explicit statement Heraclitus sets forth appropriate measure as a condition of the existence of the natural world. "The cosmos," he says, "was not created by any one of the gods or of mankind." This suggests that it is not subject to the arbitrariness or capriciousness of gods or men. It is, rather, a fixed stable structure, which "was ever and is and shall be everliving. Fire, kindled in measure and quenched in measure (ἁπτόμενον μέτρ καί ἀποσβεννύμενον μέτρα)."[52] True measure is essential to the existence of the world and is fixed into its very structure. For without measure the world cannot exist. This, I believe, is what Heraclitus means when he says that, "The sun will not transgress his measure (Ἥλιος γὰρ οὐχ ὑπερβήσεςαι μέτρα); otherwise the Furies, ministers of Justice, will find him out."[53] Should the sun not observe that proper measure which is its mean, the Furies would exact their penalty, namely the destruction of the world. It is, perhaps, significant that though Heraclitus does not (in the fragments we have) deal explicitly with the mean as a moral principle, he connects it here with justice. In so doing he implies that the order which rules the natural world is a form of justice related to that which holds sway in the moral world, and both demand the observance of the μέτριον, the proper measure between destructive extremes. If the sun is too cold or too hot it will destroy the earth, and if man in his life fails to observe the mean he will destroy society. Such is the moral view which is suggested by the fragment we have quoted.

Some ground for this claim may be found in fr.112, "Moderation is the greatest virtue (σωφρονεῖν ἀρετὴ μεγίστη), and wisdom is to speak the truth and to act according to nature, paying heed thereto." The term σῶφρον, translated as "moderation," is not necessarily synonymous with the mean, but may be a kind of general expression for temperance. However, virtue and wisdom are joined in this statement, and wisdom in part, is action in accordance with nature. Since nature follows the mean, then human action which imitates nature should also be in accordance with the mean. From this it follows that Heraclitus' σῶφρον is not merely temperate in some undetermined way, but that he lives in accordance with the mean. This view is further strengthened by fr.116 in which Heraclitus proclaims that every man can be a σῶφρον. If it is morally obligatory for every man to follow the mean, then it must be within each man's capacity. We see here that in some respects Heraclitus is anticipating Aristotle, basing both the philosophy of nature and moral philosophy on a common principle. This is a point which will assume great importance in our analysis of Aristotle.

In Democritus we find the mean dealt with in exclusively ethical terms. Some of the statements are of a general character that seems no further advanced than the early Greek folk-wisdom. So, for example, he says that "Immoderate desire is the mark of a child, not a man."[54] But even in this general statement Democritus already employs the term ἀμέτρος. It is evident that he connects lack of moderation with the absence of the appropriate measure which constitutes the mean. We can also find a significant step in the direction of Aristotle when Democritus deals with the mean as something other than a fixed point determined by simple calculation. Only a morally good man can be relied upon to know what action is appropriate in given circumstances. "Thrift and fasting are beneficial; so too is expenditure at the right time. But to recognize this is the function of a good man (γινώσκειν δέ ἀγαθοῦ)."[55] Thrift (φειδώ) and expenditure (δαπάνη) are opposed; carried to excess they can easily become the extremes of miserliness or prodigality. But there is no fixed arithmetic mean which can be set down as a guide to the proper use of money in all circumstances. We are dependent on the practical moral guidance of the "good man" who is alone able to determine where the mean lies, i.e., what degree of expenditure or thrift is appropriate in any given situation. He alone can set forth the right measure. This seems to be a significant foreshadowing of Aristotle's view that the mean is always relative to the particular person and circumstances. Democritus' ἀγαθός, the good man, is an early version of Aristotle's φρόνος, the man of practical wisdom. Though we can find in the fragmentary comment of Democritus little more than a hint, it, nevertheless strongly suggests the doctrine which is fully worked out in Aristotle's ethical theory.

The progressive approach to a level of technical philosophic development can be seen in another statement of Democritus. "In all things equality is fair, excess (ὑπερβολή) and deficiency (ἔλλειψις) not so, in my opinion."[56] Not only do we have here a clear statement of the doctrine of the mean, but we have also the very terms, ὑπερβολ and ἔλλειψις which Aristotle regularly uses for the extremes of too much and too little. Whatever the status of these terms in Democritus they achieve a fixed technical meaning in Aristotle's usage. Moreover, Democritus, anticipating Aristotle, affirms the dependence of happiness on life in accordance with the mean. Only by avoiding the extremes and following the middle way, says Democritus, can a man achieve that inner stability and serenity which is a condition of true happiness. "Cheerfulness is created for men through moderation of enjoyment (μετριότητι τέρψιος) and harmoniousness of life. Things that are in excess or lacking (τὰ δὸ ἐλλείποντα καὶ ὑπερβάλλοντα) are apt to change and cause great disturbance in the soul."[57] The term for cheerful εὔθυμος, means literally "a good state of the soul." It is closely related to εὐδαιμονία, Aristotle's term which is usually translated as "happiness." Aristotle's "happiness" goes beyond Democritus' "cheerfulness," since it involves not only moral virtue which is achieved by living in accordance with the mean, but also intellectual virtue. However, Democritus makes clear that avoidance of the extremes is, at least, a necessary condition of happiness, if not a sufficient condition. Again we seem to have a fairly mature and sophisticated approach to the doctrine which Aristotle subsequently worked out in detail.

While for Heraclitus the mean was primarily a principle of the operation of nature, for Democritus it seems to be exclusively a moral principle. These pre-Socratic philosophers continue the main lines of Greek thought which are already found in the early poets. Nature and morals were joined in the thought of Hesiod and separated by some of his successors. I have tried to show that in Heraclitus there is a suggestion of their being joined together again. In any case, we shall see that this is one of the keys to understanding the doctrine of the mean in Aristotle. Many of his interpreters are misled into thinking that the mean is only a moral principle for Aristotle. They ignore his extensive use of the mean as a principle of nature, and in so doing make it impossible to arrive at a proper understanding of the unified doctrine of the mean which operates in both Aristotle's philosophy of nature and in his moral philosophy. But before we can turn to Aristotle we must examine the most important of his predecessors, Plato. In Plato we shall discover additional dimensions of the doctrine of the mean and an additional major source of influence on Aristotle.

V

That Plato has a fully formed version of the doctrine of the mean can be established beyond any possible question. The large number and wide variety of texts in the *Dialogues* which set forth this teaching provide more than ample proof.[58] What is puzzling is that the doctrine has usually been associated with the name of Aristotle, rather than Plato, despite the fact that Plato placed such importance on it. The mean is ordinarily thought of as a characteristic principle of Aristotle's moral philosophy, and is identified with Plato only infrequently. A. E. Taylor holds that even in so advanced and complex a dialogue as the *Philebus,* "Plato is giving reflective philosophical expression to the traditional wisdom of life which, from Solon on,[59] had preached the excellence of τὸ μέσον and is definitely formulating the doctrine commonly known to us as the 'Aristotelian' identification of the virtuous with the 'right mean'..."[60] He goes on to say that the Platonic origin of the doctrine is clear, but that it is ordinarily attributed to Aristotle by the modern reader because we do not know our Plato well-enough; while "Aristotle in his *Ethics* usually treats allusions to the Platonic dialogues as too easily recognizable by his auditors to need documentation, much as Ruskin could still make constant appeals to the text of the English Bible without express citation."[61] Taylor's explanation may well be correct, so long as we grant his assumption that Aristotle's version of the doctrine of the mean is substantially the same as Plato's. But if Aristotle's doctrine differs from Plato's in significant respects then we need hardly be surprised that it has usually been attributed to him rather than Plato.

Various scholars have argued exactly this point. Wittmann takes the position that Aristotle is distinguished from all of his predecessors, including Plato, by the fact that he alone elevated the mean to the level of a general ethical principle. According to Wittmann, earlier use of the mean was restricted. It was thought to be descriptive of particular virtues, but not the principle of all virtue. Plato, he claims, understood the mean as relevant particularly to justice, but not to other virtues.[62] This claim will be shown, subsequently, to be a complete error. Other more serious efforts have been made to distinguish Aristotle's doctrine of the mean from Plato's. It has been argued that Plato's ethics relies on measure rather than the mean as its basic principle. In substance this distinction claims that Plato was looking for a strict rule of mathematical measure which would apply universally to all men, while Aristotle gave up all hope of exactness and universality. Instead he saw the mean as leading to gross determinations which are only roughly reliable and that vary with each individual and each set of special circumstances. Werner Jaeger is the most prominent scholar holding this view. He consistently differentiates between the early Aristotle, who was still pursuing the Platonic ideal, and the mature Aristotle who had abandoned this conception of moral principles. Thus, Jaeger holds that in the dialogue Eüdemus Aristotle followed a completely Platonic line, "whereas Aristotle in his later ethics differs from Plato in that he seeks not for an absolute good but for the best of man (ἀνθρώπινον ἀγαθόν)."[63] Again in Aristotle's

Three. A History of the Doctrine of the Mean in Early Greek Thought...

Protrepticus Jaeger sees evidence that "Aristotle's ethical inquiries were originally entirely dominated by Plato's problem of the measurability and measure of moral phenomena." He goes on to argue that Aristotle's change consisted simply in rejecting the universal norms, and recognizing no measure but the autonomous conscience of the ethically educated person ('the good man'), a measure which can claim no 'exactness' in the epistemological sense."[64] This interpretation depends on viewing Plato's ethics as tied closely to his theory of Ideas and particularly to his conception of the Idea of the Good, while Aristotle's mature ethics is seen as based on a rejection and refutation of Plato's Idea of the Good. More generally this comes down to the claim that for Plato ethics is ultimately dependent upon metaphysical considerations, while for Aristotle ethics is a practical science devoid of all metaphysical foundations.[65] At first glance this seems to be a correct representation of the differences between Platonic and Aristotelian versions of the mean. All that is attributed to Aristotle is supported by well-known passages in the *Nicomachean Ethics*. He does attack Plato's Idea of the Good and dissociates himself from it. He does say explicitly that in ethics we can only hope to find probable principles, not mathematical certainties. And he does introduce an element of subjectivity by making the mean dependent on φρόνιμος, the man who has practical wisdom and moral sensitivity, while at the same time admitting that the mean will vary according to the characteristics of each individual moral agent and his particular circumstances. In our later discussion of Aristotle we shall see that these elements of his doctrine of the mean must be considered in the total context in which they occur, otherwise they can be readily misunderstood. Our immediate interest, however, is with Plato, and in what follows I shall try to show that the very characteristics which are supposed to distinguish Aristotle from Plato are found in Plato's version as well.

In Plato's works we find many general statements which caution against the dangers of excess. These statements introduce an atmosphere which places Plato solidly in the main tradition of Greek ethical thought. But they are only a small first step toward a more fully and philosophically formulated doctrine. In the *Menexenus* Socrates attaches himself firmly to the ancient tradition when he says, "of old the saying, 'nothing too much,' (μηδὲν ἄγαν) appeared to be, and really was, well said."[66] We have here nothing more than a repetition of an ancient slogan, but it is significant that this slogan merits the unqualified approval (assuming that the *Menexenus* is genuine) of the Plato who is popularly thought of as an absolutist. The statement in the *Menexenus* is paralleled by similar general praise of the middle way in other dialogues. One such instance is Socrates' appeal to Callicles to "change your mind, and, instead of the intemperate and insatiate life, choose that which is orderly (κοσμίως) and contents itself with what it has for its daily needs."[67] The term κοσμίως is not one of the specific terms used for the mean, but it points to a general receptivity on Plato's part to the principle that there is a necessary relationship between virtue and right proportion, which right proportion is in many places clearly identified by Plato with the mean. In the very same discussion with Callicles, Socrates later on makes an even more explicit connection between the properly ordered or proportional life and the good. He argues that what "makes a thing good is its appropriate order (κόσμος) inhering in each thing... and... the soul which has an order of her own [is] better than that which has no order."[68] These brief preliminary general approaches to the mean are followed in Plato by far more extensive and less ambiguous statements.

Much has been written relating the ethical doctrine of the mean to the medical doctrine. It is well established that Greek medical theory rested largely on the principle that disease is an imbalance in the body, and that the task of the physician is to restore the body to its proper proportions. Plato and Aristotle viewed the soul by way of an analogy with the body. To them health of soul, like health of body requires the achievement of right measure or the mean.[69] This point is made very clearly by Plato in the *Timaeus* where he takes the view that, "Everything that is good is fair, and the fair is not without proportion (τὸ δὲ καλὸν οὐκ ἄμετρον)."[70] He goes on to argue that the healthy body must be properly proportioned, the healthy soul must pursue the mean, and the union of the body and soul requires right measure.

From this medical source Plato moves on to a general principle of the mean which is in no sense so narrowly restricted as some commentators claim. It is significant that the texts concerning the mean occur primarily in the dialogues that were written from the time of the *Republic* to the end of Plato's literary career. At the height of his philosophical maturity Plato gave repeated expression to his conviction that the good life is one which pursues the middle way between the extremes. This was not merely an unreflective parroting of the poets and dramatists. It was the carefully and consciously developed position of a great philosopher. What clearer expression do we need than that contained at the very end of the *Republic?*

In a kind of final summation of what constitutes the good life Plato's Socrates proclaims that, a man can best shun evil if he will teach himself to "know how always to choose in such things the life that is seated in the mean (ἀλλὰ γνῷ τὸν τοιούτων βιόν αἱρεῖσθαι) and shun the excess in either direction, both in this world so far as may be and in all the life to come, for this is the greatest happiness for man (οὕτω γὰρ εὐδαιμνενστατος γίγνεται ἄνφωτος)."[71] Here Plato introduces the technical term μέσον; he sets forth the mean as having almost unlimited relevance to the good life; finally, he relates it to happiness (εὐδαιμονία), thus presenting us with all the elements of the doctrine with which we are familiar in Aristotle's version.

In the *Laws,* Plato's last major work this same note is sounded. As we shall see shortly, there are many specific applications of the doctrine of the mean in the *Laws.* However, our present interest is directed toward the clearest general statement of that doctrine which occurs in the *Laws.* All three participants in the conversation are in agreement "that true life (τὸν ὀρθὸν βίον – the right life) should neither seek for pleasure, nor, on the other hand, entirely avoid pains, but should embrace the middle state (τὸ μέσον) which... is a state which we... rightly ascribe to God."[72] This statement should not be seen as merely restricted to recommending a middle way between too much pleasure and too much pain. Since the desire for pleasure and the avoidance of pain are the main motives for ordinary human action, a rule concerning the pursuit of the mean between these extremes is a rule with respect to all human conduct. This is substantiated by Plato's identification of such a life as true *imitatio dei,* a claim which could hardly be made for anything less than a complete moral life.[73] Finally, we can dispel any lingering doubt about Plato's commitment to the mean as a general moral principle if we consult his treatment of this topic in the *Statesman.* The Stranger and the young Socrates agree that we must "assert the real existence of excess beyond the standard of the mean (μέτριον), and of inferiority to the mean, whether in words or deeds." Moreover, "The chief difference between good men and bad [is] found in such excess or deficiency."[74] Here we have the principle of the mean announced without qualification or limitation. We are told clearly that good men are those who live in accordance with the mean, while bad men miss the mark, either exceeding the mean or failing to come up to it.

These passages seem to establish clearly that Plato, in his mature philosophy (as represented in the *Republic, Laws, and Statesman)* affirmed the doctrine of the mean as a basic principle of the moral life. I shall now try to show that he both follows his predecessors and goes beyond them. We shall see that there are numerous specific applications of the mean in Plato's works, and that these seem to be similar in character to the folk-wisdom which we discussed earlier; they strike us often as more nearly moralistic slogans than philosophic statements. Insofar, Plato could justly be said to be merely reflecting and reproducing the established traditions of Greek moralizing. When we see these slogan-like applications of the mean in their total context, however, they assume a different character. For they can only be properly understood if we remember that, unlike many of his predecessors, Plato elevated the mean to a general moral principle, and the particular instances of the doctrine which occur in the *Dialogues* acquire a new significance when they are understood as applications, and exemplifications of this principle. Finally, the general principle itself will be shown to have far wider relevance than just to morality. The doctrine of the mean turns out to be a basic element in Plato's theory of truth and of being.

Let us turn first to a brief summary of the specific applications of the mean which are recommended by Plato. The very art of communication is best served, he holds, by observing the mean. Socrates quotes Prodicus approvingly to the effect that the principles of the art of rhetoric require "That a speech should be neither long nor short, but of a convenient length (ἀλλὰ μετρίων) –i.e., the right measure of mean."[75] But the largest number of practical applications are to be found in the *Laws,* since it is in that work that Plato sets forth detailed rules for the conduct of life in society. We find that the whole range of human activity is thought to be best when it is in accordance with the mean, up to and including death and burial. Thus, a son pays homage to his father by providing for him "The most moderate funeral," neither spending so much as to be ostentatious, nor, so little as to be miserly.[76] Moreover, one should restrain his sorrow and his joy, allowing excessive expression to neither, but restricting both laughter and tears to their proper limits, i.e., that ordained by the rule of the mean.[77]

In marriage the advice of the wise is always to pursue the middle way. People of extreme temperaments or conditions should marry persons of opposite temperament or conditions so that both they and their children will be properly balanced. A rich man should marry into a poor family; a man of honor and social position should marry his social inferior; a man of violent temper should marry into a quiet calm family. Both the families concerned and society as a whole will gain from such alliances, "for the

Three. A History of the Doctrine of the Mean in Early Greek Thought... 93

equable and symmetrical (τὸ ὄμμετρον καὶ σύμμετρον i.e., the properly proportioned) tends infinitely more to virtue than the unmixed (ἄκρατος - the extreme).[78] In dancing, as in all pleasurable activities, special praise is reserved for men of moderation, whose who dance with restraint, observing due measure, even when they are celebrating their own prosperity. Such men are called "Emmeleiai," those who observe the proper order and achieve true harmony.[79] Just as we should be moderate in our own pleasures, so ought we observe the mean in our relations with the gods. Offerings to the gods should be strictly limited by the rule of right measure, for "a moderate man should observe moderation (ἔμμετρα τὸν μέτριν ἄνδρα) in what he offers."[80] Offerings of land, horses, gold, silver, ivory, copper and iron are to be prohibited, while gifts of wood or cloth are recommended, and even these are to be modest.

The mean is also the proper rule for economic activities. According to the *Laws,* retail trade is to be allowed to earn only a fair profit, which is to be determined by the guardians of the law in accordance with right measure.[81] The rule with respect to retail profits is only a reflection of a more general attitude toward property. The extremes of wealth or of poverty are injurious both to the individual and to the state. A virtuous man will avoid these extremes, as will a virtuous society. This rule applies to all our material possessions, even to the body itself. Here Plato stands against those tendencies in Greek culture which made a cult of bodily development. Many, he says, will disagree, but it is his view that, "Honor is not to be given to the fair body, or to the strong or the swift or the tall, or to the healthy body ... any more than to their opposites; but the mean states of all these habits (τὰ δὸ ἐν τῷ μέσῳ ἁπάσης ταύτης τῆς ἕξεως) are by far the safest..."[82] The connection is immediately made in this passage between the body and other material possessions. For he concludes with the admonition that the same rule of the mean applies to money and property. Excessive wealth or poverty also endanger the health of the state. Both in the construction of the ideal state in the *Republic* and in the legislation for an actual state in the *Laws,* Plato points out the dangers of economic extremes. "The community which has neither poverty nor riches will always have the noblest principles."[83] Consistent with this is the view that the size of the state should be severely limited, following a middle course between the extremes of unlimited geographical expansion and reduction to a degree which is not viable.[84]

All these particular instances of the mean can only be properly realized in a state which itself is formed in accordance with the mean, not only in its economic activities, but in its social and political structure. Extreme forms of government are evil and destructive. In spite of a widely-popularized picture of Plato as believing in a totalitarian dictatorship (albeit of the philosopher-king), the actual legislation in the *Laws* shows us a very different conception of government. Not a tyrannical dictatorship, nor an unrestricted democracy, but a state which is mid-way between these is the Platonic recommendation. "The mode of election... is in a mean between monarchy and democracy, and such a mean (μέσον) the state ought always to observe."[85] This is identified by Plato with avoiding in the state the extremes of slavery or freedom, which are equally undesirable. In fact, he views the decline of the Persian state after Cyrus as due to the abandonment of this middle-way of political organization.[86]

From particular instances of the mean we moved to a general rule of the mean in economic, social, and political organization. But this is insufficient. For ultimately the character of the state and of its citizens depend on the laws by which they are governed. If, as we have tried to show, the mean holds a crucial place in Plato's moral and political philosophy, then it should be the key principle in legislation. That this is so is evident in a significant passage in Book III of the *Laws,* a passage which sets the tone for the detailed legislation which only begins in Book IV. If the state is to sustain itself and to make available to its citizens the highest opportunity for a truly good life, then the legislators must be guided by the understanding that, "If anyone gives too great a power to anything, too large a sail to a vessel, too much food to the body, too much authority to the mind, and does not observe the mean (τὸ μέτριον), everything is overthrown and, in the wantonness of excess runs in the one case to disorders, and in the other to injustice, which is the child of excess.... And it requires a great legislator to know the mean and take heed of the danger."[87] This will be the work of the truly great legislator that he knows the mean and sets down laws which institute the mean as the rule of the individual and communal life in the state. That Plato has given such a central place to the doctrine of the mean seems to be established beyond any reasonable doubt. We need to determine still whether he offered any philosophic grounds for this principle or whether (as some contend) he forgot his philosophy when he became a moralist and simply relied on the established conventions of Greek society.

Three. A History of the Doctrine of the Mean in Early Greek Thought...

On the one hand, the mean may seem to be simply a result of experience, trial and error, and shrewd observation of human life. However, even in the contexts where this kind of explanation seems justified, a careful reading will show that Plato had more in mind. He moved consistently toward the understanding and explication of the doctrine of the mean as a basic philosophic principle. In a memorable passage in the *Republic* we can see how Plato has drawn together and summarized his particular observations concerning the mean. He here expresses them in a general statement which has elements both of common-sense experience and philosophic insight. Explaining the rise and course of tyranny Socrates notes that in society extreme forms of behavior tend to be self-destroying. An excess of liberty, unrestrained and undirected results in tyranny. Rulers act like subjects, and subjects like rulers. Fathers are controlled by their children, rather than children by their fathers. Even the animals in such a society are given unlimited freedom so that it becomes difficult to know whether they are ruled by men or rule over men. Such an excess of liberty destroys itself, and from this extreme of so-called democracy tyranny arises. From these observations Socrates is led to conclude that, "in truth, my excess is wont to bring about a corresponding reaction to the opposite in the seasons, in plants, in animal bodies, and most especially in political societies."[88] Here Plato is affirming that the mean is a principle of nature as well as of human society. All things—plants, animals, the very seasons, as well as man, are at their best when they observe the mean. Only in the right proportion, in accordance with due measure, do they find their fulfillment. The principle is rational, since, as he notes, excess brings about its own destruction. If this observation is correct, then a rational man seeking liberty will restrain himself to that measure of liberty which is viable. Too much liberty, like too little liberty, inevitably brings about the destruction of all liberty. The same is true of every other excess.

What is especially significant is that Plato proposes here to view human action and human society through an analogy with nature. This may explain, in part, why the doctrine of the mean receives its fullest expression only in Plato's later dialogues. As he moves away from the direct influence of the teaching of Socrates to a growing concern with the natural world he is led to see in the mean a basic principle of all existence. Whatever violates the rule of right measure destroys itself instead of fulfilling its nature. From this perspective the medical sources of the mean which we cited early in our discussion now take on new importance. For we have in them the first steps toward the generalized principle of the mean as a rule of both nature and man. The human soul must operate under the same principles of health as the human body, and health in the human body is only one instance of health or well-being which reflects the rule and the demand of the whole of nature.[89]

The mean, or right measure, is more than an empirical principle. It rests on basic claims that Plato makes with respect to knowledge and being. In one of the central passages of the Republic Plato discusses the qualities which are essential to the philosopher. What especially distinguishes the philosopher from other men is his devoted striving after truth. To be successful in this striving a man must be properly attuned to truth, and this attunement consists in right measure or the mean. Socrates reminds Glaucon, "assuredly we should not say that the want of harmony and seemliness in a nature conduces to anything else than the want of measure and proportion." But in a philosopher the absence of measure is critical, since "truth is akin to measure and proportion."[90] The mean is not merely a convenient practical rule, not merely a bit of folk wisdom. In the center of one of his most important discussions of his most important topic, namely, the nature of the philosopher, Plato stresses that the truth is like right measure. And to be in harmony with truth, to be open to the opportunity of grasping the truth, the philosopher must himself be a man of harmony and measure, i.e., a man whose nature is in tune with the rule of the mean. To grasp true being, the Ideas, is the aim of the philosopher, and for this he must have "a mind endowed with measure and grace (ἔμμετρον... καὶ εὔχαριν), whose native disposition will make it easily guided to the aspect of the ideal reality in all things."[91] In the light of such an explicit statement it is impossible to accept the view that in Plato's thought the mean was never elevated to the status of a general principle. It is now clear that it is not only a general rule with respect to morality, but also a basic postulate of Plato's epistemology and metaphysics. We shall see subsequently that in his extensive application of the principle of the mean Aristotle was deeply influenced by Plato. In the case of both philosophers the doctrine of the mean cannot be understood only as a moral rule. I have tried to show in our discussions of Aristotle (referred to above) that most of the familiar difficulties in the conventional interpretations of his version of the mean arise from the tendency to deal with it in isolation from its metaphysical and epistemological setting.

But we need first to complete our discussion of Plato by considering his treatment of the mean in the *Philebus,* for it is here especially that moral and metaphysical considerations are brought together. Most scholars have recognized strong Pythagorean influence in the *Philebus,* particularly in the discussion of the πέρας and the ἄπειρον the limited and the unlimited. For our purposes there is no need to trace out these Pythagorean sources of Plato's teaching, since the main elements are clear enough in the text of the *Philebus*. Of prime significance is the fact that in the discussion of a purely ethical problem, namely, whether pleasure is true good, Plato finds it necessary to introduce metaphysical questions. He approaches the moral problem by first dividing and classifying all things that exist (πάντα τὰ νῦν ὄντα),[92] and concludes that actual existence depends on measure, mediating between the unlimited and the limited. Each actual existent involves the imposition of limit on the limited, of a determinate form on the indeterminate. Unless this were done in accordance with the rule of right measure (i.e., the principle of the mean) the actual world would be intolerably grotesque. It is to measure and proportion (ἔμμετρον καὶ ἅμα σύμμετρον) resulting from the proper mixture of the unlimited and the limited that "we owe the seasons of the year and the rest of the blessings of life."[93] Without this element of measure there could be no ordered, intelligible, reliable world, nor a human society worthy of the name. In fact, Plato explicitly ties true being to this principle of measure. In his classification of existence, Socrates had introduced as his first two classes the unlimited and the limited. We have been discussing the third class, which is a mixture of the first two in accordance with measure. "And," says Socrates, "when I speak of the third class, understand me to include under one name any offspring of these, being a birth into true being, effected by the measure which the limit introduces (γένεσιν εἰς οὐσίαν ἐκ τῶν μετὰ τοῦ πέρατος ἀπειργασμένων μέτρων)."[94]

We saw earlier that in the *Republic* truth is conceived as related to measure and proportion, and here, early in the *Philebus* a similar relationship is established between being and measure. The threads are drawn together and joined at the end of the *Philebus*. The good is understood as a compound of truth, right measure and proportion, and beauty. Without truth it could have no reality. But truth depends upon measure and proportion. Finally proportion is the essential part of beauty. Measure stands quite properly at the center, for "measure and proportion... everywhere prove to be beauty and virtue."[95] For this reason Plato concludes in the *Philebus* that neither pleasure nor intelligence stands first in the order of goods. At the top of the hierarchy is measure, the mean, the fit or appropriate (μέτρον, μέτριον, καίριον) and whatever else is of this kind. Second are those things that are direct effects of measure, such as beauty and perfection.[96] Underlying this ranking is the same rationale which we noted in the *Republic*. Failure to achieve the mean is always self-destructive. Excess and defect destroy that which they are supposedly intended to realize. This is equally true in the world of nature and in the life of man. "Any blending that in any way fails of measure and proportion must inevitably spoil its ingredients and most of all itself. 'Tis no blend at all, but a veritable unblended confused mess that regularly brings confusion on its subject."[97] Here we have Plato's last word on the subject. Moral and metaphysical considerations, the study of nature and the study of man, all lead him to give first place to the rule of right measure.

Finally, we must recognize that in his views concerning the way in which the doctrine of the mean is to be applied to particular cases Plato comes very close to what we find later in Aristotle. Early in our discussion of Plato we referred to interpretations which make much of the distinction between measure and the mean, assigning the former to Plato and the latter to Aristotle. The ethic of measure is supposed to be controlled by mathematically exact rules, while the ethic of the mean abandons all pretense of exactness. Moreover, the ethic of measure is thought to be objective, while the ethic of the mean has a strong subjective base, since it depends on the judgment of the man of practical wisdom. Like many of the other supposed distinctions between the Platonic and Aristotelian doctrine of the mean, this one is also unfounded. Plato understood clearly how difficult it is to give any exact determination of the mean in any particular moral situation. Like Aristotle he also appealed to the judgment of the man of moral education and sensitivity.

Plato was keenly aware that there is a gap between legal ideals and moral actualities. The legal ideal is a code of law which is exact, specific, detailed and unambiguous. It should spell out exactly what the law requires, leaving no room for the frailties of individual human judgment. Ambiguity may be desirable in a poet, but it is unacceptable in a legislator. "The legislator must give not two rules about the same thing, but one only." If you are legislating about funerals, "you in the capacity of legislator must not barely say 'a moderate funeral,' but you must define what moderation is, and how much; unless you are definite, you must not suppose that you are speaking a language that can become law."[98] The legal ideal is well stated, but Plato knows that the complexities of human life resist reduction to such precise rules.

Three. A History of the Doctrine of the Mean in Early Greek Thought... 99

In actual practice the legal and moral ideals are synonymous. The purpose of the law is to educate the citizen in virtue, i.e., to produce virtuous men. It is for this end alone that the state is properly governed by law.[99] But the very character, of the moral life is such that few instances lend themselves to decision by way of the kind of exact rule at which the legislator properly aims. In the last analysis, Plato acknowledges that both moral and legal decision rest heavily on the judgment of the best and most virtuous men. Neither the rule of the mean nor any other moral rule can be applied mechanically. "Now it is difficult to determine accurately the things which are worthy or unworthy of a freeman, but let those who have obtained the prize of virtue give judgment about them in accordance with their feelings of right and wrong."[100] This is a long way from being a mathematically exact, objectively determined rule of right measure. Even if we were to grant that Aristotle was more keenly aware of the problem, there is no ground for saying that Plato ignored the subtleties of moral choice in favor of rigid and mechanical rules. Nor was he unaware that relatively few men are endowed with the capacity either to know the mean or to abide by its rule. "The class of men is small — they must have been rarely gifted by nature, and trained by education, — who when assailed by wants and desires, are able to hold out and observe moderation (καρτερεῖν πρὸς τὸ μέτριον δτνατὸν ἔστιν)."[101] Because he knew this, Plato, like his pupil Aristotle, depended on the law to guide and educate the citizenry and on wise and virtuous men to show by way of legal and moral rules (i.e., the principle of the mean) what was appropriate in each particular case. Plato elevated the mean to the status of a central philosophic principle, moral and metaphysical, but did not lose sight of the problems which arise when we move from abstract theory to the inexactitudes of practical decision. In this, as in many other regards, Aristotle followed the lines set down by his teacher.

NOTES

[1] These introductory remarks are based on the introduction to my paper, "The Doctrine of the Mean in Aristotle and Maimonides: A Comparative Study," in *Studies in Jewish Religious and Intellectual History Presented to Alexander Altmann*, (U. of Alabama Press, 1979); it also occurs as a short part of the introduction to Chapter 5 of my *Interpreting Maimonides: Studies in Methodology, Metaphysics, and Moral Philosophy*, (U. of Chicago Press, 1990).
[2] Cf. Kant, *Die Metaphysik der Sitten*, Cassirer edition, Vol. 7, pp. 244-5. Concerning the respected position of the doctrine of the mean Kant says, "Wenn das die Weisheit ist, die zu erforschen wir zu den Alten (dem Aristoteles), gleich als solchen, die der Quelle näher waren, zuruckkehren sollen: virtus consistit in medio, medium tenuere beati, est modus in rebus, sunt certi denique fines, quos ultra citraque nequit consistere rectum, so haben wir schlect gewält, uns an ihr Orakel zu wenden."
[3] Edward Von Hartmann, *Das sittliche Bewusstsein* (Berlin, 1886), p. 111. My translation.
[4] S. Schindele, 'Die aristotelische Ethik," *Philosophisches Jahrbuch der Gorres - Gesellschaft*, Vol. 16, 1903, p. 150, My translation. Cf. *Gompers, Greek Thinkers* (New York, 1912), vol. 4, pp. 247-8.
[5] Cf. George Grote, *Aristotle*, 3rd. edition (London, 1883), pp. 513-515.
[6] F. R. Earp, *The Way of the Greeks* (Oxford University Press, 1929), p. 42.
[7] R. Eucken, *Über die Methode und Grundlagen der aristotelischen Ethik* (Berlin 1870), pp. 9-10.
[8] Gomperz, *op. cit.*, p. 257.
[9] Harald Schilling, *Das Ethos der Mesotes* (Tübingen, 1930), p. 11: "Das Mass ist die griechische Tugend, wie des einzelnen so des Staates, und weil Aristoteles so klar erkannt, so scharf erfasst hat ist er der griechische Ethiker, der griechische Staatsrechtlehrer par excellence." Quoted from Theobald Ziegler, *Die Ethik de Griechen und Römer*, (Bonn, 1886), p. 134.
[10] Werner Jaeger, *Aristotle: Fundamentals of the History of His Development* (Oxford, 1934), p. 44, fn.1; cf A. E. Taylor, *Aristotle* (London, 1919), p. 105.
[11] μέτ φυλάσσεσθαι καί δὸ ἐπὶ πᾶσιν ἄριστος. Hesiod, *Works and Days*, 694.
[12] Max Wundt, *Geschichte der Griechischen Ethik* (Leipzig, 1908), Vol. I, p. 74; p. 215.
[13] Cf., Earp, *op. cit.*, pp. 43, 46.
[14] Cf., Michael Wittman, *Die Ethik des Aristotles* (Regensberg, 1920), pp. 61-62; Cf. also, Schilling, *op. cit.*, pp. 12-13. The views which conflict with this interpretation of Aristotle will be discussed below in their proper place.
[15] Homer, *Odyssey*, XV, 65ff. ἀμίνω δὸ αἴσιμα πάντα. The word αἴσιμα, derives from αἴσα, the goddess of destiny, and refers to that which is appropriate or in due measure because it is in accord with the will of the gods.
   In this and subsequent quotations from the Greek poets and dramatists I follow the text and translation of the Loeb editions, unless otherwise noted. In some cases I have made minor changes in the Loeb translations in order to emphasize the force of a particular word or phrase.
[16] *Ibid.*, XXI, 204.
[17] Solon, fr. 6.

Three. A History of the Doctrine of the Mean in Early Greek Thought... 101

[18] Theognis, 557-60. Cf. 693-4, where he notes how difficult it is to maintain "due measure when good things are to thy hand."
[19] Theognis, 475; 497; 839-40.
[20] Theognis, 401; 657.
[21] Theognis, 614-616. Note that in both instances the μέτριον the man of measure, is identified with the ἀγαθόν, the good man.
[22] Theognis, 219-20.
[23] Theognis, 331.
[24] Theognis, 335-6.
[25] Cf., the entries under "Theognis" in Troy W. Organ, An *Index of Aristotle* (Princeton 1949), p. 165. The last entry should read 1243a17 instead of 1234a17. There are no additional citations in Bonitz's *Index Aristotelicus* which are clearly ascribable to Theognis.
[26] Phocylides, Fr. 12. I follow here Jewett's translation.
[27] Pindar, *Olympian Odes*, I:55f
[28] Pindar, *Pythian Odes*, II:34.
[29] Pindar, *Nemean Odes*, XI:29 ff.
[30] *Ibid.*, 45-47.
[31] Pindar, *Pythian Odes*, XI:51 ff.
[32] Pindar, *ISTHMIAN odes*, VI:71. μέτα μέν γνώμα διώκων, μέτρα δὲ καί κατέχων.
[33] Cf., Archilocus, fr. 66. Though none of the specific terms that refer to the mean are used in this passage, the general direction of Archilocus' thought is, nevertheless, unmistakable.
[34] Aeschylus, *The Persians*, 821 f Cf., also Fr. 159 (Nauck). For other instances where he noted the danger of arousing the anger of the gods through human excess, *cff.*, *Prometheus*, 887 *ff.*; *Persians*, 362, 532 ff., 724 f.; Agamemnon, 378 ff., 921 ff., 947.
[35] Aeschylus, *Eumenides*, 696 ff.
[36] Aeschylus, *Agamemnon*, 468 ff.
[37] Aeschylus, *Eumenides*, 526-534.
[38] Cf., Sophocles, *Ajax*, 127 ff.; *Antigone*, 710 ff.
[39] Sophocies, *Oedipus at Colonus*, 12llff. For the phrase τοῦ μετρίου παρείς I have adopted the translation proposed in Liddell & Scott under the entry παρίημι
[40] Euripides, *Orestes*, 682-710.
[41] Euripides, *Children of Hercules*, 202 ff.
[42] Euripides, *Iphigenia at Aulis*, 977 ff.
[43] Euripides, *Children of Hercules*, 387-8.
[44] Euripides, *Iphigenia at Aulis*, 919 ff.
[45] Euripides, *Andromache*, 866.
[46] Euripides, *Suppliants*, 865 ff.
[47] Euripides, *Ion*, 629-632; cf. *Ion*, 490.
[48] Euripides, *Suppliants*, 238-245.
[49] Euripides, *Hyppolytus*, 252ff. I follow here the translation of Rex Warner (London 1949). Cf , *Iphigenia at Aulis*, 552.
[50] Euripides, *Medea* 125-130. Even in this strained translation the main point is clear enough.
[51] Heraclitus, fr. 10 (Diels) as quoted and translated in Oxford University Press edition of the *Works of Aristotle*, Vol. III, *De Mundo*, 396b2Off.

[52] Heraclitus, fr. 30. In this and subsequent quotations from Heraclitus and Democritus I am following the Greek text and the numbering of H. Diels, *Fragmente der Vorsokratiker*, 6th edition, and the English translation of Kathleen Freeman, *Ancilla to the Pre-Socratic Philosophers (Oxford* 1952), unless otherwise noted.
[53] Heraclitus, fr. 94.
[54] Democritus, fr. 70.
[55] Democritus, fr. 229.
[56] Democritus, fr. 102.
[57] Democritus, fr. 191, 11.1-4, Cf., fr. 233: "If one oversteps due measure, the most pleasurable things become most unpleasant."
[58] There are more than thirty passages in nine of the *Dialogues* in which the doctrine of the mean occurs explicitly. I shall make some reference to most, if not all, of these passages, either in the text or the footnotes of this essay.
[59] I have tried to show above that the teaching of the mean considerably antedates Solon, and that it occurs as early as Homer and Hesiod.
[60] A. E. Taylor, *Plato: Philebus and Epinomis* (London 1956), Introduction, p. 40.
[61] *Ibid*, pp. 40-41. Cp. also, A. E. Taylor, *Plato: The Man and His Work* (London 1949, sixth edition), pp. 269, 399, 415. In each of these passages Taylor strongly affirms that in the *Politicus* and especially in the *Philebus* we have the "direct source" of Aristotle's doctrine of the mean. It is interesting to note that Taylor is not in agreement with other commentators when he offers a specific passage as the Platonic source to which Aristotle alludes. In *Plato*, p. 415, he says that Aristotle's allusion at *Ethica Nicomachea*, 1104b12 is to *Philebus* 26de. Burnet in his edition of Aristotle's *Ethica Nicomachea* interprets the passage as definitely alluding to *Laws* 653a, with echoes of *Republic* 401e. W. D. Ross, in his notes to the Oxford Aristotle edition concurs with Burnet, as do Grant and Stewart in their notes. It seems that Aristotle's allusions are not so easily recognizable, even to scholars, and that choosing a particular passage in Plato as the passage which Aristotle intended is a hazardous and uncertain business.
[62] Michael Wittmann, *Die Ethik des Aristoteles* (Regensburg 1920), pp. 61-62: "Nur in bestimmten Fallen hat man bisher vom Gedanken der rechten Mitte Gebrauch gemacht, nicht aber sollte das allgemeine Wesen der Sittlichkeit erfasst werden... So hat Plato speziell die Gerechtigkeit, Isocrates die Tapferkeit als ein Vermeiden von Extremen dargestellt."
[63] Jaeger, *op. cit.*, p. 48. Cf., Schilling, *op. cit.*, pp. 12-13, 14. 64 Jaeger, *op. cit.*, p. 88, fn. 1.
[65] Cf, Jaeger, *op. cit.*, p. 396; Schilling, *op. cit.*, p. 3; Schindele, *op. cit.*, vol. 15, pp. 126-7.
[66] *Menexenus*, 247e. Unless otherwise noted all translations of passages from Plato are from the fourth revised Jowett edition (Oxford 1953). Greek quotations from Plato follow the version of the Oxford Classical Texts.
[67] *Gorgias*, 493c.
[68] *Gorgias*, 506e. Cf., *Republic*, 402e ff. for another instance where the ideal of κόσμος is set forth as parallel to the mean.
[69] Cf., A. E. Taylor, *Aristotle, op. cit.*, pp. 76-77. Jaeger, *op. cit.*, p. 43 says, "This explanation of disease... as lack of symmetry was taken over by Plato from contemporary

medicine, on which he based his whole science of ethics or therapy of the soul." Cf., also, R. C. *Lodge, Plato's Theory of Ethics* (London 1928), pp. 443-446.
[70] *Timaeus*, 87c. *ff.* Cf., also, *Timaeus*, 82a. Concerning the soul Plato says in *Timaeus*, 89e, "We take care that the movements of the different parts of the soul should be in due proportion."
[71] *Republic*, 619a. Translated by Paul Shorey, Loeb Classical Library edition.
[72] *Laws*, 792cd, 793a.
[73] On the problem of *imitatio dei* as a principle in Plato's ethics see Otto Apelt, *Platonische Aufsätze* (Berlin 1912), p. 109.
[74] Statesman, 283e. Translated by Harold A. Fowler in the Loeb Classical Library edition.
[75] *Phaedrus*, 267b.
[76] *Laws*, 717de.
[77] *Laws*, 732c.
[78] *Laws*, 773a-d.
[79] *Laws*, 816b.
[80] *Laws*, 955e. ff.
[81] *Laws*, 920c.
[82] *Laws*, 728cd.
[83] *Laws, 679b;* cf. *Republic,* 42le - 422a. In *Critias,* 112bc, there is a picture of the ideal state of antiquity in which, again, one of the characteristics is the pursuit of a middle way between wealth and poverty, ostentation and meanness.
[84] *Republic,* 423c.
[85] *Laws,* 756a-767a.
[86] *Laws,* 694a ff.
[87] *Laws,* 69lcd.
[88] *Republic,* 563e-564a, Shorey translation in Loeb Classical Library edition. Cf., the entire passage
beginning with 562b.
[89] *Timaeus,* 87c. ff. to which reference was made earlier bears out the validity of this claim.
[90] Republic, 486d, Shorey translation.
Αλήθειαν δὲ ἀμετρίᾳ ἡγεῖ ξυγγενῆ εἶναι ἢ ἐμμετριὰ; Εμμετρία.
[91] *Ibid.*
[92] *Philebus,* 23c.
[93] Philebus, 26ab, tr. By A.E.Taylor, op. cit., cf. note 59 above.
[94] *Philebus,* 26d, Jowett tr.
[95] *Philebus,* 64e, Taylor tr.,
μετριότης γάρ καὶ συμμετρία κάλλος δήπου ἀρετὴ οανταχοῦ ζυμβαίνει γίγνεσηαι
[96] *Philebus,* 64ab.
[97] *Philebus,* 64de.
[98] *Laws,* 719de.
[99] Cf, *Laws,* 630b-631.
[100] *Laws, 919e.,* Cf, 658ef and 663cd.
[101] *Laws,* 918d.

4

A NEW VIEW OF MAIMONIDES' METHOD OF CONTRADICTIONS

It is a standard view of contemporary Maimonides scholarship that we can only grasp Maimonides' true doctrine in the *Guide of the Perplexed* if we give most careful thought to the author's own instructions to his readers. Among these instructions most attention has paid recently to the stress that Maimonides seems to place on the presence of contradictions in his book and on the correct way of understanding those contradictions. This concern is, of course, by no means a new one. The major medieval commentators on the Guide were fully aware of the fact that it is no ordinary book and that it must be read with special care. There is a general agreement with the judgment of Shlomo Pines that, "the Guide belongs to a very peculiar literary genre, of which it is the unique specimen"[1]. The medievals, like our contemporaries, were aware of the problem of contradictions in the book. They were sensitive to the author's instructions to his readers, and they were concerned in the case of seemingly contradictory statements to determine what it was that Maimonides was affirming to be true.

It is to be expected that all this should have been noted, since no author could have been more direct and more explicit about these matters. What is surprising, as I shall attempt to show in this essay, is how much has been overlooked by both medieval and modern commentators and bow much they have taken for granted that is in no way supported by the text. Maimonides demanded of his readers a close and careful reading which weighs the force and significance of every word, but we shall show that the commentators have not given him such a reading (at least with respect to the issues we are considering in this study). Furthermore, Maimonides required his readers and all who would deal with the subject matter of his book to be thoroughly trained in the basic elements of logic and to make constant use of their knowledge of logic as an indispensable tool for a correct critical reading of his very complex book[2]. Yet, as we shall show, the commentators, both medieval and modern, have failed to pay attention to certain elementary logical principles and distinctions, nor have they taken note of the special terminology which Maimonides introduced into his discussion of the so-called method of contradictions. The result is a failure to confront the text of the Guide in the way in which the author expected of his readers. Much that has been written about contradictions in the Guide turns out to be doubtful if not simply wrong. Inattention to Maimonides' terminology and to the clues which he has provided us can only lead to misunderstanding.

Maimonides begins his celebrated account of the seven causes in the following way. "One of seven causes should account for the contradictory or contrary statements to be found in any book or compilation"[3]. The most important point to note is that he speaks of "contradictory or contrary statements". We should pay attention first to the fact that he is speaking about "statements" and then that he specifically refers to those that are contradictory or contrary. Now, as we shall show, these are technical terms in logic, and specifically in Maimonides' own logic. Yet, hardly any of the commentators (none that I can identify) consider the significance of this sentence.

Consider the most obvious points. First, is the important rule that logical opposition is restricted here to statements. There may be other peculiarities or inconsistencies that we will confront in this book, but they will not be of the logically formal type that occurs in the opposition of statements to each other. Second, Maimonides does not speak loosely or in a general way only about contradictions, but he specifically mentions "contradictory or contrary statements". It is a commonplace of the Aristotelian logic that is adopted by Maimonides that contradictories and contraries behave in quite different ways. Contradictories cannot both be true or both be false. If one is true, the other is necessarily false, and vice versa. Contraries cannot both be true, but may both be false, and subcontraries (which I believe he included here in his term "contraries") cannot both be false, but may both be true. It is already evident how much error we hazard if we allow ourselves, as has been generally done especially by the contemporary commentators, to ignore completely these distinctions and to speak only about contradictions in the Guide.

Four. A New View of Maimonides' Method of Contradiction

That Maimonides was aware of the exact technical meaning of these terms is evident from his *Treatise on Logic*[4]. Since that treatise is devoted to an explication of logical terms, it does not deal directly with the way in which contradictories are related to each other. Yet, there can be no possible doubt that Maimonides was familiar with the relations between these types of statements as they were set forth in what came to be known as the square of opposition. These relations were already set down by Aristotle in his logical works and from there they entered into the logical tradition as standard items[5]. Most important for our purpose is to note that this same account of the relations of propositions within the square of opposition is present in al-Farabi in his discussion of the passage in Aristotle to which we just referred[6]. As we know, Maimonides held al-Farabi in the highest esteem, especially as a logician. In a statement that has been frequently quoted, he advises his translator, Samuel ibn Tibbon, to ignore all works on logic except for those of al-Farabi, which are alone of the very highest quality in Maimonides' opinion[7]. We can, therefore, be confident that Maimonides was thoroughly familiar with al-Farabi's teaching concerning the opposition of propositions. When we add to this the fact, already noted, that the relations of propositions as set forth in the square of opposition had become a standard part of logic in the intellectual world which Maimonides inhabited, there can be no doubt that he knew and accepted as correct these rules. It seems to follow then, as a matter of course, that when we find statements in the *Guide* that are in whatever way inconsistent with each other, it is a serious mistake simply to classify them all as contradictions. Yet, this is in fact what the commentators generally do, and this includes Leo Strauss and his followers. What is required of us is to determine whether we are dealing with contradictories, contraries, subcontraries, or some other form of opposition or inconsistency. Failing to make this determination and to treat the problem before us in accordance with the rule of logic, we are almost certain to fall into error in our interpretation of the Maimonidean text.

When we study the work of Leo Strauss, who more than any other scholar has made us aware of the importance of inconsistencies in the *Guide*, we discover to our great astonishment that he pays no attention to the rules of logic and to the basic logical distinctions which are essential for understanding Maimonides. He speaks only about contradictions and ignores the other forms of opposition and inconsistency. He stresses, no doubt with full justification, the importance of contradictions, but then sets down a rule for dealing with them which ignores the canons of logic and Maimonides' own careful instructions. He holds that, "Contradictions are the axis of the *Guide*... While the other devices used by Maimonides compel the reader to guess the true teaching, the contradictions offer him the true teaching quite openly in either of the two contradictories"[8]. Strauss goes on to instruct us how to determine which of the contradictories Maimonides considered to be true. "We may therefore establish the rule that of two contradictory statements in the *Guide* or in any other work of Maimonides that statement which occurs least frequently, or even which occurs only once, was considered by him to be true"[9].

This claim may be a good rule for reading an esoteric work, but it certainly does not conform to the canons of logic or to Maimonides' own clear instructions. The student dealing with such complex subjects as those dealt with in the Guide must take particular care to abide by the rules of logic and not to suppose that he knows anything with certainly if it is not supported by logical evidence. "For if you stay your progress because of a dubious point; if you do not deceive yourself into believing that there is a demonstration with regard to matters that have not been demonstrated; if you do not hasten to reject and categorically to pronounce false any assertions whose contradictories have not been demonstrated; if, finally, you do not aspire to apprehend that which you are unable to apprehend—you will have achieved human perfection... If, on the other hand, you aspire to apprehend things which are beyond your apprehension; or if you hasten to pronounce false, assertions the contradictories of which have not been demonstrated or that are possible, though very remotely so... you will not only not be perfect, but you will be the most deficient among the deficient..."[10]. Maimonides' own rule is clear enough. In the case of contradictories, we can only proceed correctly if we know which is true, since it follows necessarily that its contradictory is false. However, we can only know with certainty which is true if we have a rigorous demonstration. For Maimonides demonstration is a strict logical category. It is not an esoteric procedure at all, but one well established in the philosophical tradition to which he belongs. It is difficult to find any ground which would justify substituting Strauss' rule for that which Maimonides himself set down. In dealing with any case of inconsistent propositions, our first task is to determine the nature of the inconsistency. If they are contradictories, then we are faced with the challenge of determining whether either of them can be demonstrated to be true. If they are contraries, we need to deal with the possibility they may both be false, and if they are subcontraries that they may both be true. Furthermore, as we shall soon see, there are in the Guide other modes of opposition or inconsistency which do not fit into any of these standard logical classifications, and these too must engage our attention.

Of special importance to us are not only those points of logic with respect to which Maimonides is in full agreement with the classical tradition, but even more those points with respect to which he differs from that tradition. Among these the most striking is his treatment of singular propositions. These are propositions which are neither universal nor particular in the standard sense of those terms, but instead have as their subject a single individual. Maimonides' examples of such singular propositions are, "Zayd is an animal" or "Bekr is wise". In the history of logic from the time of Aristotle on these singular propositions have been a source of trouble since they do not seem to fit precisely into any of the established classifications.

Some logicians construe them as universals, since the predicate is applied to the entire subject which is treated in this case as a class having one member. Others treat them as particulars. Among the Arab logicians, al-Farabi classifies singular propositions as particular, while Avicenna classifies them as universals[11]. The debate has gone on through the centuries, but Maimonides goes his own way here. He takes an independent stand for which there is no clear precedent. He distinguishes singular propositions from all other types and makes a special point of not assimilating them to any other form of proposition. However, he tells us nothing at all about how to integrate these propositions into the standard system of logic, nor does he give us any information about how to deal with cases of opposition between singular propositions. They evidently are not to be treated like standard cases of contradictions or contraries[12]. What makes this topic especially important is the fact that all propositions that have "God" as their subject are singular propositions. If, as Maimonides tells us, the *Guide* has as its subject "the science of the law in its true sense", and this includes *Maaseh Merkavah*, then it follows that the subject of the book must deal extensively with God, as it in fact does. It is obvious that we face very difficult problems of interpretation if we do not have a proper logical understanding of how to classify and deal with singular propositions. It is evident that whenever we have statements of which "God" is the subject, and those statements are in some way opposed or inconsistent, we have no straightforward rule for resolving the problem. Certainly, we cannot with any confidence just make use of Strauss' rule for resolving contradictions in Maimonides. It may well be that if the subject-matter of "divine science", which is the way to the highest wisdom, can only be expressed in singular propositions, something other than ordinary logic will be required of those who would master it.

Our suspicions are confirmed to some degree when we take note of an additional peculiarity in Maimonides' terminology. After setting forth his account of the seven causes "which should account for the contradictory or contrary statements to be found in any book or compilation"[13], Maimonides goes on to discuss which of the causes are applicable to which types of books. He reviews briefly various types of sacred literature and then turns to the works of the philosophers and to his own work. Remarkably, in the case of the works of the true philosophers and of his own work he makes no reference whatsoever to contradictions or contraries. Instead, he introduces a new term which Pines translates as "divergences". "As for the divergences *(ikhtilāf)* occurring in the books of the philosophers, or rather of those who know the truth, they are due to the fifth cause... Divergences that are to be found in this Treatise are due to the fifth cause and seventh. Know this, grasp its true meaning, and remember it very well so as not to become perplexed by some of its chapters"[14].

What is of critical importance here is both the fact that in the case of the works of the philosophers and, what interests us most, his own work, he makes no mention whatsoever of the standard types of logical opposition. He says nothing about contradictions or contraries in his work, despite the fact that he begins this section with an account of how we are to explain any contradictions or contraries that we find in various types of literature. Shall we conclude that there are no contradictions or contraries in Maimonides' own book? Or is it rather the case that he is directing our attention to other types of actual or seeming inconsistencies in the *Guide* while telling us nothing about contradictions that we may find in that book? At this point, we cannot answer with any certainty. What is clear, however, is that we must pay particularly close attention to this new term he has subtly and with almost no warning introduced into the discussion. Since we know that Maimonides has written his book in such way as to test the competence of his readers, it is reasonable to suppose that taking note of this new term and reflecting on its implications is part of that test. Very few of the most eminent and justly respected of the medieval or modern writers on Maimonides seem to have met the challenge of this particular test.

The term "divergence" confronts us with special problems. In the history of logic prior to Maimonides the term has no established use. It appears that only one of the earlier, Arab logicians made use of the term at all, and his usage is so broad as to have robbed the term of any technical significance[15]. The term is not used by al-Farabi upon whom Maimonides depended so heavily in the field of logic. We can only conclude that he deliberately has introduced a non-technical term in order to make the careful reader aware that in his book we must look for and deal with types of inconsistency which are not standard logical forms.

I am inclined to believe that Maimonides has already given us earlier clues that are intended to catch our attention and alert us to what lies ahead. Twice in his introductory remarks he uses forms of the term *ikhtilāf* and on both occasions it is specifically in connection with his own work. The translators have not taken care to convey the exact term that is used in Arabic. The first occasion is in the general introduction where he notes that his book is written for "one who has philosophized and has knowledge of the true sciences". He instructs that type of reader in some of the oddities that he should expect to find in the Guide and explains that in certain chapters one should look for hints and clues of a particular sort. Then he adds, "Such a chapter may contain strange matters regarding which the contrary of the truth sometimes is believed"[16]. The term which is translated as "contrary" is *khalāf*, and I believe that if we take seriously Maimonides' stress on the care with which he has chosen each word, we should translate the phrase as "that which diverges from the truth" rather than as "the contrary of the truth". The latter has a specific technical meaning and Maimonides did not choose to use his own technical term for "contrary", i.e. *taddād* or one of its derivatives[17]. What is of interest to us is that in this early reference to what may be jarring to the attentive reader of his book, Maimonides speaks of cases in which people sometimes believe what diverges from the truth. We are not informed of the nature of this divergence, but the terminology itself is enough to alert us to the likelihood that he is not talking about standard cases of logical inconsistency.

The second case is also in reference to his book. Maimonides asks an oath of his readers not to offer their own explanations of the Guide to others. If they believe him to have said anything original, they should keep it to themselves. Moreover, a reader who thinks Maimonides is in error, he urges, "should not hasten to refute me, for that which he understood me to say might be contrary to my intention"[18]. Here again the term which is rendered as "contrary" is *khaljif* and, I believe, would be better translated as "may diverge". In this case, ibn Tibbon does in fact render it by its Hebrew cognate, hilluf. Again Maimonides seems to be informing us that there are modes of inconsistency with his own intentions which are important and which must command our attention, but which do not share the characteristics of contradictories or contraries. Finally, in his discussion of the reasons for inconsistencies in the Talmud he speaks of "contradictions or divergences *(ikhtilif)*" to be found in that work.[19]

Before we turn to a discussion of a number of cases of supposed contradictions, it may be instructive to note briefly that among the medieval commentators Kaspi was perfectly clear about the distinction between contraries and contradictories[20]. In contrast, Shem Tov in his comment on the opening of the discussion concerning the causes of contraries or contradictories in various types of books makes the error of eliminating the distinction between the two. He says, "Contradictories and contraries are such that they cannot both be true, but it is possible that both should be false". Now it is correct that contraries are such that both may be false, but it is certainly not the case with respect to contradictories. This may explain, in part, why the comments of Shem Tov about particular cases of contradictions in the Guide tend to be singularly unilluminating. Furthermore, both Shem Tov and Efodi are careless in their quotations or paraphrases of Maimonides' carefully chosen language. Where Maimonides speaks, as we have already noted, about the "divergences" which may be found in his book, they substitute for "divergences" contradictions *(setirah)*. In this case, ibn Tibbon, who is not always meticulously careful in matters of terminology, correctly has *hilluf.*

Since Maimonides informs us that the divergences in his book are due to the fifth or the seventh cause, it is important to look at them carefully. The fifth cause is purely a matter of didactic strategy. In teaching any given subject matter the teacher must take account of the level of the student's knowledge and intellectual development. This requires him at times to give an initial account which is not fully accurate, or even one which in some degree misrepresents a particular point. Later, when the student is ready to understand at a deeper level, the earlier account is corrected. It is obvious that we do not have here instances of genuine contradictions at all, but only a teaching device adopted by the skillful teacher for the benefit of his pupil. No terms for the opposition of propositions are used in the discussion of the fifth cause, i.e., there is no mention of contradictories or contraries.

Four. A New View of Maimonides' Method of Contradiction

In the case of the seventh cause, however, we must pay very close attention to exactly what Maimonides says, since whatever genuine contradictions, contraries, or divergences we find in the *Guide* are by the author's own testimony due to this cause. As we study that brief paragraph carefully, we come to the frustrating conclusion that the author has told us very little. Let us examine the text. "In speaking about very obscure matters it is necessary to conceal some parts and to disclose others". We are not informed what the nature is of the obscurity that we are dealing with here. Is it identical with the obscurity of subject matter which occupies us in the case of the fifth cause? Is it different, and if so, in what way? Maimonides tells us nothing to clarify this point. Nor does he tell us what it is about that particular form of obscurity that requires us to conceal some parts and to disclose others. He goes on to say that sometimes "this necessity requires that the discussion proceed on the basis of a certain premise, whereas in another place necessity requires that the discussion proceed on the basis of another premise contradicting the first one". We are not informed about the nature of this "necessity" or how the author determines when to employ one premise and when to employ its contradictory. It is worth noting that, among the medieval commentators, both Shem Tov and Efodi cite the above sentence concerning basing the later discussion on a premise that contradicts the first one, and then add on their own words, *"kefi ha'emet"*, thus adding to what Maimonides actually says without any clear justification.

Finally, we are cautioned that "the vulgar must in no way be aware of the contradiction; the author accordingly uses some device to conceal it by all means". Again, we are given no understanding of why the contradiction must be hidden from the vulgar. What undesirable effects will it have on them if they should learn about the contradiction? Maimonides gives us no help at all in clarifying this very obscure account of the seventh cause.

The usual assumption is that we are dealing here with the exposition of doctrines which will seem heretical to all but the most highly sophisticated readers. We must not risk corrupting the simple innocent faith of the vulgar, hence, we must conceal any premise that would endanger their spiritual health. Moreover, we must never let them discover that we are basing our real doctrines on such dangerous premises. Finally, we must conceal from them the contradiction inherent in this entire procedure, otherwise we again risk corrupting them. While it is likely that Maimonides has in mind something of this kind, we must, nevertheless, stress that the text of the account of the seventh cause tells us nothing about this matter which is explicit. This account may be correct, but if so it will have to be justified by an analysis of what Maimonides actually does in his book. Let us turn then to an examination of some actual instances of "divergences" in the Guide in the hope that we may be able to achieve a somewhat better understanding of this very complex topic.

We begin with some cases of contradictions in the Guide which were noted by Leo Strauss. In the course of his very elaborate discussion of prophecy, Maimonides stresses the uniqueness of the prophecy of Moses, its incomparability to all other instances of prophecy, and the fact that we are not able to give a proper account of it. In this connection, he asserts that, "As for the prophecy of Moses our Master, I shall not touch upon it in these chapters with even a single word, either in explicit fashion or in a flash[21]. Yet, we know that he does in fact discuss various aspects of Mosaic prophecy. Strauss points out that in the Guide we are explicitly taught that unlike all the other prophets the prophecy of Moses had no element of the imagination in it, but was purely intellectual. On this basis, Strauss observes that "Undoubtedly Maimonides contradicts himself regarding Moses' prophecy"[22]. This is a typical instance of speaking about contradictions loosely and with no regard for the technical meaning of the term. Whatever we have here, it is not a contradiction in any literal sense. How would Strauss go about even applying his own rule to the resolution of this contradiction"?

What we have here is a statement followed by an action which is inconsistent with that statement. Now a statement can only be contradicted by another statement, not by an action. This is why Maimonides was so very careful to speak about the seven causes which "should account for the contradictory or contrary statements to be found in any book'. Truth or falsity are properties of statement, never of actions. Consequently, it is misleading to speak about Maimonides' action having contradicted his earlier statement. Admittedly, there is something not in order here; however, it is not a logical contradiction, but a difficulty of another sort. I take this to be one instance of what Maimonides meant by "divergences". We have here an inconsistency which engages our attention by, in effect, stopping the smooth flow of the text. The author does something that he said he would not do. We are forced to stop, to reflect, to determine whether he has actually done what he said he would not do, or whether he only seems to have done so, and to try to understand what has happened here.

Four. A New View of Maimonides' Method of Contradiction

This is certainly not a case of biding something from his readers by using esoteric rhetorical devices. Any reader, however unskilled, will certainly be aware that Maimonides does have many things to say about Mosaic prophecy, even after he assures us in strong language that he will not say a single word about that subject. Perhaps what is operating here is an instance of the fifth cause. For didactic purposes Maimonides needs to make clear early on that no one can give a full and adequate account of Mosaic prophecy. It will be difficult enough to understand fully the account of the lesser levels of prophecy, but the unique prophecy of Moses transcends our capacity to understand. This point has to be stressed in a way which leaves no possible doubt. Yet, even to characterize other modes of prophecy we are forced to speak of them in contrast with the prophecy of Moses, and in this very process we shall be saying something about Moses as well. With enough understanding developed in the course of study and reflection, it will become clear to the reader that even when Maimonides does speak about Mosaic prophecy, he does not given any clear account of it. To take just one point, a point which Strauss discusses, we can make no sense out of the claim that there is no element of imagination in Moses' prophecy. He does after all employ metaphors and similes which are the work of the imagination. We might even say that when Maimonides appears to be speaking about the prophecy of Moses he is not really doing so, since he says nothing that is fully intelligible. However we finally understand the inconsistency about the prophecy of Moses, it is certain that it is not a contradiction, but some other form of difficulty which Maimonides includes under his term "divergence".

We have a similar case with respect to the problem of Maimonides' treatment of prayer, where again Strauss claims to have found a contradiction. "The demonstrated teaching that positive attributes of God are impossible stems from the philosophers (I, 59, III, 20); it clearly contradicts the teaching of the Law in so far as the Law does not limit itself to teaching that the only true praise of God is silence but it also prescribes that we call God 'great, mighty, and terrible' in our prayers"[23]. Admittedly, there is something not quite in order here, but it is not a formal contradiction. To start with a point that we already made earlier, an action or an imperative cannot contradict a statement. Like actions, imperatives have no truth value. They cannot be either true or false. But to contradict a statement is just to imply its falsehood. Hence, it makes no sense to speak of the law requiring a particular form of prayer as contradicting the statement that God has no positive attributes. Moreover, even if it were a contradiction it would not be a contradiction internal to Maimonides, but rather between the teaching of the Law, on the one hand, and the teaching of Maimonides on the other. We need to take a more careful look at the whole issue.

Admittedly, prayer constitutes a problem for Maimonides just because we can never say anything positive about God which is philosophically acceptable[24]. The intellectual ideal would be the worship which expresses itself only through silence. Yet, not only are we commanded by the Law to worship God in certain fixed linguistic formulas, but the need of the human spirit is such that it cannot help but express itself in words. In allowing, within his system, for both the denial of divine attributes and the duty to pray Maimonides presents us not with a contradiction, but again with a form of divergence. The two parts do not go together smoothly, and the attentive reader is forced to reflect on the implications of this inconsistency. For the untutored masses the problem need not arise at all, since they find no particular problem in the fixed formulas of prayer which praise God in positive terms and seem to affirm that He possesses positive attributes. The intellectually sophisticated will feel the problem once they have grasped the teachings of Maimonides concerning God's attributes.

How can thoughtful readers go about dealing with this inconsistency which cannot be treated as simply a logical problem in which we have to determine which of two contradictories is true and which false? They can recognize it as a divergence which is explicable by the seventh cause, and in the process they can gain insight into how Maimonides solves for himself the problem of prayer. It is clear that Maimonides might have chosen to affirm his doctrine of divine attributes and simply to have rejected categorically all possibility of prayer. Or he could have maintained a stance of simple piety with regard to prayer, and given up or remained silent about the doctrine of attributes. In holding to both simultaneously, he seems to affirm that there must be place within a single system for the demands of religious piety and the demands of philosophical truth. To present this complex notion directly to the unphilosophical reader would involve the risk of tearing him away from the life of piety. If he recognizes the inconsistency, he may never be able to return to the life of faith, but he will also not be intellectually qualified to lead the life of the worship of God through the intellect alone. Consequently, it is important to keep him from being aware that while the religious act is based on the premise that one can speak meaningfully and in positive terms about God, the philosophical analysis denies that premise. For the philosophical reader the discovery of the tension between the teaching of the Law and the teaching of philosophy will pose the problem as to which should prevail. While Maimonides enunciates the ideal of worship which makes no use of language, he also recognizes that this presents an impossible demand not only for the common man, but even for the philosopher. His solution is to retain both the language of worship and the truth about divine attributes within a single system. These elements of the system live in dialectical tension, and it is a great art to keep them in balance. Yet, as we reflect on the "divergence" between the requirement to worship and philosophical truth within the work of Maimonides, we learn a profound lesson. Contradictions must be resolved if we know with certainty which of the contradictories is true and which false. Intellectual honesty leaves us no choice but to affirm the one and reject the other[25]. About this Maimonides is absolutely uncompromising. When we do not have a genuine contradiction, but, as in the case of prayer, a divergence between the religious commandment and the philosophically demonstrated principle, it is then that Maimonides teaches us the great art of balancing the two. To know how to keep them in balance and to live with the tension is precisely what is required of the religious man who seeks and discovers philosophical truth. We should never forget that it is to just such a person that Maimonides addressed his great work.

Another type of divergence arises with respect to the principle that we have a duty to imitate God. Maimonides treats this as a duty which defines the ideal of human conduct. "For the utmost virtue of man is to become like unto Him... as far as he is able; which means that we should make our actions like unto His, as the Sages made clear when interpreting the verse, "Ye shall be holy"[26]. This theme is repeated in the Guide and is the foundation of Hilkhot De'ot which Maimonides construes as a fulfillment of the commandment to imitate the ways of God *(lehidammat biderakhav)*. Yet, he also expresses repeatedly the conviction that there is "absolutely no likeness in any respect whatever between Him and the things created by Him'[27]. How can we imitate God if there is absolutely no likeness whatsoever between God and man? The puzzle grows even more complicated when we realize that Maimonides extends this doctrine to include a denial of any relations between God and man. "There is no relation in any respect between Him and any of His creatures"[28]. Now, of course, it is only with respect to actions that we are told to be like God and we know that Maimonides was tolerant with respect to attributing to Him attributes of action. But this does little to solve our problem since even imitating God's actions suggests that there is a relation of similarity between God and man. Furthermore, "likeness" and "similarity" are symmetrical relations. This means that if in any respect man is like God, then, at least in that same respect, God is like man.

By now it is no longer necessary to point out that there can be no contradiction between a statement and a commandment. Hence, we do not have here a case of direct contradiction or contrariety, but a divergence of some sort. Yet, it is immediately evident that the premise on which the commandment to imitate God rests is problematic. We must assume that if we are so commanded it presupposes that there is some meaningful way in which the commandment can be fulfilled as, in fact, the Sages pointed out. This in turn rests on the premise that there can be some likeness between human action and divine action, and in that respect some likeness between man and God. We might formulate this premise as, "God is a being who has some similarity to man". It is opposed by the philosophical statement that, "God is a being who has no similarity whatsoever to man". We see immediately the nature of our problem. We have two opposed statements, but since they are singular propositions whose subject is "God", we have no rule for dealing with them. Maimonides, as we saw earlier, refuses to follow his predecessors in treating them either as universals or as particulars. We have here a classic case of "divergence". There is something logically wrong, but we cannot characterize it accurately and we have no device for getting it straight within the established rules of logic.

Perhaps we have some guidance from the fact that Maimonides, despite the vigor of his denial of relations between God and man, is nevertheless more tolerant of this kind of predication about God than of almost any other. He says that, "Relation is an attribute with regard to which it is more appropriate than with regard to the others that indulgence should be exercised if it is predicated of God"[29]. This indulgence would appear to be in some measure an opening to an understanding of our problem. We are again probably dealing with a case of divergence due to the seventh cause. The philosophic understanding of God rests on the premise of His absolute uniqueness. The religious understanding which aims at the ordering of the political community rests on the premise that man and God can resemble each other since men are required to be God-like in their behavior. It is important to protect the vulgar from any awareness of the divergence between these two premises, since rejection of the religious premise invites socially destructive behavior. When the learned discover the problem they will be able to rely on their training in logic to help them see that these two premises not being contradictories, are not necessarily mutually exclusive. As in the case of prayer, they will recognize that they are dealing here with the tension between an imperative of action and a philosophical conclusion. Although they rest on premises that are in some fashion opposed, we are not forced to reject the one in favor of the other. Here again the model is that of Maimonides himself who exemplifies for us the way in which a Jew who is a philosopher finds his way through the divergence by balancing, in an ongoing tension, the demands of both worlds.

A particularly difficult problem arises in connection with the assertion that God is the cause of the world. This is certainly a commonplace of Maimonidean teaching. "God... is the principle and the efficient cause of all things other than himself". "God is the efficient cause of the world, its form, and its end"[30]. Such statements can be found throughout the Guide. Moreover, they represent a truth which Maimonides claims to have proved beyond question. The demonstrations of God's existence are essentially based on establishing that God is the ultimate cause of the world. This conclusion follows necessarily from a set of seemingly rigorous philosophical arguments. Yet, it conflicts with other doctrines of Maimonides. Cause is a relation and we have already seen how vigorously Maimonides argues against the claim that there can be any relations between God and the world. He not only argues against this claim, but believes that he has also demonstrated its contradictory. In that case, it would appear that we have before us demonstrations. One asserts that, "God has at least one relation with the world, namely, cause". The other denies that God has any relation with the world whatsoever. These are, of course, singular propositions, and it may thus be that the propositions are neither contrary nor contradictory, but divergent. In that case, we cannot resolve the problem by determining which is true and which false. For the vulgar to discover that there can be any problem about understanding God as the cause of the world would be intolerable. Confronting opposed propositions might only undermine completely their faith in God the Creator. The learned, however should not fall into this error. They should understand that discourse about God is not limited by the known rules of logic, and that there may well be cases in which it is permissible, even necessary, to affirm seemingly inconsistent propositions in which the subject is "God".

It is evident that Maimonides thought in just such terms. We need only consider what he himself does with respect to the issue of God's providence and/or governance of the world. Here we have one of the most important and comprehensive of all cases of divine causality. It is complicated not only by the difficulty of arriving at an unambiguous account of Maimonides' views, but no less by the problems that we have just pointed out concerning any claims that might be made about divine causality[31]. The difficulties are openly set forth by Maimonides in a passa,, that might well serve as a model for any commentator on this subject. "For the governance and the providence of Him, may He be exalted, accompany the world as a whole in such a way that the manner and true reality of this accompaniment are hidden from us; the faculties of human beings are inadequate to understand this. On the one hand, there is a demonstration of His separateness, may He be exalted, from the world and of His being free from it; and on the other hand, there is a demonstration that the influence of His governance and providence in every part of the world, however small and contemptible, exists. May He whose perfection has dazzled us be glorified"[32]. We are in the situation in which we have demonstrations for opposed propositions that refer to God. Note that in this passage Maimonides does not speak of contrary or contradictory propositions, only of the fact that we have proved with seeming certainty that God is completely separate from the world and also that He is present in the world as its cause. If this is not a case of contradiction, then it is certainly a case of divergence. How shall we deal with it?

Affirming opposed statements about God, even if they are not formally contradictory is an offense to the intellect. Consistency is the very stuff of which all rationality is made. Yet, we are being asked by Maimonides to accept the claim that he has demonstrated inconsistent propositions about God. What we have here is remarkably similar to what we find in the section of Kant's *Critique of Pure Reason* that deals with the antinomies. There, too, the claim is made that both a thesis and its antithesis have been demonstrated, a situation which is intolerable, but inescapable. For Kant this is one of the ways in which he establishes that metaphysics is impossible, but also that we have a natural disposition to do metaphysics which persists against all counterforces. This is the point of the opening sentence of the Preface to the first edition of the first *Critique.* "Human reason has this peculiar fate that in one species of its knowledge it is burdened by questions which, as prescribed by the very nature of reason itself, it is not able to

Four. A New View of Maimonides' Method of Contradiction

ignore, but which, as transcending all its powers, it is also not able to answer". The problem is that once we are dealing with that which transcends all actual and all possible human experience we no longer have any control over the subject matter. That is why it is possible to demonstrate, or seem to demonstrate, both a thesis and its antithesis when dealing with such subjects. Kant's solution, as implied in the very title of his book, is to discover the limits of reason and then to effect the Copernican revolution of the intellect which is his special contribution to philosophical thought.

I do not want to turn Maimonides into a Kantian, but I do believe that we are able to get some insight into Maimonides from a Kantian perspective. He, too, sees that once we come to talk about God we no longer have the concepts and the controls which are necessary for philosophic clarity and reliability. Yet, we are dealing with subjects about which we cannot afford to remain agnostic. We cannot just say that we do not know and leave it at that, since in our very lives we will behave and think in such way as to have taken a stand. There are times, as in the case of providence and divine causality, when we may even have to affirm inconsistent propositions, simply because we can neither refute them nor can we give them up. This is why he can only end his comments on this subject with an expression of praise to God, "May He whose perfection has dazzled us [i.e. left our intellect stunned] be glorified". Perhaps it is helpful to remember that Kant in full awareness of the implications of his work informs us that, "I have therefore found it necessary to deny knowledge, in order to make room for faith[33]. Maimonides was certainly not fully anticipating the Kantian revolution, but he did have an acute sense of the limits of human knowledge and of our human need to go beyond what is known in those cases where demonstration is not available or not possible.

This becomes evident in a passage that has not occupied sufficiently the attention of students of the *Guide,* although it seems to overturn in one stroke much that Maimonides has repeatedly affirmed. Maimonides treats the existence of God as a demonstrated truth. Having set forth the proofs for God's existence based on the premise of the eternity of the world, he concludes, "All these are demonstrative methods of proving the existence of one deity, who is neither a body nor a force in a body, while believing at the same time in the eternity of the world"[34]. If we can prove the existence of God while affirming the eternity of the world, it appears to be self-evident that we can prove his existence while affirming the creation of the world in time. Even at Sinai the first two commandments were heard by every one according to the Sages, and this is interpreted by Maimonides to mean that since the existence of God and his unity are demonstrated truths, they were apprehended by all the people without the mediation of prophecy. For, "with regard to everything that can be known by demonstration, the status of the prophet and that of everyone else who knows it are equal; there is no superiority of one over the other"[35]. There is then no question that the unity and the existence of God have been demonstrated.

Yet, there is one passage in which Maimonides throws doubt on any claim to prove the existence of God, just on the ground that such beyond the limits of human experience and thus beyond the capacity of the human intellect. "For it is impossible for us to accede to the points starting from which conclusions may be drawn about the heavens; for the latter are too far away from us and too high in place in rank. *And even the general conclusion that may be drawn from them, namely, they prove the existence of their Mover, is a matter the knowledge of which cannot be reached by human intellects.* And to fatigue the minds with notions that cannot be grasped by them and for the grasp of which they have no instrument, is a defect in one's inborn disposition or some sort of temptation. Let us then stop at a point that is within our capacity, and let us give over the things that cannot be grasped by reasoning to him who was reached by the mighty divine overflow so that it could fittingly be said of him: With him do I speak mouth to mouth"[36].

Here we seem to have an actual instance of a contradiction. One statement affirms that there are no proofs for the existence of God, while the other affirms that there are some proofs for the existence of God. A universal negative is opposed by a particular affirmative, and these are true contradictories. In that case, we would be forced to conclude that one is true and the other false, but we do not know which is which. Did Maimonides think that he had in fact demonstrated the existence of God, or did he think that his proofs were invalid and that no demonstration is possible? We seem to have no convincing answer to this question. If we were to invoke the criterion proposed by Strauss, we would conclude that Maimonides denies that it is possible to prove God's existence, since that statement occurs only once in the Guide while its contradictory occurs many times. Should this not lead us then to conclude that most of the philosophic conclusions which are drawn by Maimonides are also unsound, since many of them derive from the proofs for the existence and the unity of God? What, for example, about the strong defense of God's incorporeality against all literal readings of Scripture and the rabbinic aggadah? This doctrine depends directly on the proofs for existence and unity. If we follow the Straussian directive we are likely to undermine the entire structure built by Maimonides and to return to a pre-scientific pre-philosophical mode of religious thought. But this would only turn the whole Maimonidean enterprise into an absurd charade for which we could find no intelligible purpose.

Here again we can be helped by greater care with the logical analysis of the issues and closer attention to Maimonides' instructions. We only can construe the propositions in question as contradictories if we formulate them with the term "proofs" as their subject. If, on the other hand, we decide that the correct formulation should have "God" as the subject, the entire situation is changed. Then they would read, "God is a being whose existence can be proved" and "God is a being whose existence cannot be proved". These are obviously singular propositions, and require a different analysis. We are now faced not with a set of contradictories, but with some form of divergence. We do not have any logical tools for dealing with this difficulty, but we can give some account of what is before us. Proving the existence of God is essential for the entire philosophical structure that Maimonides wants to erect. It is also essential to protect the purity of faith from contamination by any element of divine corporeality. Without such proof there is no basis for the claim that Maimonides' metaphorical reading of anthropomorphisms in the Bible is correct and that any literal reading is mistaken. Hence, there is more than ample reason for him to use every intellectual device available to prove the existence of God. This effort is, moreover, fully supported by the great philosophical tradition of Aristotelianism with which Maimonides associates himself. Several proofs are presented, and their reliability is invoked over and over, in order to be certain that all segments of the population, learned as well as vulgar, are protected from the destructive effects of erroneous doctrines about God. Yet, at some point it must be made clear to those of true intellectual sophistication that in the end no argument for the existence of God is completely sufficient. We force the intellect to carry us far as we can possibly go in acquiring a rational understanding of these ultimate things and rational certainty about them. In the end, however, we are, at the most critical point, dependent on faith in the prophecy of Moses. This is made known in the isolated passage which we quoted above, a passage which escaped the attention of most readers and even evoked disbelief from some translators.

This is a classic instance of a divergence which is explained by the seventh cause.

There are other inconsistencies, particularly about God, which display basically the same structure. There is, for example, the tension between the doctrine that God acts out of free choice and the opposed claim that He acts out of an inexorable inner necessity. Maimonides construes the verse which God speaks to Moses, "And thou shalt see my back", to mean, "thou shalt apprehend what follows from Me, has come to be like Me, and follows necessarily from My will—that is, all the things created by Me..."[37]. Here we have the explicit statement that all things that are created by God follow necessarily from His will. Yet, elsewhere Maimonides identifies as "the First Cause of all things, I mean God's will and free choice"[38]. The tension between these two conceptions is present throughout the *Guide*. It is, of course, the tension between the God of Aristotle who is the first cause which acts only out of necessity, and the God of Scripture, the creator of the world who acts out of complete freedom and in accordance with His own purposes. The divergence between the two notions is built into the very fabric of Maimonides' thought. He needs the Aristotelian first cause in order to be able to give a scientific account of the world in which there is a fixed natural order. He needs the freely acting Creator-God in order to provide for biblical prophecy, commandments, reward and punishment, all the elements that constitute the religious understanding of man, society, and history. He has no absolute intellectual ground for affirming the one at the expense of the other. instead he retains them both in an ongoing tension. The alert reader will recognize the problem, see quickly that because of the special character of singular propositions we do not have a standard form of contradiction or contrariety here, and then try to penetrate just how it is that Maimonides goes about dealing with this divergence.

A parallel instance occurs with regard to the tension between human freedom and God's foreknowledge. In the discussion of the subject in the *Mishneh Torah,* Maimonides begins by setting down human freedom as an absolute condition for any divine commandments to be binding on man. It is both a moral and metaphysical requirement that men have free will. At the same time, it is also an absolute condition of God's knowledge that it include knowledge of all future events. These propositions appear to be mutually exclusive. If man is truly free, then no decision has been made about what he will do until he himself makes the choice. How then can

Four. A New View of Maimonides' Method of Contradiction

God know in advance? If God does know in advance, how can there be any free choice? The only answer that Maimonides can give is that divine knowledge cannot be understood on the model of human knowledge. In some mysterious way God can know future events without causing those events to occur necessarily. We do not understand how this works, but we know with certainty that God has foreknowledge and that men are free. He adds that this is not only a matter of religious tradition, but of established scientific knowledge[39].

In the Guide we have the same tension, but it emerges in a somewhat different form. When the emphasis is on God's justice, then the principle of human freedom is stated in absolute terms. It is set down as a fundamental principle of the Torah of Moses that "man has an absolute ability to act-, I mean to say that in virtue of his nature, his choice, and his will, he may do everything that it is within the capacity of man to do..."[40]. When, however, the subject is God as cause of the world and the events in it, we have a quite different statement. Here we are given an account of the deity as, "He who arouses a Particular volition in the irrational animal and who has necessitated this particular free choice in the rational animal..."[41]. So, we have both man as absolutely free and God as necessitating each free choice. The notion of a free choice which is necessitated by an outside force seems itself to be a contradiction in terms. We are again dealing with a subject with respect to which there is the claim that inconsistent propositions have been demonstrated. In H. Teshuvah, Maimonides is open and straightforward about the seeming inconsistency. He makes no effort to hide it, nor does he attempt to resolve it. In the *Guide* he is less open about the matter, and separates his various statements so that they may not be noticed by an ordinary reader. It is, however, his expectation that these opposed statements will be noticed by the careful reader. They will engage his attention and he must decide how to deal with the issue. Having no ground for affirming one proposition and denying the other, his only option may be to do what Maimonides recommends in the Mishneh Torah, namely, to affirm both as true without being able to give an account of how it can be so.

Maimonides would be a far easier writer to understand if he had not strewn so many obstacles in our path. If he needed to include a deliberate collection of inconsistencies in his book, it would have been far easier to cope with if they were all of a standard logical type. If we were dealing with cases of contraries, subcontraries, or contradictories, we would know just how to approach them with the standard tools of Aristotelian logic.

Things would be quite clear indeed if in addition we had certain knowledge as to which of the various propositions was true and which false. It is not just a matter of perversity on the part of Maimonides that he does not make things easy for his readers. Nor is it simply a matter of his deliberate esotericism. It is above all the nature of the subject matter with which he is dealing. It is a subject matter which does not lend itself to neat and easy solutions, as the whole history of western philosophy will bear witness. Maimonides had as profound a grasp of the complexities of this subject matter as any philosopher in our tradition. He was a thinker of rigorous honesty and was incapable of self-deception. He knew full well the difference between probability and certainty, between demonstration and conjecture. He was clear about 'where knowledge ends and faith or commitment begin. As a result, he saw it as his obligation to present his readers not only with his certainties, but also with his doubts, not only with demonstrations, but also with conjectures. The reader who is competent to follow the labyrinthine structure of his argument and who pays close attention to his language and his instructions will emerge with a deep understanding of what Maimonides thought was philosophically or scientifically knowable and what was a matter of faith.

What we may learn above all is the method of high intellectual responsibility which Maimonides practiced. The notion that the secrets of the Guide will be revealed to us by a simple method of discovering so-called contradictions and determining in some mechanical way which of them he was affirming stems from a failure to appreciate the depth of sophistication and the high level of seriousness with which Maimonides did his work. I believe that in this respect he was a profound and subtle disciple of Plato (whether he had actually read much Plato, or not). In the *Phaedo,* Plato sets forth a basic principle of philosophic method. Socrates evokes from his young friend Simmias the following remarkable summary of the true way of the philosopher. "I think, Socrates, as perhaps you do yourself, that it is either impossible or very difficult to acquire clear knowledge about these matters in this life. And yet he is a weakling who does not test in every way what is said about them and persevere until he is worn out by studying them on every side. For he must do one of two things; either he must learn or discover the truth about these matters, or if that is impossible, he must take whatever human doctrine is best and hardest to disprove and, embarking upon it as upon a raft, sail upon it through life in the midst of dangers, unless he can sail upon some stronger vessel, some divine revelation, and make his voyage more safely and securely"[42]. One must never give up the search for rational demonstration or empirical evidence too soon. Neither should we suppose that nothing less than demonstration is ever useful as a guide to our thinking. The challenge is to settle for no less than demonstrative certainty whenever that is available, but lacking that ideal answer we must still exercise our full intellectual powers to achieve the best answers we can. They will inevitably fall short of the ideal, but they will reflect the deepest understanding at which we can arrive after sincere and intense struggle with the hardest and most important questions that man has to confront. That this is the method to which Maimonides is committed is evident from all that he has written. He states it explicitly when he tells us that the man who aspires to perfection attains a rank at which he pronounces the... correct opinions to be true; and in order to arrive at this conclusion, he uses the veritable methods, namely, demonstration in cases where demonstration is possible, or strong arguments where this is possible. In this way he represents to himself these matters, which had appeared to him as imaginings and parables, in their truth and understands their essence"[43].

NOTES

[1] Shlomo Pines, "The Philosophic Sources of The Guide of the Perplexed", which serves as the Translator's Introduction to his translation of the Guide published by the University of Chicago Press, 1963. See p. lxxix. All quotations in English from the Guide will be from this edition.
[2] With regard to the obligation to read with meticulous care and to pay attention to every word, see Guide, P. 15. For emphasis on the importance of logic as a necessary prerequisite, see Guide, "Epistle Dedicatory", p. 3, and 1, 34, p. 75. 3 Guide, Introduction to the First Part, P. 17.
[3] *Guide,* Introduction to the First Part, p. 17.
[4] See Israel Efros, *Maimonides' Treatise on Logic,* (New York, American Academy for Jewish Research, 1938), Chapter IV.
[5] See *De Interpretatione,* 7, 17b 17-37.
[6] *Al-Farabi's commentary and Short Treatise on Aristotle's De Interpretatione,* translated bv F.W. Zimmerman, (Oxford University Press, 1981), pp. 65-66. See also *Al-Farabi's Short Commentary on Aristotle's Prior Analytics*, translated by Nicholas Rescher. (University of Pittsburgh Press, 1963), pp. 55-57.
[7] Letter to Samuel ibn Tibbon, in *Kovetz Teshuvot ha-Rambam,* (Leipzig, 1859), p. 29d.
[8] Leo Strauss, "The Literary Character of *The Guide for the Perplexed"*, in *Persecution and the Art of Writing,* (Glencoe, The Free Press, 195Z), p. 74.
[9] *Ibid.,* p. 73. As evidence in support of this thesis, Strauss offers Maimonides procedure in the *Treatise on Resurrection* where he relies on an isolated passage in the Book of Daniel against the many other scriptural passages which seem to speak against resurrection. Even if Strauss' reading of Maimonides on this point is sound (a claim which I would not be prepared to grant), it in no way serves to establish the rule which he proposes.
[10] *Guide,* 1, 32. pp. 68-69. That Strauss was familiar with this passage goes without saying. See, e.g., his reference to it in "How to Begin to Study the *Guide of the Perplexed"*, in the Pines' translation of the *Guide,* p. xxxix. What is instructive is that despite his full awareness of this statement of Maimonides and others like it, he did not follow it but substituted instead his own rule for determining which of two contradictories Maimonides believed to be true.
[11] Cf. al-Farabi, *Short Commentary on Aristotle's Prior Analytics,* op. cit., pp. 53-54. On Avicenna see Ibrahim Madkour, *L'organon d'Aristote dans le Monde Arabe,* (J. Vrin, Paris, 1969), p. 171: "Comme Aristote, Ibn Sînā assimile les singulières aux universelles et les indéterminées aux particulières".
[12] For a discussion of this subject see Efros, op. cit., pp. 21-23. Discussing the importance of Maimonides' work in the light of the earlier logical teachings, Efros makes the wise observation that, "perhaps the significance of our work lies not where it agrees... but where it shows discrimination in daring to disagree". At least with respect to his treatment of singular propositions, Maimonides does not follow an established school.
[13] *Guide,* Introduction, p. 17.
[14] *Ibid.,* pp. 19-20.
[15] Only the early logician, ibn al-Muqaffa, used *ikhtlāf,*(as a logical term. However, he used it to mean opposition in general and also with qualifiers to mean the various types of contraries

and contradictories. See F.W. Zimmerman, "Some Observations on al-Farabi and Logical Tradition", in the Walzer Festschrift, *Islamic Philosophy and the Classical Tradition*, (University of South Carolina Press, 1973), pp. 530-531. It appears doubtful that the terminology of ibn al-Muqaffa would have been known to Maimonides.

[16] *Guide*. Introduction, p. 10.

[17] It is worth noting that ibn Tibbon in his translation does exactly the same thing when he renders the phrase *hefekh ha'emet*. In other contexts the term *hefekh* is used by him to mean "contrary" in the technical sense. Thus he begins his version of the passage on the seven causes with reference to the causes of *hasetirah 'o hahefekh*.

[18] *Guide, Introduction*, p. 15.

[19] *Ibid., p.* 19.

[20] See *Maskiyyot Kesef*, p. 9, in *Shelosha Kadmonei Mefarshei Hamoreh*, (Photocopied edition, Jerusalem, 1961).

[21] *Guide*, II, 35, p. 367.

[22] "How to Begin to Study *The Guide of the Perplexed*", op. cit., PP. xxxvi-xxxvii.

[23] *Ibid.,* p. xlviii.

[24] For a more extended discussion of this problem see, M. Fox "Hatefillah b'Maheshavto shel Harambam". *Hatefilla Hayhudit: Hemshekh Vehiddush,* Gabriel H. Cohn. ed,, (Jerusalem. 1978), pp. 142-167.

[25] On the matter of total commitment to accept as true whatever is established by demonstration, see, e.g., *Guide*. 11, 25.

[26] *Guide*, I, 52, p. 118.

[27] *Ibid., 1,* 35. This theme recurs with frequency. See, e.g., I, 55, p. 128 where Maimonides says that we must "of necessity deny, with reference to Him, His being similar to any existing thing".

[28] *Ibid.,* I, 52, p. 118. See I, 55. p. 128, where he asserts that "we must likewise of necessity deny, with reference to Him, His being similar to any existing thing".

[29] *Ibid.,* I, 52, p. 118.

[30] *Guide,* I, 16, p. 42: I, 69. p. 167.

[31] For a more comprehensive discussion of the treatment of divine Causality, in the *Guide,* see M. Fox, "Maimonides' Account of Divine Causality", to appear in the special Maimonides volume of the Proceedings of the Ninth World Congress of Jewish Studies.

[32] *Guide.* I, 72, p. 193.

[33] *Critique of Pure Reason,* Preface to the Second Edition, 8 xxx.

[34] *Guide,* II, 1, p. 249.

[35] *Ibid.,* II, 33, p. 364.

[36] *Ibid..* II, 24, p. 327. This is the translation of Pines. He notes that his version differs from that of ibn Tibbon. This translation is fully justified by the original text. Munk gives essentially the same translation and makes a point of noting that it follows the reading in all the available manuscripts and that it is also translated this way by al-Harizi. He suggests that the translation of ibn Tibbon is motivated by a desire to make this passage harmonize with all the statements that affirm proofs for the existence of God. The emphasis is my own.

[37] *Guide,* I, 38, p. 87.

[38] *Ibid.,* II, 48, p. 409.

[39] H. Teshuvah. 5: 5 and 6:5.

[40] *Guide,* III, 17. p. 469.
[41] *Ibid., II,* 48, p. 410.
[42] *Plato, Phaedo,* 85 CD. An extensive discussion of this question of Plato's philosophic methodology is contained in, M. Fox, "The Trials of Socrates: An Interpretation of the First Tetralogy". *Archiv fuer Philosophie,* 6 (3/4), 1957, pp. 226-261.
[43] *Guide,* I, 33, p. 72.

5
PROLEGOMENON

Dr. Abraham Cohen, author and editor of *The Teachings of Maimonides,* was a scholar of established reputation and recognized achievement. Apart from his original works, he made a major contribution to learning through his service as General Editor of the *Soncino Books of the Bible.* In this role as editor he produced scholarly commentaries on all the books of the Hebrew Bible, an achievement which was possible only for a man who had a deep and comprehensive mastery of the vast and complex biblical literature. His equal mastery of rabbinics was demonstrated in his *Everyman's Talmud* and in his contributions to the Soncino edition of the Babylonian Talmud in English. In the present volume Cohen approaches Maimonides in a way which was fully consistent with the scholarship of his day. However, our situation has changed considerably in the more than forty years since the book first appeared. The general cultural, intellectual, and philosophical climate has undergone a major revolution, and the study of Maimonides must now also be viewed in a radically new perspective. An analysis of this new situation in Maimonidean studies and its implications for our understanding of that great thinker will occupy a central place in this Prolegomenon. To Cohen and to most of his generation Maimonides appeared as a typical medieval philosopher, distinguished from others primarily by his Jewish faith and his incredibly vast and creative rabbinic learning. His problem was understood as the parallel of other medieval thinkers, primarily that of reconciling a revealed religion with the claims of a purely rational philosophy. It was thought that anyone with proper scholarly equipment and interest could find out easily enough just what Maimonides was saying in his various works.

131

Admittedly, the *Guide of the Perplexed* is a long and difficult book, one which Cohen thinks that, "Few readers are likely to have the patience or inclination to go through... from cover to cover."[1] In his view this is not so much a result of the intrinsic difficulty of this book, but rather a consequence of the fact that a work written in the twelfth century poses special problems for a twentieth-century student. It seemed perfectly reasonable to Cohen to alleviate the difficulties by composing the present work which has two objectives. First, it tries to give a systematic picture of the doctrines of Maimonides, presenting them in an orderly and structured pattern, though Maimonides himself had presumably failed to do so. Cohen studied not only the *Guide* but all the other works of Maimonides which had any relevance to philosophical or theological issues. He attempted in this book to bring together from the entire Maimonidean corpus a unified exposition of the system of Maimonides. Second, this book seeks to introduce the student to the thought of Maimonides by presenting him with an anthology selected with discrimination from his various works. The anthology is so structured as to allow Maimonides to speak for himself, with only brief transitional explanations by Cohen.

Given the probability that today's readers are no more diligent or scholarly than those of forty years ago the anthology stands as a contribution of lasting value. It makes available selections from a number of works of Maimonides, including some which are still not available in English. A reader seeking to acquaint himself with the style and direction of Maimonides' thought can surely make an excellent start with the selections in this volume. What we can no longer accept without question is Cohen's version of what Maimonides said and his conception of how the parts of the system (if there is a system) fit together. Here we must give consideration to the effects of Maimonidean scholarship during, the last forty years and to newer ways of studying his works.

A major development in the study of Maimonides in the last few decades has been the work of Professor Leo Strauss, whose studies force us to reject the easy certainties about Maimonides which have long been accepted. In two outstanding essays[2] Strauss laid new foundations for the study of Maimonides, especially the *Guide of the Perplexed*. Strauss has emphasized the fact that the *Guide* is an esoteric book, that is, a book whose surface doctrine hides another very different set of teachings. In his own introduction to the *Guide,* Maimonides himself makes this point very clear. He speaks repeatedly of the "secret" doctrine which must be set forth in a

Five. Prolegomenon

way which is appropriate to its secret character. Rabbinic law, to which Maimonides is determined to be faithful, had prohibited any direct public teaching of the secrets of the Torah. One was permitted to teach them only in private to selected students of proven competence, and then only the "chapter headings" might properly be taught. Abiding by this ruling, Maimonides intends to offer in his *Guide* no more than such chapter headings, and to arrange the presentation in such a way that none but the most highly qualified students will be able to follow his explanations. For this reason, as he tells us, even the chapter headings (i.e., his teaching) "are not set down in order or arranged in coherent fashion in this Treatise, but rather are scattered and entangled with other subjects that are to be clarified. For my purpose is that the truths be glimpsed and then again concealed...."[3] Such an exposition must be carefully constructed so as to protect the simple-minded from doctrines which they cannot understand and which would only harm them, while making the truth available to students who have the proper personal and intellectual preparation. Maimonides tells us explicitly that he used the following method, among others. "In speaking about very obscure matters it is necessary to conceal some parts and to disclose others. Sometimes in the case of certain dicta this necessity requires that the discussion proceed on the -basis of a certain premise, whereas in another place necessity requires that the discussion proceed on the basis of another premise contradicting the first one. In such cases the vulgar must in no way be aware of the contradiction; the author accordingly uses some device to conceal it by all means."[4] It is one of the mysteries of our intellectual history that these explicit statements of Maimonides together with his instructions for how to read his book have been almost universally ignored. This is not the place to consider the reasons. For us it is enough to have been warned by Strauss so that we may exercise appropriate caution and not repeat the mistakes of our predecessors in the study of Maimonides.

Once we begin to read Maimonides in the way that he requires of us we can no longer be comfortable about the ease with which Cohen and most other scholars attributed particular doctrines to him. Only the most painful study makes it possible for us even to hazard an opinion concerning the views of Maimonides, and such an opinion is reliable only if it emerges from a sensitive confrontation with the obstacles and subtleties of the texts. We can best grasp the nature and scope of our problem if we give some consideration to the, variety of opinions that recognized scholars have offered with respect to major problems in the interpretation and teaching of Maimonides.

We begin with the question of whether Maimonides was a model of traditional piety or, as some assert, a veiled heretic. That the latter charge is not utterly fantastic can best be understood if we remember the great controversy which arose shortly after his death, and which tore apart major Jewish communities in Europe and the East. In some places his philosophic writings were banned so that it was a serious violation for anyone to study them. Intense feelings built up to a tragic climax in the burning of the *Guide* in a public ceremony in France some thirty years after his death.' In a variety of ways the controversy continued for centuries. It is well known that only a generation ago there were *yeshivot in* eastern Europe where the study of Maimonides' *Guide* was considered *prima facie* evidence of severe heretical tendencies. No doubt, that attitude can still be found in various circles today.

Even when he was not accused of personal impiety there were always those who attacked particular doctrines of Maimonides as contrary to the fundamentals of the Jewish faith. Every student of the *Mishneh Torah* is familiar with the often-bitter criticisms of R. Abraham ben David of Posquières, some of which are on theological points. Rabad suggests, for example, that the views of Maimonides on resurrection and the world-to-come are contrary to the established teachings.

He even expresses doubt concerning the legitimacy of Maimonides' views on the incorporeality of God.[6] In the same standard editions of the *Mishneh Torah* in which the glosses of Rabad are printed we also find the *Kesef Mishneh* of R. Joseph Karo, the sixteenth century author of the' *Shulhan Aruk.* Karo consistently defends Maimonides against the attacks of Rabad, not only with respect to issues in law and jurisprudence, but also in the controversies concerning matters of theology and the fundamentals of faith. This pattern continues through the ages; to one group Maimonides is a heretic or at least propounds heretical views, while to another his teachings are a model of conventional orthodoxy. Nahmanides, in his commentary on the Pentateuch, attacks Maimonides at some points almost without restraint. In a familiar passage, Nahmanides goes so far as to say that certain views expressed in the *Guide* are so far wrong that "they directly contradict the teachings of Scripture so that it is forbidden to listen to them and certainly forbidden to believe them."[7] We know, of course, that the same Nahmanides was often a defender of Maimonides against attacks of the very sort which he himself launched. What is perhaps less known is that Maimonides found another vigorous defender against these attacks in R. Yom Tob b. Abraham of Seville. This great fourteenth-century Talmudist composed a small book, the *Sefer ha-Zikaron,* for the specific purpose of explaining and defending the views of Maimonides which had been criticized by Nahmanides.[8]

Even among recent and contemporary writers the battle continues. Ahad ha-Am represented Maimonides as a pure rationalist who imposed reason on faith and, when necessary, adjusted the norms of rabbinic law in order to force them into conformity with the demands of reason. His famous essay on Maimonides is entitled, "Shilton ha-Sekel" ("The Supremacy of Reason"). This view of Maimonides is strenuously opposed by Aharon Kaminka who claims that for Maimonides reason, philosophy, and science were all subordinated "to the absolute supremacy of his strongly held faith in the truth and eternity of the Torah of Moses and the talmudic tradition which derives from it. That faith welled up from the depths of his heart... and it alone can explain the integrity of all the remarkable achievements of his life."[9] Kaminka presents peculiar evidence for the complete orthodoxy of Maimonides and for the claim that while he assimilated philosophy into the tradition, it never dominated his thinking or his teachings. He is certain that if Maimonides had deviated in any slight degree from the norms of rabbinic doctrine this would have been detected at once and he would not have been accepted as the unexcelled authority in matters of law and faith. It is characteristic of the blindness or tendentiousness of much Maimonidean scholarship that Kaminka was able to ignore the mass of familiar animadversions on Maimonides, since to recognize them would have forced him to abandon his own thesis. In contrast to Kaminka, Tschernowitz casts serious doubts on the orthodoxy of Maimonides, asserting that he was so committed to the primacy of worldly learning that not only did he make philosophy the judge of what should be an article of faith, but "with respect to every matter of law with which he dealt, if there was any contradiction between scientific knowledge and the traditional view he almost always decided in favor of science.... Maimonides, the philosopher, is clearly visible behind the walls of his own structure of traditional Jewish law."[10] Finally, any study of the writings of Leo Strauss on Maimonides or of some of the more recent work of Shlomo Pines reveals, between the lines (if not openly), the conviction that the true views of Maimonides were very far indeed from conventional orthodoxies. The main purpose of his esoteric style in the *Guide* is, according to this view, to make it possible for him to express his heretical ideas without injuring either the social structure or the naive and useful faith of simple-minded believers.[11]

An extension of the controversy over the orthodoxy of Maimonides emerges in differences over the question concerning his relationship to Aristotle and Aristotelian philosophy. It may seem strange to some to suggest that there is any question here open to discussion, since it is a commonplace of the textbooks that Maimonides was completely under the dominance of the philosophy of Aristotle. The only generally recognized exception is his stand on the creation of the world *ex nihilo* against the Aristotelian doctrine of the eternity of matter.[12] Yet an examination of scholarly discussion reveals deep disagreement on this question as well. In one of his earliest scholarly studies Harry A. Wolfson, among the greatest historians of medieval philosophy, argues that Maimonides can only be understood as an Aristotelian. He "is a true convert to Aristotelian philosophy. To him the thorough understanding of Aristotle is the highest achievement to which men can attain." His primary purpose was to show that scriptural and rabbinic teaching was in harmony with the philosophy of Aristotle. "Maimonides was not a rabbi employing Greek logic and categories of thought in order to interpret medieval Aristotelian, Jewish religion; he was rather a true medieval Aristotelian in using Jewish religion as an illustration of the Stagirite's metaphysical supremacy."[13] Wolfson concludes that Maimonides' personal piety should not be questioned. He was without doubt a meticulously observant Jew, but his personal piety was in no way derived from or connected with his Aristotelian philosophic system. Husik goes even further in this direction radically with the claim that though the doctrines of Aristotle radically oppose the teachings of the Hebrew Bible, Maimonides was a devoted Aristotelian and tried to achieve a harmony between Greek philosophy and Torah.[14]

This widely accepted interpretation of Maimonides can be found in a variety of forms and in many places, particularly in regard to Maimonides' ethics. Because he taught the doctrine of the mean, it is often taken for granted that his ethical theory was essentially Aristotelian in origin and in its content. For M. Lazarus, in his *The Ethics of Judaism,* and David Rosin, in his *Die Ethik des Maimonides,* there is no question as to the almost pure Aristotelianism of Maimonides' ethics. Their understanding of Maimonides is by far the most common one. Yet, no less a philosopher than Hermann Cohen differs sharply from them. Cohen's famous and

Five. Prolegomenon

controversial essay, "*Charakteristik der Ethik Maimunis,*" is a major attempt to demonstrate that Maimonides' ethics were completely independent of Aristotle's and that he is, in fact, fundamentally opposed to Aristotle. Cohen holds that if Maimonides' ethics were not independent of Aristotle his doctrine would be self-contradictory, unphilosophical, and could, as a result, have no place in his system. One of the main burdens of Maimonides' thought, according to Cohen, is his battle against materialism. His great achievement is the victory of idealism over materialism, and for this very reason he cannot be thought of as supporting the essentially materialist views of Aristotle. Even Maimonides' doctrine of the mean is thought by Cohen to differ radically from the Aristotelian doctrine. Because Maimonides often used Aristotelian terminology, people have been misled into thinking that he was a follower of Aristotle's philosophy. Cohen claims that this was only a stratagem employed by Maimonides in order to gain a favorable hearing for himself. Given the dominance of Aristotle over medieval thought it would have been intellectual suicide to oppose him openly. The trick, which Maimonides mastered superbly, was to sound like an Aristotelian while undermining all the foundations of the Peripatetic philosophy.[15]

These differences concerning the interpretation of Maimonides are not necessarily related to the private commitments or personal views of the scholars in question. We find that Zvi Diesendruck, who was a professor at the Hebrew Union College, a Reform rabbinical seminary, and Yaakov Moshe Charlap, a model of old Orthodox piety in the religious quarter of Jerusalem, both agree with Hermann Cohen that Maimonides was no Aristotelian. They take this position not only with respect to his ethics but include practically the whole of his philosophy. Diesendruck argues that "the entire philosophy of Maimonides is one continuous endeavor to overcome Aristotle in the most essential points.... Maimonides differs from him in all matters of importance in metaphysics as well as ethics; in these fields he regards the Aristotelian teachings as erroneous and even dangerous."[16] Though there is no reason to think that Rabbi Charlap knew the work of Professor Diesendruck, he follows a remarkably similar line of argument. Granting that Maimonides incorporated some elements of Greek philosophy into his works, Charlap proclaims as a fact beyond all doubt that these elements were totally transformed and Judaized before Maimonides gave them a place in his writings. The terms Charlap uses for this process of intellectual transformation are the exact terms normally used for the process of religious conversion into the Jewish faith.[17] As we allow the pendulum to swing again to the opposite extreme we find one more contemporary writer affirming Maimonides' Aristotelianism and with it his complete heresy. Yaakov Becker pictures for us a Maimonides who is strikingly similar to Leo Strauss', though he gives no direct indication that he has studied or been influenced by the work of Strauss. His Maimonides is an esoteric writer determined to set forth in one work two opposed systems of thought. One is to be a system of traditional Jewish beliefs intended for the protection of the untutored masses, while the other is an Aristotelian philosophy which is *the* truth and which contradicts the religious tradition at almost every crucial point. We have here a special version of a "double-truth" theory, with Maimonides hiding his true doctrines from the eyes of the vulgar. In Becker's view, "Maimonides never resolves the contradictions between the Torah of Moses and the philosophy of Aristotle. On the contrary, he expands and deepens them. His war against Aristotle was only apparent. At the profoundest levels of the *Guide of the Perplexed* he continually deepens the abyss between these two world views. He makes absolute distinctions between them, while justifying each as appropriate for different spheres of human life."[18] Becker goes on to show, to his own satisfaction, that for Maimonides the true philosophy was that of Aristotle. His God, like Aristotle's, is in no significant respect the God of the Torah. He is not the creator of the world; he is not the power that sustains the world; there is no providence; and God has no relationship whatsoever to the world. Such is the interpretation of Becker.

What shall we make of such a welter of contradictory opinions about Maimonides? Our first conclusion must be that we can no longer rest easy with the comfortable certainties that characterized the work of Abraham Cohen in this volume, and which seem typical of most other writers on Maimonides. Students of the history of philosophy will rightly point out that this problem of interpretation is not peculiar to Maimonidean scholarship. Many major philosophers have evoked similarly contradictory interpretations. As one example, we need only think of the range of opinions regarding the relationship of Aristotle to Plato. Yet it can be argued (and, I believe, demonstrated) that hardly ever has there been such deep disagreement over so many issues and over so many centuries about the views of a single philosopher. If Maimonides does not differ in kind from other philosophers, he surely differs in degree. The reasons are not difficult to isolate. First, we must consider the effects of his literary style on which we commented earlier. Any esoteric writer is subject (by his own deliberate choice) to wider ranges of interpretation and misinterpretation than a straightforward writer. In the case of Maimonides we must always find out not only what he seems to say, but also whether he is actually saying what he seems to say. We must depend on hints and on our own capacity to construct an ordered system where there appears only to be disorder. It is no surprise that such writing evokes wildly contradictory interpretations.

The problems of interpreting Maimonides are compounded by the range of subject matter about which he wrote, the varying purposes for which he wrote, the diverse styles which he employed, the number of years which separate his earliest and latest works, and the question of the interrelationships of his various works. We can illustrate the nature of our difficulties by considering an example of the problem which faces us when we try to see Maimonides' teaching from the perspective of all the relevant passages in his writings. It is well known that in his ordering of the commandments of the Torah the number "14" plays a very significant role. His *Sefer ha-Mitzvot* (Book of the Commandments) sets forth a series of fourteen "roots", i.e., general principles for identifying, enumerating, and classifying the commandments. His great legal compilation, the *Mishneh Torah* is a codification of the commandments divided into fourteen books. Finally, in the *Guide* he informs us that he has "divided all the commandments into fourteen classes."[19] Knowing how careful a writer Maimonides was, it would be reasonable to assume that these three classifications of the commandments into fourteen groups are in some fashion related, if not identical. Yet, a first reading shows them to be quite different from each other, and if there is a relationship it is by no means obvious. In any case, we might expect that scholars would have dealt with the problem and solved it. Instead we find casual discussions and contradictory opinions with little careful attention to the texts. What is most disturbing is that these discussions and opinions are found in the works of men whose scholarly distinction is beyond all question. We find that Isidore Epstein, one of the greatest of Jewish scholars in England, says that the fourteen-fold division of the commandments in the *Guide* is a classification and summarization of the fourteen books of the *Mishneh Torah*.[20] Yet, as we shall see shortly, the differences are very great and very obvious, so much so that no one, least of all a responsible scholar, should be guilty of identifying the two Classifications as alternate versions of the same scheme. Other scholars, however they may differ in background and method, tend to treat the three fourteens in a very casual way, though this hardly seems faithful to what we know of Maimonides and his literary method. Isaac Herzog, the late Chief Rabbi of Israel, says of the three fourteens that, "This is, of course, sheer coincidence. There is no sort of logical correspondence between the respective divisions."[21] This is an opinion which Rabbi Herzog repeats in several other studies. The same view is expressed by Irving Levey, a well-known scholar in the Reform movement, when he asserts that, "Mere coincidence has thrown the number 'fourteen' into great prominence in the works of Maimonides."[22] And one of the outstanding contemporary scholars in the field of Jewish philosophy shares this opinion. S. Rawidowicz writes that the only thing these three classifications of the commandments have in common is the number "fourteen," but holds that there is no other significant connection among them, neither in their theoretical foundations nor in their practical consequences.[23]

In contrast with these views we have the analysis of Leo Strauss. He is never willing to believe that there is anything purely coincidental in the writings of Maimonides. Certainly, we should not dismiss as coincidental something as obviously connected as this threefold classification of the same set of commandments into fourteen groups. Strauss argues that it is Maimonides' deliberate plan to give the impression that the three fourteens are essentially the same in order to mislead the casual student. It would appear that he succeeded even with diligent students, as the example of Epstein would testify. Strauss would have us study these three cases carefully, note the precise differences, and from them (and other relevant evidence) determine just what Maimonides has hidden under the outer surface of the fourteens." Unhappily, Strauss does not carry his analysis further, so we do not know his solution to the problem.

For our purposes it might be fruitful to examine the texts somewhat more closely in this case, in order to see how complex and subtle the problem is. In Chapter 35 of Part III of the *Guide* Maimonides sets forth his division of the commandments into fourteen classes. Since he explicitly seems to relate this division to the fourteen books of the *Mishneh Torah* it is natural that we should assume the connection. However, when we study his text carefully we are overwhelmed by remarkable incongruities and inconsistencies. Of the fourteen books in the *Mishneh Torah* only nine are specifically mentioned in the classification in the *Guide*. A discerning student must ask himself why five of the books are omitted, and what principle determined which are omitted and which included. Further, we note that, remarkably enough, the first book of the *Mishneh Torah,* the "Book of Knowledge," is not mentioned, although Maimonides seems to view it as the foundation for all that follows in his code. On the other hand, the first three classes of commandments in the *Guide* are each associated with one section of the "Book of Knowledge." If the structures of the classifications were parallel then each class in the *Guide* should be the counterpart of one book in the *Mishneh Torah,* whereas here we find three classes associated each with one section of one book of the *Mishneh Torah*. Sometimes Maimonides refers to the individual sections by their full names, *e.g., Hilkoth Yesodei ha-Torah* (Laws of the Foundations of the Torah). At other times he refers to the content of such a section, but not to its full name. So, for example, he tells us that included in the first class, in addition to the commandments that are listed in *Hilkoth Yesodei ha-Torah, are teshuba and taaniot* (repentance and fasts). Why does he not refer specifically to the full names of the sections of the Code which bear these titles, *i.e., Hilkoth Teshuba and Hilkot Taaniot?* Is he suggesting in the *Guide* that he now wants to include only certain portions of those sections, but not all of them? Or is there some other less compromising explanation? Again we note that two sections of the same book in the *Mishneh Torah* are assigned to two different classes in the *Guide,* and that conversely sections from different books in the former are assigned to a single class in the latter. Thus, the Laws concerning Forbidden Foods are in the thirteenth class in the *Guide* and the Laws concerning Prohibited Sexual Relations are in the fourteenth class, though they are both contained in a single book, *Sefer Kedusha* in the *Mishneh Torah.* (It is worth noting that this book is among those whose names are omitted by Maimonides in this part of the *Guide.*) In turn we find, for example, that the fourth class in the *Guide* includes commandments from, at least, four different books of the *Mishneh Torah*.

In this Prolegomenon I cannot attempt even to suggest a solution to this set of problems. What is important for any serious student is to be aware of the complexity that we must cope with in almost every Maimonidean text. That complexity is multiplied if we try to see the various works of Maimonides and their parts in any kind of intelligible and coherent interrelationship. To ascribe such a problem as the three fourteens to mere coincidence, as some very responsible scholars have done, is a far too simple and far too crude a solution. To assure us that the repetition of the fourteens is deliberate, as Strauss has done, is a necessary first step in taking the texts seriously. The real achievement, however, is to solve the puzzle, to explain what Maimonides had in mind, to account for the similarities, differences, inconsistencies and obscurities which have turned this seemingly simple scheme of classification into a dark and impenetrable mystery. We have here one striking example of the kind of demands that must be made on contemporary students of Maimonides, and we can see why the easy certainties of our anthologist and his colleagues can no longer be ours.

Our grasp of the difficulties which confront us in the effort to understand Maimonides' teachings will be even clearer if we consider some additional problems of interpretation. A question which is central to the thought of Maimonides in the opinion of almost every commentator is the problem of our knowledge of God. There is no doubt that Maimonides considered the true knowledge of God to be a necessary condition for the attainment of the highest human perfection. The very first obligation of a Jew that he records in his *Mishneh Torah,* in the first section of the first chapter of the first book, is that we are commanded to know that God exists and that He is the necessary basis for all else that exists. Similarly, the first commandment listed in his *Sefer ha-Mitzvot* is the commandment to believe in the existence of God. Chaim Heller, in his scholarly edition of the text of that work, suggests that according to the reading in the Arabic text it would be appropriate to render this commandment as speaking of *knowing,* rather than believing, that God exists. This same theme permeates much of the *Guide* and seems to reach its climax in the very last chapter where the true knowledge of God is presented as the ultimate end of man. Philosophers and prophets agree on this, according to what Maimonides says in that last chapter.

Yet there are some very troubling, questions which no student can afford to ignore. How can we be commanded to know anything, especially something as arcane and inaccessible as the ultimate truth about the world? If I truly have knowledge of God, and knowledge here clearly means intellectual apprehension, then I have penetrated the secret of the very ground of all being. To strive for this goal may be every man's duty, but it is strange, to say the least, to insist that we are all *commanded* to reach the goal. Immanuel Kant taught us the principle that ought implies can, that is, that whatever a man is truly obligated to do he is able to do. Conversely, we are not obligated to do that which we are incapable of doing. How puzzling then that Maimonides, who often asserts that only a small intellectual elite is capable of achieving true knowledge of the highest matters, should make the highest knowledge of all obligatory for all men. The confusion grows greater if we consider further aspects of the question.

In Part I, Chapter 15 of the *Guide* Maimonides seems to be saying that whoever makes the effort to know God succeeds, and we can properly be commanded to make such an effort. Moreover, in the first two chapters of Part II of the *Guide* Maimonides claims to have presented rational demonstrations of the existence, unity, and incorporeality of God. If these are, in fact, valid demonstrations, as he apparently believed them to be, then they are such that any man should be able to grasp them. For every man is, as a man, endowed with rational powers, which means, among, other things, with the power to follow a rational argument. That man is endowed with such intellectual powers in his very nature is established in the very first chapter of the *Guide,* since this is how Maimonides interprets the biblical statement that man was created in the image of God. So far, then, it appears reasonable to command man to know God.

As we continued to study the texts, however, a typical set of Maimonidean contradictions emerges, and our earlier certainties are no longer easily tenable. In the *Mishneh Torah,* in the same first chapter which commands us to know God, we are surprised to discover that Maimonides also says that the genuine truth about God's nature is beyond all human knowledge. Even Moses, who stands above all other men in his capacity to apprehend God, was incapable of truly knowing Him.[25] The point is repeated and elaborated in the *Guide* with a specific reference to this earlier passage in the *Mishneh Torah.* Speaking of Moses' expressed desire to know God fully, Maimonides points out that Scripture tells us that his plea was denied by God who hid from him this ultimate knowledge. "When I say He hid from him, I intend to signify that this apprehension is hidden and inaccessible in its very nature."[26] If Moses could not know God truly, then surely no other man can achieve such knowledge. In fact, Maimonides goes on in the very next sentences to warn that when man has reached his intellectual limits any effort to go beyond is only destructive. So it now appears that we cannot really know God and we are mystified by the commandment which says that we must.

When we consider what Maimonides says, that we *can* know of God our situation seems even less promising. We are told explicitly that we can gain no positive knowledge whatsoever of God. We know Him only through negative attributes. This means that we can only know what He is not, but never what He is. In fact, even when we speak of God as having certain positive qualities we must interpret them negatively. Thus, to say that God is living is only to say that He is not dead. "Of this thing [*i.e.*, God] we say that it exists, the meaning being that its nonexistence is impossible."[27] It is a strange kind of knowledge indeed which is purely negative. In fact, Maimonides seems to be saying that no man is able to fulfill the commandment to know God, which makes us wonder whether there is any meaningful sense in which it can be a commandment at all. Yet there is no doubt that be explicitly and repeatedly records and codifies such a commandment.

Now we are, of course, familiar with the fact that Maimonides considers this kind of knowledge of God to be significant. At least, he certainly says in various places that it is significant knowledge. However, as he develops his theory of negative attributes Maimonides seems to present the paradoxical doctrine which affirms that the less we know about God the more we know about Him, so that our ideal should be to negate everything that is predicated of Him in order to know everything about Him. "Accordingly the negative attributes make you come nearer ... to the cognition and apprehension of God.... Desire then wholeheartedly that you should know by demonstration some additional thing to be negated, but do not desire to negate merely in words. For on every occasion on which it becomes clear to you by means of a demonstration that a thing whose existence is thought to pertain to Him should rather be negated with reference to Him, you undoubtedly come nearer too him by one degree.... On the other hand, the predication of affirmative attributes of Him, is very dangerous.[28] What can we claim to know about the God, whom we are commanded to know, if all we can do is state what He is not? If we deny only *some* positive qualities, then we leave open the possibility that the innumerable remaining positive qualities may properly be predicated of God. If, on the other hand, we deny in principle *every* positive quality, without undertaking the impossible task of identifying and enumerating them, then we would appear to be in danger of the blasphemous heresy that God is nothing. It seems to help little if we call Him by such names as the Holy Nothingness. While there is every reason to think that Maimonides did not want to fall into this trap, it is extremely difficult to find a way out of it.

Conventional commentators try to resolve the dilemma, if they recognize it at all, by appealing to Maimonides' doctrine that we predicate positive terms of God analogically, rather than literally, and that what we can affirm of Him are the so-called attributes of His actions which we see in our own experience. Though Maimonides explicitly introduces the notion of the analogical use of terms with respect to God, it is not very helpful, as he himself seems to recognize in other places. The key to the problem is that a term used as a common predicate for two subjects must be used either unequivocally or equivocally, that is, it must either have the same meaning in both cases or a different meaning. If I say that God is wise and compassionate and that Mr. Cohen is wise and compassionate, I must determine whether the predicates mean the same thing in both cases. If they do, then I can rightly claim that I understand God's wisdom and compassion on the model of Mr. Cohen's wisdom and compassion. Of human wisdom and compassion I have direct experience, and I can, therefore, justly claim to know something about God, namely, that He is wise and compassionate in the same way that men are. However, this alternative has been explicitly closed to us by the doctrine which denies that I can ever have such positive knowledge of God. For this reason, then, I must say that I use these terms with totally different meanings in the case of God, and meanings which I cannot specify. It follows that when I speak of God as wise and compassionate I am not saying anything intelligible, since I have no idea of what these predicates mean and can put no content into them. Thus, analogy is not much help, and we are back to the negative attributes with which we began. This is acknowledged by Maimonides, although he earlier introduced the idea of analogical terms. He says that, "It has already been demonstrated that anything that we think of as a perfection—even if it existed as pertaining to Him—in accordance with the opinion of those who believe in the attributes, nevertheless would not belong to the species of perfection that we think of, save only by equivocation, just as we have made clear. Accordingly you must of necessity go over to the notion of negation."[29]

    The familiar Maimonidean solution to all this is usually taken to be the notion that though we do not know any positive attributes of God we do know His actions or their consequences in the world. We speak of these as if they had been done by God just as a man would have done them. So when there is a great natural catastrophe which harms people and property we speak of God as being angry, since only great anger would move a man to behave in this way. At best this is only a way of speaking, but it adds no illumination and no knowledge. However we may find it convenient to speak, it seems that we have no knowledge of God since in principle this knowledge is beyond us. It is even doubtful whether on Maimonides' own grounds we can properly speak of God's actions, for to speak of His actions leads ultimately to affirming positive attributes and thus to the same compromises of His absolute unity which Maimonides has taken the greatest pains to avoid.

Here again we have seen how difficult it is to gain a clear understanding of the teachings of Maimonides. There is no doubt that he records the duty to know God as the very first commandment. Nor is there any doubt that he repeatedly speaks in many places in his works about the knowledge of God as the true perfection of man. He treats it as an ideal toward which every man should direct his supreme efforts, and identifies the realization of that ideal with the summit of man's self-fulfillment. Even the most casual reader could cite numerous passages from various books to show that this is the teaching of Maimonides. Yet when we examine it in the total context and full development of his own analysis we seem forced to conclude that this ideal is not only impossible, but empty of content and meaning. There are real hazards here. First, there is the serious danger of misunderstanding and misinterpreting Maimonides. Given certain predilections, it is not very difficult to read him in such a way that he turns out to be a crypto-heretic. Considering all that we know of the man and his life, his piety and his meticulous commitment to the law, this hardly seems like a tenable position. However, with some ingenuity it is an interpretation which can certainly be worked out and made plausible. It is just as easy to read the texts in such way that he emerges as a man of unquestioned and conventional orthodoxy. What must be stressed is that no responsible scholarly reading of Maimonides may be so tendentious as to ignore what does not fit into the reader's preconceived scheme. With great effort and with penetrating intellect he must be read as he asked us to read him. Only then can we hope that a reliable and sound understanding will be open to us. In addition to the danger of misinterpreting Maimonides there is the danger which deeply concerned him that casual readers might misunderstand him and be corrupted by their misunderstanding. He tried strenuously to avert this danger by composing his books, especially the *Guide*, in the way he did. Nevertheless, the hazards are there, and casual students may well reach destructive conclusions on the basis of their limited and confused understanding of this great thinker.

Five. Prolegomenon

Granted that Maimonides is a difficult and puzzling writer who demands inordinate efforts of his readers, we certainly must ask whether for us today that effort is justified. Have we any reason, apart from purely historical curiosity or antiquarian interest, to study Maimonides with enthusiasm today? Does his thought have any contribution to make to contemporary man? Is there, at least, some element of continuing relevance to general philosophic concerns or to specifically Jewish interests? We must recognize and acknowledge without hesitation that much of what Maimonides wrote seems to have outlived its usefulness to us. In his Preface, and again in his Introduction, Cohen stresses this point. "The spirit of the book [*i.e., The Guide*] is immortal, but much of its actual content is obsolete... It does not answer the perplexities of the religious mind today."[30] That the science of Maimonides' twelfth-century world is out of date surely cannot be seriously questioned. Traditionalists who are reluctant to admit that anything in Maimonides could be obsolete might take comfort from the fact that no less a rabbinic authority than Meir Lebush Malbim faced this issue squarely more than a century ago. In the introduction to his commentary on the Book of Ezekiel, Malbim discusses Maimonides' interpretation of the vision of the chariot in the first chapter. As he puts it, "Maimonides' interpretation has been refuted because the foundations on which he built it have been refuted. The astronomy, natural science, and ancient philosophy which were the foundations and supports of his interpretation have been completely undermined and destroyed by the scientific research which has developed in recent generations. This research has built its astronomy and structured its natural sciences on new foundations which are stronger and more reliable."

We might well argue that not only Maimonides' science, but his philosophy and theology as well are completely obsolete. Recent philosophical developments in the western world, especially logical positivism and linguistic analysis, cast grave doubts on the meaningfulness of many traditional philosophic questions, and on the validity of their solutions. Similarly, the "new theology" claims to cut the ground out from under classical theological concerns and methods. What is left then for a twelfth-century Jewish thinker to teach us today, if his science is wrong, and his philosophy and theology open to the charge of meaninglessness or irrelevance?

One could defend the view that the stance of contemporary philosophy is by no means the last word, and that there is much of continuing value in earlier metaphysical studies. However, it would require far more space than is available in this brief essay to work out such a claim. Abandoning that effort for the present, it will be more fruitful to concentrate on the significance of Maimonides for contemporary thought in the fields of ethics, the philosophy of religion, and especially of Judaism. It seems to me clear that he has much to teach us about these matters which continue to be of interest and value.

We can learn first, and most importantly, from Maimonides an uncompromising and fearless intellectual honesty in all matters having to do with religion. At a time when the forces of closed-minded intellectual timidity have managed to gain a position of some prominence, even in certain Jewish circles, the example of Maimonides is of great interest. While protecting the integrity of the system of Jewish law, he left room for the intellect to develop its own best understanding concerning the fundamental questions of faith. In his interpretation of the Bible he battled against literalist fundamentalism, finding his justification in the long-established tradition of nonliteral midrashic interpretation. The Law is necessarily fixed, because the integrity of society demands that the precepts of the Law must be obligatory. But the human effort to grasp the ultimate nature of things must, in Maimonides' view, never be totally constricted or suppressed. We can command patterns of behavior, and we rightly expect men to subordinate their private inclinations to legal norms. It is dangerous and self-defeating to command conformity in the formulation, understanding, or apprehending of ultimate philosophical or theological matters. Here the mind of man must be left free to find its own way. If, by chance, we were to succeed in preventing man from thinking, we would also have succeeded in robbing him of what is essential to his humanity.

It may seem strange to ascribe such intellectual openness to the same Maimonides who set down a rigid dogmatic structure of thirteen obligatory principles of faith, and who was extremely severe in his explicit condemnation of any Jew who denies even one of these principles. How can he be held up as a model of commitment to freedom of thought? The answer is, as usual, that we must look at the principles of faith in the total context of Maimonides' thought, otherwise we are bound to misunderstand their purpose and their force. In the same *Commentary on the Mishnah* in which the seemingly rigid creed is set forth, we find that Maimonides distinguishes sharply between the fixity of the norms of law which regulate our behavior and the flexibility which is proper in the formulation of theoretical principles. "I have said many times that when there are differences of opinion among wise men about principles of faith which do not lead to any definite actions, then it is not proper to issue a fixed decision in accordance with any one view."[31] Maimonides is saying here that the formulations of the practical *halaka* must be fixed and that differences of opinion must be resolved so that men will know what behavior is required of them. On the other hand, what we might call the theoretical *halaka*, the expressions of the principles of faith, do not demand fixity and agreement. So long as we know the law and observe it, we are free to carry on unrestricted speculation about all those complex theoretical matters which are necessarily subject to diverse views. Now it is known that hardly any aspect of Maimonides' thought engendered so much subsequent debate and diversity of opinion as did his creed. Later thinkers attacked individual articles, or the entire formulation. Some denied that there are thirteen principles of faith and substituted some lesser number. Others rejected the very notion of principles of faith since they argued that we can properly make no distinction among the commandments since all are of equal dignity. Even the principle that God is incorporeal was questioned by Rabad in a famous gloss in the *Mishneh Torah*. He disputes Maimonides' contention that the belief in God's incorporeality is one of the essentials of faith. Says Rabad: "Greater and better men than he [i.e., Maimonides] have accepted the doctrine of corporeality based on their reading of various scriptural and aggadic texts. It is clear from the rest of this gloss that Rabad did not himself believe that God is corporeal nor did he want to encourage that opinion in others. He was only denying that the issue could be settled dogmatically, since there is some ground on which to base divergent opinions. We can see then that by his own expressed rules of method Maimonides had to leave such matters open, for there are educated and reasonable men who differ in their understanding and conclusions.

We must try to resolve the apparent contradiction between this commitment to freedom of thought and the fierce uncompromising rigor with which the thirteen principles of faith are presented by Maimonides. The solution lies in the deep concern that Maimonides had for the protection of the social order, and for making available in that order the maximum opportunity for men to achieve the highest and most reliable knowledge of the highest things. Without an ordered society there can be neither the personal security nor the leisure which men need in order to engage in philosophical or theological speculation. Therefore, he insists on the absolutely binding force of the divine law which directs and regulates the behavior of men. Moreover, though the highest human fulfillment is in the attainment of true knowledge, comparatively few men are inclined to the requisite and demanding philosophic activity. Therefore, the unreflective masses must be provided with a set of sound opinions which will guide them in their thinking and confirm them in right action. We should, however, never confuse this utilitarian imposition of opinion or belief as a social necessity with any attempt to restrict thoughtful men in the process of serious inquiry. The latter must not only be allowed, but encouraged, for theirs is the only road to true human perfection. The point is set forth by Maimonides a number of times, of which the following is a typical example. "Just as it behooves us to bring up children in the belief, and to proclaim to the multitude, that God... is one and that none but He ought to be worshipped, so it behooves that they should be made to accept on traditional authority the belief that God is not a body; and that there is absolutely no likeness in any respect whatever between Him and the things created by Him; and that His existence has no likeness to theirs.... This measure of knowledge will suffice for children and the multitude to establish in their minds that there is a perfect being, who is neither a body nor a force in a body, and that He is the Deity, that no sort of deficiency and therefore no affection whatever can attain Him."[33] This way of imposing belief on the masses has a kind of social utility which justifies it, but it must never be permitted to limit free speculation on the part of those whose intellect leads them to think about these matters. Much later in the *Guide* Maimonides distinguishes sharply between the masses whose beliefs are imposed by 'tradition and the independent mind of the man of true knowledge and, hence, true piety. He speaks of his desire "to confirm men in the intention to set their thought to work on God alone after they have achieved knowledge of Him, as we have explained. This is the worship peculiar to those who have apprehended the true realities; the more they think of Him and of being with Him, the more their worship increases. As for someone who thinks and frequently mentions God, without knowledge, following a mere imagining or following a belief adopted because of his reliance on the authority of somebody else, he is to my mind outside the habitation and far away from it and does not in true reality mention or think about God."[34] Once we understand the force of such passages we can see that Maimonides was in fact deeply committed to free inquiry and did not consider it desirable to impose dogmatic orthodoxies on all men. For our age nothing less is acceptable, and it would

Five. Prolegomenon

benefit contemporary authoritarian dogmatists greatly if they allowed themselves to be taught by the greatest mind of the Jewish Middle Ages.

Just as we can profit from an imitation of Maimonides' lack of dogmatism so can we learn much from him about the possibilities and the limits of reason in general. We saw earlier that there are some ambiguities with respect to his conception of the role of reason in the solution of crucial human problems. We alluded to one of the typical views earlier when we mentioned the title and content of Ahad ha-Am's essay, "The Supremacy of Reason." This conception of Maimonides as pure rationalist is echoed by Abraham Cohen in his Preface to this volume when he says, "His philosophy may be antiquated, but his insistence on the supremacy of reason and his emphasis on knowledge as the essential preparation for religious comprehension are of eternal value"[35] That Maimonides placed an extremely high value on reason is indisputable, yet it is a mistake to overlook the fact that he also recognized clear limits to reason. This comes out in two ways that are important for our own time.

The first significant lesson is that man cannot limit himself only to that which is rationally certain, for in doing so he finds it impossible to deal with some of the most urgent of human concerns. A widely held view among contemporary philosophers is that we have no ground for belief about any matter unless it is empirically verifiable or rationally demonstrable. Unhappily, most of the deepest issues that require decision on our part are neither verifiable nor demonstrable. Should we then resign from the human community or from all personal and intellectual responsibility because we cannot answer with demonstrative certainty the questions which are before us? The way of Maimonides is worthy of consideration. He did not find reason fully adequate to deal with all basic questions. He recognized clearly that there are matters for which we can find no help in logic or in the natural sciences, matters which cannot be dealt with either by rational metaphysical speculation or empirical inquiry. Yet he did not on this ground abdicate all responsibility. Intellectual honesty requires that we first determine the boundaries of our rational capacity to deal with certain questions. Listen to the clear and unambiguous way in which he presents his position. "All that Aristotle states about that which is beneath the sphere of the moon is in accordance with reasoning; these are things that have a known cause.... However, regarding all that is in the heavens, man grasps nothing but a small measure of what is mathematical... the Deity alone fully knows the true reality, the nature, the substance, the form, the motions, and the causes of the heavens.... And to fatigue the minds with notions that cannot be grasped by them and for the grasp of which they have no instrument, is a defect in one's inborn disposition or some sort of temptation. Let us then stop at a point that is within our capacity, and let us give over the things that cannot be grasped by reasoning to him who was reached by the mighty divine overflow so that it could be fittingly said of him: With him do I speak mouth to mouth."[36]

Reason has its limits and an intelligent man should recognize those limits. But responsible human life often forces us to take a stand on questions for which rational inquiry offers us no certain answers. We are not free to remain neutral or to take no stand, simply because too much is at stake. Neither should we deceive ourselves into supposing that we have taken a stand on the grounds of rational demonstration or scientific evidence when we have not. From Maimonides we can learn how to see our limits, be intellectually honest, and yet commit ourselves when we must, in the full awareness that we have chosen to go beyond reason. It is essential to know why we have done so and to be clear about the ground we have substituted for reason. Maimonides' treatment of the problem of the creation of the world versus the doctrine of the eternity of matter is the best possible model for us to follow. Avoiding every temptation to self-deception, he shows us with remarkable force and clarity how to approach the resolution of such an issue. He can produce no demonstrative evidence for either thesis, yet it is urgent that he take a stand. In this case he does so on purely religious grounds, making clear what those grounds are, why he has chosen them, and above all that should reason ever prove to be adequate to the question he would be ready to give his allegiance to any rationally demonstrated position without being limited by a fixed prior reading of Scripture. Whoever imitates Maimonides will neither abandon rational and empirical evidence, nor will he be so imprisoned by his desire to know all things that he claims certainty without evidence.

There is a second and related lesson to be learned from this aspect of Maimonides' thought. If we are today no longer very much troubled by some of the classical metaphysical problems which deeply occupied him and his generation, we are very much concerned with moral problems that are similar to his. Questions of personal conduct, relations to other men, obligations to society and to the state—such questions are essentially the same today as they were then, in spite of the changes in the conditions and circumstances of our lives. Moral philosophy is perhaps the greatest

Five. Prolegomenon

intellectual failure of western man. Since antiquity our best minds have devoted themselves to the task of creating a rational morality, of finding in reason the grounds of obligation as well as the content of our duty. Our vast literature in the field of ethical theory is one continuing testimony to our inability to cope with the problem by reason alone. Yet we continue to try because the alternative seems to be moral chaos. I consider it to be one of the greatest of all Maimonides' achievements that he saw this problem clearly and without illusions. Maimonides teaches explicitly that morality is not derived from reason and that moral statements are neither true nor false. Yet he does not conclude from this that what is open to us is only moral anarchy. Because he is under no illusions concerning the capacity of reason to deal with moral questions, he sees that a move must be made in another direction. Morality is too important for the individual and for society to allow ourselves the luxury of demanding either rational certainty or nothing. Maimonides frankly acknowledges that we must turn here to tradition, religion, social convention, or some thing similar. Speaking of the last eight of the ten commandments (the first two being, in his view, rationally demonstrable) he says that, "As for the other commandments, they belong to the class of generally accepted opinions and those adopted in virtue of tradition, not to the class of the *intellecta*."[37] *His* treatment of morality is complex and subtle, and as a faithful Jew he locates its source in the divine commandments. Contemporary Judaism would do well to reflect on the way of Maimonides. Contemporary philosophy would do equally well. It is not my contention that we must adopt the Maimonidean commitment to morality as divine commandment, though this is surely one viable option. It is important that we consider his arguments against the presumed rational foundations of morality, and face with intellectual honesty the need to base our moral rules on some other foundation. Maimonides can save us here from much of the confusion, much of the cant, and much of the self-deception which surrounds current moral discourse.

In this brief Prolegomenon I have tried to suggest both some of the problems and some of the benefits of the study of Maimonides. Readers of Cohen's anthology can get important first insights into the teachings of the great medieval sage. Beginning with these insights, one may hope that they will be led to further disciplined study in the full awareness that they are dealing with one of the most subtle and most rewarding of all great thinkers. In studying Maimonides properly we are engaged in more than a purely historical exercise. We open up valuable perspectives on some of the most aggravated problems of our own time. Moses Maimonides, when properly understood, is both the greatest of the teachers of Torah and a true guide of the perplexed.

29 Elul 5728 MARVIN FOX
Professor of Philosophy
The Ohio State University

Notes

[1] Introduction, p. vii

[2] See especially, Leo Strauss, "The Literary Character of the *Guide for the* Perplexed" in Essays on *Maimonides,* ed. Salo W. Baron (Columbia University Press, 1941). Reprinted in Leo Strauss, *Persecution and the Art of Writing* (The Free Press, 1952). See also, Leo Strauss, "How to Begin to Study the *Guide of the Perplexed"* in the Shlomo Pines translation of the Guide (University of Chicago Press, 1963). All quotations from the Guide in this essay are from the Pines translation.

[3] Guide, Introduction to the First Part.

[4] *Ibid.*

[5] For a recent useful study of the controversy, see Daniel Jeremy Silver, *Maimonidean Criticism and the Maimonidean Controversy, 1180-1240* (Leiden, 1965).

[6] Glosses on *Hilkot Teshuba,* III, 7; VIII, 2 and 7.

[7] Commentary of Nahmanides on Genesis, 18:2.

[8] Yom Tob b. Abraham, *Sefer ha- Zikaron,* ed. Moshe Yehuda Blau (New York, 1957).

[9] A. Kaminka, "Ha-Emuna v'ha-Bikoret ha-Siklit b'Mif'alo shel ha-Rambam," *Haarez,* No. 4788, (5695) pp. 17-18.

[10] H. Tschernowitz (Rav Tzair), "Lu lo Kam k'Moshe," *M'oznayim,* III, Nos. 4-5, pp. 396-397.

[11] See the Strauss essays referred to above, N. 2, and Pines' Introduction in his translation of the Guide.

[12] Cf., below, pp. 50-54.

[13] Harry A. Wolfson, "Maimonides and Halevi: A Study in Typical Jewish Attitudes toward Greek Philosophy in the Middle Ages," *Jewish* Quarterly Review, 11, 191 I1912, pp. 306, 314.

[14] Isaac Husik, *A History of Medieval Jewish Philosophy,* (Philadelphia, 1944) pp. 299-300.

[15] Hermann Cohen, "Charakteristik der Ethik Maimunis," *Moses ben Maimon,* Band I (Leipzig, 1908) pp. 85,102, 109, 111-113.

[16] Zvi Diesendruck, "The Philosophy of Maimonides," *CCAR Yearbook,* XLV, 1935, P. 358.

[17] Y. M. Charlap, *Mei Marom: Misabib l'Shmona Perakim* (Jerusalem, 5705) pp. 13, 85-86.

[18] Yaakov Becker, *Mishnato ha-Pilosofit shel ha-Rambam* (Tel Aviv, 1955) pp. 19-20.

[19] *Guide,* III, 35.

[20] 1. Epstein, "Maimonides Conception of the Law and the Ethical Trend of his Halachah," *Moses Maimonides: Anglo-Jewish Papers in Connection with the Eighth Centenary of His Birth,* ed. I. Epstein, (London, 1935) p. 64.

[21] I. Herzog, ibid., P. I43.

[22] Irving Levey, "Maimonides as Codifier," *CCAR Yearbook,* XLV, 1935, pp. 368-396.

[23] S. Rawidowicz, "Sefer ha-Petiha l' 'Mishneh Torah," *Metzudah,* (5715) P. 137.

[24] Strauss, *Persecution, op. cit.,* p. 63.

[25] *Hilkoth Yesodei ha-Torah, I,* 9 and 10.

[26] *Guide,* I, 21.

[27] *Ibid.,* I, 58.

[28] *Ibid.,* I, 60.

[29] *Ibid.,* I, 60; cf., I, 54: I, 56.

[30] Below, p. 17.

[31] Commentary on *the Mishnah, Sotah,* III, 3.

[32] *Hilkoth Teshuba*, 111, 7.
[33] *Guide*, I, 35.
[34] *Ibid.*, III, 3 1.
[35] Below, p. viii.
[36] *Guide*, II, 24.
[37] *Guide*, II, 33.

6

THE GUIDE OF THE PERPLEXED

The Guide of The Perplexed. By Moses Maimonides. Abridged edition with Introduction and Commentary by Julius Guttmann. Translated by Chaim Rabin. London: East and West Library, 1952, 233 pp.

  The appearance of a new edition of Maimonides' *Guide* would be an event of great importance in any age. It is of particular importance, however, that the East and West Library has in the past few years published popular editions of a number of Jewish philosophical classics culminating with this edition of the *Guide of The Perplexed.* Theological discussion has recently begun to flourish again in English speaking Jewish communities. There is a noticeable concern among rabbis and thoughtful lay people with philosophical and theological questions, and it is good at such a time to have the works of the greatest Jewish thinkers of other ages available for ready reference.

  This edition of Maimonides' *Guide* has many virtues and, inevitably, some defects. The translation, which is new, seems to be reasonably accurate, though there are some glaring errors and occasional infelicities. A typical instance of bad translation can be found at the very beginning of the text (p. 52), where we find the following sentence: "The word Image, on the other hand, is applied to *physical form,*[1] i.e. the essential feature of a thing by which it becomes what it is..." Even a cursory reading would make it clear that the term "physical form" is impossible here. The sentence refers to "image" as man's essence, and is concerned (as the following sentences show) to make clear the distinction between man's physical form which is accidental, and his intellect which is his essence. As the text (even in this translation) goes on to say, "it is because of this intellectual perception that the words in *the image of God He created him are used".* This is not an isolated instance, but in spite of a few such errors the translation is certainly adequate.

Apart from errors there are also many unnecessarily awkward and cumbersome renditions of very simple sentences. Thus, (choosing again from the beginning) we find with reference to the Hebrew word *to'ar* the following: "That is a term which cannot, God forbid, under any circumstances whatsoever be applied to the Almighty Lord". (p. 51). The same sentence is rendered by Friedlander much more simply and just as accurately. His translation reads, "This term is not at all applicable to God". In spite of the translator's claim in his Preface that he has sought to preserve the simple and direct style of Maimonides, he manages more frequently than is necessary to make simple sentences complex and lucid expressions obscure.

The abridgement is very well done.[2] Typical sections from each of the parts of the *Guide* have been included. They have been selected wisely and judiciously, and have been arranged in such a way as to form a fairly continuous argument. In order to make the book easier for the general reader, many complicated arguments are omitted as much would be incomprehensible, without a fairly good knowledge of the philosophic tradition on which Maimonides built. In addition, Professor Guttmann's excellent notes are helpful and illuminating. Unfortunately they are too few in number and too limited in scope. Any reader, and particularly the general reader to whom the book is directed, needs considerable help in his first study of Maimonides. A popular edition such as this would have been immeasurably better if it had provided the reader with a very full commentary, instead of a relatively small number of occasional notes.

Excellent as this abridgement is there are some serious questions about the adequacy of any abridgement of a classic work. A great book has a certain integrity which is expressed in its systematic structure and in the interrelationships of its parts. An abridgement may offer the reader some idea of the author's main doctrines, but it makes impossible more than a verbal grasp of the meaning of these doctrines. Unless we can see a theory or an argument in its total context we can neither reliably judge its adequacy nor, apprehend its inner meaning. This is particularly the case with Maimonides. In the light of his reluctance to commit metaphysical truths to writing, and his assertion that he is offering only outlines or chapter headings, and that these have been deliberately mixed up so that only an acute student can find his way through the maze, it would seem almost futile to try to understand Maimonides properly in any abridgement. Arguments which are difficult enough when studied in their full version

Six. Review. Julius Guttman: Guide of the Perplexed by Moses Maimonides

become impossibly cryptic when they are cut. In the abridged version the light, which the various parts of the book shed on each other is considerably darkened, and the reader often finds himself struggling to make sense out of views that are senseless in the form that he is studying them. We may well recall Maimonides' own words of instruction to his readers:

> If you want to get the greatest benefit from reading this book and not to miss any of its points, bring the various chapters of it to bear on the interpretation of each other. Nor should you be satisfied, in reading any particular chapter, with merely understanding its general argument, but try to get at the full import of each word employed in the course of exposition, even if it has nothing to do with the subject of that chapter. The expressions used in this treatise have not been chosen at random, but are carefully thought out and meticulously marshaled, so as not to fall short of the full explanation of any difficulty. Anything in it, which seems out of place, in fact, contributes to the elucidation of some subject discussed in another place. Therefore, do not treat such passages with suspicion, which would only be an insult to the author and you would deprive yourself of benefit. Rather, study carefully every point that demands it and go on pondering over it; for just these will resolve for you the greatest difficulties of the Law which disturb the minds of most intelligent people.

These are rules of procedure which ought to be followed in the serious study of any serious book.

In addition to the text and the notes, the book's value is much increased by the fine quality of Professor Guttmann's Introduction. He has succeeded in explaining some of the basic principles of Maimonides' philosophy with such clarity that the average reader should feel much more at home even in the more abstruse sections of the Guide. Guttmann's comments are carefully tied to the actual selections in the text. The main topics which Maimonides takes up are discussed in this introduction with care and lucidity. Every reader, but especially those who approach Maimonides for the first time, will find in Professor Guttmann's introductory remarks some reliable guidance for his own perplexities over the *Guide of The Perplexed.*

No review of a new edition of Maimonides' great philosophical work would be complete without some attempt to determine the meaning of the book for our own time. Contemporary Jewish theological discussion has tended to move so strongly in the direction of the mystical and the irrational that Maimonides' extreme rationalism is a balancing force of much value. Even sophisticated theologies sometimes reflect current intellectual fashions in an uncritical way. Much contemporary Jewish theology gives the impression of having swallowed whole the irrationalist doctrines which are currently influential. Careful and widespread study of Maimonides' teachings might well serve to modify, considerably, these irrationalist tendencies. Judaism is sufficiently rich and sufficiently complex to make it possible to include within its proper limits, a synthesis of these extremes.

While applauding the beneficent effects of Maimonides' faith in reason, we must also acknowledge the limits and limitations of that faith. In his Introduction Professor Guttmann notes these limitations, in passing, but his commitment to and admiration for Maimonides overshadow his criticism. As a result, it seems to this reviewer that Guttmann has, in a number of instances, smoothed over very real difficulties without actually resolving them.

Perhaps the most striking of these difficulties is the paradoxical character of Maimonides' rationalism. He holds that the highest end of all human activity, the culmination of man's quest, the goal of the religious life and of every properly directed life, is the knowledge of God. "Everyone who knows Him is well beloved and drawn near; but he who does not know Him is in disfavour and rejected. The degree of favour or disfavour, drawing near or rejecting is in proportion to the degree of knowledge". (p.72) Yet, Maimonides acknowledges frequently, and occasionally almost with desperation, that man's finite intellect is incapable of knowing what God is. We can merely know that He is. Even Moses, though he is unique among men and unique among the prophets, is incapable of knowing God's essence. For Moses is still a man, and still finite. We are involved in an anguished struggle for the achievement of a goal, which is both necessary and impossible. Contemporary thinkers would be likely to see here a fundamental dialectical tension in man's being, and this might well become a starting point for an examination of man's apparently impossible situation. It is true that Maimonides does not view man in these dialectical terms. But one should not today ignore the questions which arise for us so naturally in studying Maimonides. It would have been valuable if a scholar like Guttmann had made a serious attempt to face the issues. Instead, he merely assures us (with very little supporting evidence) that, "There is no contradiction between this conviction that human perception is limited and Maimonides' faith in reason". (p. 8)

Given the belief that the knowledge of God is the proper end of man, it follows necessarily that morality will be -assigned an inferior place in the hierarchy of values. About this Maimonides is very explicit. Here again, Guttmann seems to face the issue, only to shy away from it. He stresses the essential opposition between the position of morality in the religious teachings of the Bible and Talmud and the place which it occupies in Maimonides system. "For the Bible", says Guttmann, "the moral precept is the essential expression of the will of God, and obedience to it, the true service of God. For Maimonides, morality has become an expedient, partly for the welfare of society and partly for the discipline of personality, whose ultimate perfection lies not in the moral but in the intellectual sphere". (p. 32) After this very clear insight into Maimonides' position and its attendant difficulties, Professor Guttmann again tries to show that it is still possible to find here a legitimate Jewish doctrine. He attempts to resolve the difficulty by making reference to passages where Maimonides seems to restore morality to its proper place. But this is hardly adequate, since we must ask not only what Maimonides explicitly says, but also what the actual requirements of his position are. It seems clear that, given Maimonides' views about the true end of man, morality must be assigned an inferior place in his value system. In so far as this is the case, he is in opposition to the Bible, and adherents of Maimonides must face the issue squarely. Professor Guttmann, however, seems to have walked around the issue. It is not enough for him to show that Maimonides, at some points, exalts man's imitation of God even above man's knowledge of God. He must also show how these occasional statements can be harmonized with the much more frequent and more forceful exaltation of knowledge over morality.

There is one crucial consequence of Malmonides' rationalism with regard to which Professor Guttmann does acknowledge a real and unresolved difficulty. This is in his discussion of Maimonides' explanations of the reasons for the ceremonial and ritual commandments of the Torah. As is well known, Maimonides sought to give reasons for the apparently unreasonable commandments, and to explicate the seemingly inexplicable mysteries of the Law. According to his view, the commandments of the Torah must make sense. He is unwilling to conceive of them simply as expressions of the inscrutable will of God. Consequently, he deals with the ceremonial prescriptions in accordance with an historical critical method, and explains the commandments in these terms. On his analysis, the commandments are understood as directed toward the Biblical generations in their specific historical circumstances. To save them from the excesses of idolatrous paganism, or from the dangers of the unhygienic life, or from the limitations of their own knowledge and understanding, God imposed on the Jewish people the "yoke of the kingdom of heaven" which is expressed in the 613 commandments. In this fashion Maimonides explains the sacrificial cult, the dietary laws, and much of the rest of the ceremonial law. In so doing, he anticipated (though unintentionally) by many centuries the current tendency to read the commandments out of existence by conceiving them as relevant primarily to circumstances and needs of past ages. For if the commandments are thought of in Maimonides' historical-critical way, then they lose their obligatory character when the circumstances which evoked them no longer exist.

Professor Guttmann praises Maimonides' treatment of the commandments as a consistent result of his rationalism. However, Guttmann is perceptive enough to admit that for the gain of having the commandments appear reasonable, Maimonides "had to pay with the admission that that part of the Biblical law, which was directed against paganism had now no actuality, serving as it did the eternal purpose of the Torah ... only in certain time-bound circumstances". (p. 29) This is an admission which does not seem to disturb Guttmann. But it is certainly disturbing to any one who views the legislation of the Torah as "*hukath olam*", as an eternal law. Though many men today may find it easy to reject the view that Biblical law binds Israel for all time, Maimonides certainly could not and did not dismiss this traditional belief casually. It would have been most illuminating to the student of the Guide if the introduction to this edition had considered this problem more directly, and if it would have shown how Maimonides himself dealt with it.

There is still another result of Malmonides' rationalism which we must consider, namely, the allegorical method of interpreting the Bible. It is somewhat surprising that this topic, which is dealt with in the Guide so prominently, should be barely mentioned by Professor Guttmann in his Introduction. It is especially surprising since the Introduction centers on Maimonides rationalism, and the allegorical method is one of the main results of that rationalism. What is most disturbing is that the allegorical method seems to make it possible to read into the Bible almost any doctrine one desires. At the beginning of Book 11, Chapter XXV Maimonides makes an explicit admission to this effect. This does not mean that allegory is to be used without principle and without control but rather that there are external principles by which the Torah is judged and interpreted. It appears that for Maimonides philosophical truth sets the standard for the understanding of the Bible. Consequently, whenever a Biblical statement, which is read literally conflicts with his philosophical principles, he escapes the difficulty by interpreting the passage allegorically. But this is a procedure which raises a grave question for Jewish theology. Can principles external to the Biblical revelation be admitted as the normative criteria for the understanding of that revelation? Surely the main lines of Jewish tradition would hold that philosophy should be judged by the Bible, and not the Bible by philosophy. We must admit the difficulties of understanding the Biblical text internally and in its own terms, and the even greater difficulty of formulating a set of theological principles on the basis of the Bible alone. Though the task is difficult, it seems to be the only way in which Biblical faith can be properly grounded. Maimonides' allegorical method exposes us to the danger of substituting reason for revelation. This may be philosophically sound. It may even provide a more intellectually adequate theology. But it is an extreme of rationalism which seems to contravene directly both the explicit teaching of the Bible and the rabbinic conception of the foundations of Jewish faith.

    The criticisms of Guttmann's Introduction and of Maimonides' doctrine should not be construed as a derogation. Guttmann's Introduction is an excellent way for the beginner to approach Maimonides. Perhaps its limitations derive from the fact that it was intended for just such a purpose. As for Maimonides' doctrine, it is hardly necessary to reaffirm his greatness among the small number of major thinkers in the world's history. Whether we agree or disagree with his basic orientation, it is clear that we cannot afford to ignore him. We may hope that this new edition will reawaken interest in Maimonides among all of us, whose perplexities continue to require guidance.

MARVIN FOX
Ohio State University,
Columbus, Ohio.

NOTES

[1] Italics are my own.

[2] It is unfortunate that where portions of chapters are omitted there is no indication given of this in the text. As a result, there are some obvious lacunae which the reader is likely to attribute to Maimonides' inadequacies rather than to the editor's industriousness.

7

REVIEW:
Shlomo Pines, *The Guide of the Perplexed* by Moses Maimonides

The Guide of the Perplexed. By Moses Maimonides.
Translated with an Introduction and Notes by Shlomo Pines,
with an Introductory Essay by Leo Strauss.
(Chicago: The University of Chicago Press, 1963. Pp. cxxxiv + 658. $15.00.)

    The publication of a new English translation of Maimonides' *Guide of the Perplexed* is an event of major importance to students of medieval philosophy and of Jewish thought. By common consent Maimonides is recognized as by far the greatest and most original of the medieval Jewish philosophers. But his work has been relatively inaccessible to those without a command of Arabic and Hebrew. The Guide has been translated into a number of modern languages, most notably into French by Solomon Munk. However, even the best of these translations has defects which distort the book and make it unintelligible. These defects were built on occasion from the translators' inadequate linguistic knowledge, but they stem more frequently from their failure to understand Maimonides. As Professor Pines puts it in his Introduction, "the Guide belongs to a very peculiar literary genre, of which it is the unique specimen." Not knowing this, though Maimonides himself makes it eminently clear, most translators treat the Guide as if it were an ordinary book, with the inevitable consequence that both they and their readers are misled. In the new edition now before us special efforts were made to note and take account of the peculiarities of this remarkable piece of esoteric writing. In addition to the new translation by Professor Shlomo Pines of the Hebrew University in Jerusalem, the volume contains a long introductory essay by Professor Leo Strauss as well as a very long introduction by the translator. In all three parts of the book, the translation as well as the two introductions, the qualified reader is guided to a better understanding of Maimonides' esoteric teaching as it is understood by Pines and Strauss. In the following pages, I shall discuss each part of the book separately.

On the Translation

Professor Pines' superb translation can only be fully appreciated when it is compared carefully with the Friedländer edition which began to appear in 1881, and which has since that time been considered the standard English translation of the Guide *for the Perplexed*. The new version now available to us is so far superior that it should permanently replace the Friedländer. No translation can ever be a fully adequate substitute for the original text, but Professor Pines' rendition of Maimonides' Guide comes as close to this aim as any one could hope.

He has managed to be remarkably faithful to Maimonides, avoiding the strong temptations to "improve" or "emend" which ensnare so many translators. Pines' intention was that his "translation should remain as close as is practicable to the original," and in this he has succeeded admirably. Where Maimonides is obscure the translation deliberately reproduces the obscurity, and where Maimonides is awkward or ambiguous the translation is equally awkward or ambiguous. Pines holds (correctly) that Maimonides wrote exactly as he intended, and that the English reader should be offered the book that Maimonides wrote, not a translator's revision of it. Neither felicity of style nor seeming clarity of thought were Pines' controlling purposes. He sought accuracy and has achieved it in this splendid translation.

Some examples comparing the two translations will show how far the ordinary student has been misled when he has been forced to rely on Friedländer. The old version adds phrases not in the original, drops phrases which are in the original, misconstrues key passages, and mistranslates key terms. The following instances, chosen from the Introduction and Part I, are typical of what one finds throughout. We can see here the great value of Professor Pines' work.[1]

P	F
1) Some of these terms are equivocal; hence the ignorant attribute, to them only one or some of the meanings in which the term in question is used (p, 5).	Of these some are homonyms, and of their several meanings the ignorant choose the wrong ones (p. 2).
2) It is not the purpose of this Treatise to make its totality understandable to the vulgar or to beginners in speculation, nor to teach those who have not engaged in any study other than the science of the Law—I mean	It is not here intended to explain all these expressions to the unlettered or to mere tyros, a previous knowledge of Logic and Natural Philosophy being indispensable, or to those who confine their attention to the

the legalistic study of the Law. For the purpose of this Treatise and of all those like it is the science of Law in its true sense (p.5).

study of our holy Law, I mean the study of the canonical law alone; for the true knowledge of the Torah is the special aim of this and similar works (p. 2).

These two passages, occurring in Maimonides' "Introduction to the First Part" show typical errors of Friedländer in contrast with the accuracy of Pines. In (1) F has missed the point. Maimonides says that the ignorant are unaware of the range of meanings of key equivocal terms in Scripture, not that they consistently choose the wrong meaning. In (2) P adds the phrase "a previous knowledge of Logic and Natural Philosophy being indispensable," though it is not present in the original text. Moreover, P blurs the very significant distinction between "the legalistic study of the Law" and "the science of the Law in its true sense," i.e., between *sharīā* and *fiqh*. Without this distinction it is impossible to understand the professed aim of the *Guide*.

P
3) Know that with regard to natural matters as well, it is impossible to give a clear exposition when teaching some of their principles as they are (P. 7).

F
Know that also in Natural Science there are topics which are not to be fully explained (p. 3).

F renders "topics" in place of "principles" and misconstrues "it is impossible to," reading it "are not to be," i.e., "ought not" in place of "cannot."

On some occasions F conveys exactly the wrong sense of a term and in so doing both obscures the meaning of the particular passage and misses basic distinctions which are crucial.

For example:

P
4) We saw also that if an ignoramus among the multitude of Rabbanites should engage in speculation on these *Midrashim* he would find nothing difficult in them... (p. 10).

F
We have further noticed that when an ill-informed Theologian reads these Midrashim, he will find no difficulty... (p. 5).

To identify this "Rabbanite" as a "Theologian" is a major error. For the whole point is that he is a legalistic student of the law who has neither training in nor aptitude for theology or metaphysics. He is not an "ill-informed Theologian"; he is no theologian at all. P recognizes this clearly, while F misleads the reader.

At times F seems not to be familiar with standard terminology. In I-17 and elsewhere, for example, he repeatedly contrasts Form with

Substance, when the text reads Form and Matter. As usual, P's version is correct. At the end of I-28, we see a similar instance:

P	F
5) The purpose of everyone endowed with intellect should be wholly directed to rejecting corporeality with respect to God... and to considering all these apprehensions as intellectual, not sensory (p. 61).	The primary object of every intelligent person must be to deny the corporeality of God, and to believe that all those perceptions... were of a spiritual not of a material character (p. 38).

P is both clear and accurate. P probably understood the passage, but what is the unwary reader to make out of a call for perceptions which are "spiritual" rather than "material"? Later we find F incorrectly using the term "exact sciences" where P and the text read "mathematics," e.g., in I-31.

On other occasions, F restricts certain terms to very specific meanings where the text is not at all specific. For example, at the end of I-36, P is faithful to the text when he speaks of "men who inquire into the truth and are engaged in speculation," while F reads into the text more than it says and translates this phrase as "true philosophers." Further on, at the beginning of I-51, F again reads "philosophers" where P and the text read "men of science." Similarly in 1-59 (pp. 83, F; 138, P), F speaks of "the lowest class of philosophers" while P correctly reads "a single individual among the pupils." In the very next sentence, the term "philosophers" does occur and is rendered properly in both versions, as is the case with respect to the phrase "chief of the philosophers" at the beginning of I-5. Precision and consistency obviously did not concern F. We have here a not untypical case in which four different Arabic terms are translated by F with the common term "philosopher," while P carefully renders each term by a different and exact English equivalent.

Then there, are passages in which F exhibits surprising insensitivity as be selects exactly the wrong meaning in translating certain key terms. One wonders what confusions were generated for uninitiated students who struggled to understand the following passage in F:

P	F
6) ... a mere explanation of a term—as if you said that man is a rational living being. For being a rational animal is the essence and true reality of man, and there does not exist in this case a third notion, apart from those of animal and	...or the explanation of a name, as, e.g., "man is a speaking animal"; for the words "speaking animal" include the true essence of man, and there is no third element besides life and speech in the definition of man.... that is to say that

Seven. Review. Sholomo Pines, The Guide of the Perplexed... 169

of rational, that constitutes man... It is as if you said that the thing denoted by the term "man" is the thing composed of life and rationality (p. 113).

the thing which is called man, con*sists* of life and speech (p. 68).

In describing man as a "speaking animal," F seems to have misunderstood a commonplace term in medieval Hebrew and Arabic usage. Following the ambiguity of the term λόγοσ which means both word and reason, Hebrew and Arabic usage described man by a similarly ambiguous term. Thus, in Hebrew man is often identified as *medabber*, i.e. speaking, but it is elementary that this term is to be understood as referring to man's rationality. It means λόγοον ἔχειν. To translate it literally is a gross misconstruction. P is clear and consistent on this point. In a footnote (p. 77), he points out that the Arabic adjective *nutqiyya* derives from a term which "means, like *logos* in Greek, both speech and reason." Wherever this term or its derivatives are used to speak of man's essence P consistently renders it as "reason" or "rational." F, on the other hand, uses various terms, such as "speaking," "intellectual," and "having reason." In I-34 (p. 47), he uses "intellectual"; in I-51, quoted above, "speaking"; and in I-52 (p. 69), "has reason." It should be stressed that in each of these instances the Arabic text uses exactly the same term.

F not only mistranslates individual words or phrases. He frequently gives an erroneous translation of an entire passage.

P	F
7) Furthermore his saying, "That I may find grace in Thy sight," indicates that he who knows God finds grace in His sight and not he who merely fasts and prays, but everyone who has knowledge of Him (p. 123).	The words "That I may find grace in Thy sight," imply that he who knows God finds grace in His eyes. Not only is he acceptable and welcome to God who fasts and prays, but everyone who knows Him (p. 75).

Here F has God favoring the man who knows Him, *as well as* the man who fasts and prays. But the text reads just as P has translated it, namely that prayer and fasting alone do not make a man acceptable to God. This passage caused severe attacks on Maimonides for seeming to suggest that God does not desire the ordinary worship of pious men. If we had only the F translation, it would be difficult, indeed impossible, to see here any ground for questioning Maimonides' orthodoxy.

I have presented only a small selection of passages exhibiting the variety of errors in F that are corrected in P. They are typical and have their counterparts throughout the book. On this basis, it must be evident that P must now be viewed as the English translation of *The Guide of the Perplexed*. It is not only superior to F, but also to the other translations in modern languages. Even the French translation of Munk, which is an acknowledged classic of pioneering scholarship, does not meet the standard of precision and consistency achieved by Professor Pines. Translators of other classic works would do well to imitate his method and strive to meet his very high standards.[2]

On Leo Strauss' Introductory Essay

The story is told that after James Hutchinson Stirling published his massive volume, The *Secret of Hegel*, he was congratulated by his readers for having kept the secret so well. One has a similar feeling when studying the introductory essay, "How to Begin to Study The Guide *of the Perplexed*," by Professor Leo Strauss. The essay is brilliant, tantalizing, frustrating, and at times infuriating. To be understood at all it should be read in conjunction with Strauss' other writings on Maimonides, particularly his study "The Literary Character of *The Guide for the Perplexed.*"[3] But even with this added help much still remains obscure. For Strauss has not written (nor did he intend to write) a simple and straightforward introduction for the use of the uninitiated reader. He has, rather constructed an obstacle course designed to block the forward movement of all but the most skilled students of Maimonides' Guide. Ordinary readers, beginning with this introductory essay are unlikely ever to get beyond it to the text of the Guide. Even the highly skilled reader will receive no clear and explicit analysis of the *Guide*. If he succeeds in finding his way through the Strauss essay, he will have clues, hints, suggestions, and some confusion, not a systematic and structured interpretation. Professor Strauss has left to each reader the work of interpreting the *Guide* for himself.

These comments are not meant as a criticism of Strauss, but only as a characterization of his introduction. There is no doubt at all that this is exactly the kind of introduction he intended to write. In fact, he says so explicitly at one point when he notes his "desire to give the readers some hints for the better understanding"[4] of a particular section. It is quite clear that any reader who wants more than hints will have to get them on his own. This deliberately obscure manner of introducing Maimonides' Guide is necessitated by the special way in which Strauss understands and reads that great work, for unlike most earlier interpreters he takes very seriously Maimonides' own instructions on how to read the Guide. It is strange that despite Maimonides' great pains to instruct and direct the reader on how to read the Guide, his instructions have been largely ignored. Rarely does one find a work on Maimonides, a commentary or a systematic study of his thought in which the author gives evidence that he remembers Maimonides' admonition that the *Guide of the Perplexed* is a special kind of esoteric book. As a result the book has been consistently misunderstood because it was not studied with the method that Maimonides himself set forth. It is to the credit of Leo Strauss that he has taken Maimonides seriously. In his various writings Strauss reminds us that esoteric books must be read in a special way, and especially that Maimonides' Guide is a supreme example of such a book.

What may seem regrettable is that Strauss has chosen to write interpretations which are as esoteric as the Guide itself, insisting that no other responsible mode of interpretation is open. "Above all," he writes, "an esoteric interpretation of the Guide seems to be not only advisable, but even necessary... The interpretation of the Guide cannot be given in ordinary language, but only in parabolic enigmatic speech. That is why, according to Maimonides, the student of those secrets is required not only to be of mature age, to have a sagacious and subtle mind... and to be able to understand the allusive speech of others, but also to be capable of presenting things allusively himself."[5] Professor Strauss has written an introduction which meets this standard, an introduction which is most often cryptic and allusive, explaining basic points only by way of hints and hidden clues.

For the reader such an introduction poses a major dilemma. How seriously shall we take Strauss? Shall we deal with him as he deals with Maimonides or not? Strauss insists that Maimonides wrote each word of the Guide with such meticulous care that we must assume that there are no inadvertent slips or errors. Every seeming mistake, every apparently careless or inaccurate quotation, every internal contradiction—all are clues for the skillful reader to follow. For the perceptive student they open up doors to the deeper and secret meaning of the *Guide*. This imposes a great burden on the reader since he is never allowed to take the easy way in accounting for the peculiarities of the Guide.

Does Strauss write with the same care as Maimonides? When we find that Strauss, in his introductory essay, makes errors or seems to be careless how shall we react? Are these merely the ordinary slips to which most of us are prone, or are they deliberate devices for testing the reader and directing him? Each reader will have to make tip his own mind. I believe, however, that it would be most fruitful to study Strauss' essay as if it is both deliberately esoteric and perfectly constructed. Only then can we reach a sound judgment of it. I shall point out, in what follows, only a few typical instances of the various types of apparent errors made by Strauss. But the burden of interpreting this puzzling essay must be assumed by each student in his own fashion.

The essay opens with an outline plan of the Guide, which is by no means a mere conventional résumé of its contents, but an original and creative analysis of the structure of the book and the interrelations of its parts. Strauss first divides the book into seven sections with deliberate emphasis on the significance of the number "seven." He then tells us that, "wherever feasible, each section is divided into seven subsections"; but we are never told directly at any point what considerations determine whether it is feasible or not. This leaves us mystified by Section VII which contains only two subsections and consists altogether of three chapters. Later on (p. xliv), Strauss returns to this theme, stating that "for the general reason indicated, Maimonides desired to divide each of the seven sections of the Guide into seven subsections." We must note that the "general reason" has never been clearly indicated, nor are we told what prevented Maimonides from doing as he desired. It is proper to raise these points since, as Professor Strauss himself reminds us (P. xxx), "It is one thing to observe those regularities and another thing to understand them."

Strauss begins his discussion by quoting the last sentence of Maimonides' own Introduction to the Guide and ends his essay with the same quotation. But the two versions are not identical. In the second version the order of the last two clauses is reversed and a phrase is omitted. The first version is an accurate translation of the original, while the second is not. Moreover, neither is absolutely identical with the reading in Pines' translation. A similar "error" occurs (P. xxviii) when Strauss says that the first subsection (i.e., Chapters 1-7) begins and ends with the same word, "image." But while the first word of Chapter 1 is "image," the last word of Chapter 7 is "image" only in the English translation. In the original it is the Hebrew word "*k'salmo*," i.e., "according to his image," rather than "*selem*" as in Chapter 1. Are these careless errors or do they contain clues planted deliberately to test the reader and lead him to the inner secrets of Strauss' interpretation?

In a very suggestive discussion, Strauss touches on the crucial issue of Maimonides' treatment of the doctrine of the unity of God. But, as usual, he leaves us with unanswered questions. He makes the brilliant observation (which is obvious only after he calls it to our attention) that in the Guide Maimonides quotes only once "the most important biblical text ... 'Hear, 0 Israel, the Lord is our God, the Lord is One'" (p. xlvii f.). What he does not tell us is that Maimonides omits the words "Hear, 0 Israel," and quotes only the remainder of the verse. The same is true of the quotation in Mishneh Torah, H. Yesodei ha-Torah I-7, to which Strauss also refers. Further on in the same discussion (p. xlviii), Strauss notes three instances in the Guide where Maimonides quotes from Deut. 4:35, "The Lord He is God; there is none else beside Him." In each of these instances, however, Maimonides does not quote the portion which Strauss cites, but only the first part of the same verse, "Unto thee it was shown" adding "and so on." Now these might seem like small matters in an ordinary book, but must be taken seriously in Maimonides' Guide. Does Strauss make these errors deliberately in order to test and teach us, or are they merely oversights?

There are passages in which Strauss tantalizes us with cryptic and mystifying observations. This is particularly true of the numerical symbolism which he suggests but does not work out in detail. For example, after noting (p. xxx) that I-14 and I-17 deal respectively with man and the prohibition against teaching natural science publicly, he comments that "14 stands for man or the human things and 17 stands for nature." A few lines farther on, he notes that I-26 is concerned in part with a principle for the interpretation of the Torah. This leads to the strange claim that since "26 is the numerical equivalent of the secret name of the Lord, God of Israel, 26 may therefore also stand for His Torah."

If we study this supposed symbolism we are puzzled. No explanation whatsoever is offered for the association of 17 with nature. But let us examine the other numerical symbols for which some hints of an explanation are offered. It is true that 26 is the numerical equivalent of God's name, but how can one justify a simple identification (by way of a common symbol) of God and Torah? Certainly Maimonides would not have made such an identification. Our confusion grows when we consider the implications of 14 as the symbol for man. This is not a numerical equivalence at all, since man (*adam*) equals 45. But Strauss gives us a clue when be notes that 14 is the numerical equivalent of hand (*yad*), "the characteristically human organ." Presumably this is the justification for using 14 as the symbol for man.

We know, however, that in Maimonides' works the number 14 is closely associated with Torah. The *Mishneh Torah,* Maimonides' code of Jewish law, is divided into 14 books and is known as *Yad haHazaqah,* i.e. the mighty hand. In his *Book of the* Commandments, Maimonides sets out "14 roots of the commandments." And in the Guide he divides all the commandments into 14 classes. If 14 stands for man then there is the strong suggestion that the commandments of the Torah are to be viewed as human rather than divine. This, in turn, seems to contradict the symbolism of 26 which is taken as identifying Torah with God, not with man. When we study I-14, we are even more bewildered, for the verses cited by Maimonides all seem to suggest that man (except for rare individuals) has little connection with God and hardly any superiority over the beasts. Perhaps 14 and 26 suggest the ambiguity of "Torah," as Strauss does when he speaks of Torah as "the true science of the law" in contrast to Torah is "the science of the law in the usual sense, i.e., the *fiqh*... In contradistinction to the legalistic study of the law, which is concerned with what man ought to do, the true science of the law is concerned with what man ought to think and to believe."[6] This is the distinction between the subject matter of the *Mishneh Torah* and the subject-matter of the Guide. At one point Strauss calls the latter the *Torah for the Perplexed,* in contrast to the first Torah (and Maimonides' own code, the *Mishneh Torah)* which is for the unperplexed. There is in all this the daring suggestion that Maimonides viewed the original Torah as less connected with divine matters than his own new "Torah." It is a suggestion which is developed by Strauss (P. xxxiii) when he argues that according to Maimonides some later prophets (e.g., Isaiah) achieved "a higher stage in the knowledge of God than Moses." Since "progress beyond the teaching of the Torah is possible or even necessary," it may be the case that Maimonides has reached a higher level than the Torah or the prophets. None of this is spelled out explicitly by Strauss. In fact, at times he seems to take a contrary position. What I have suggested is only one possible interpretation, an interpretation which shows that there is always a danger of merely playing a game with a text instead of understanding the author's thoughts. There are here such serious implications concerning the true views of Maimonides that it would be better either to spell them out and defend them clearly and unambiguously, or else not to present them at all. That one can deal with such matters properly only through hints and allusions is not a fully convincing claim.

Let us turn to still another problem in interpreting Strauss' introduction. In his earlier essay, Strauss urges us to take note of "little words" in Maimonides' text which are readily ignored by the unwary though they profoundly affect the meaning. "Cannot miracles be wrought by such little words as 'almost', 'perhaps', 'seemingly'?"[7] Shall we in turn pay equal attention to his own use of such words and phrases? I-le assures us, for example (p. xv), that, "No one can reasonably doubt... that II-32-48, III-1-7, and III-25-50 form sections." What is the force of "reasonably"? Since Maimonides explicitly cautions us not to take the apparent structure for the real structure of the Guide, it seems perfectly reasonable to doubt that the parts in question form sections. Does avoidance of seemingly "reasonable doubt" perhaps characterize the simple-minded reader unprepared for the adventure of exploring the hidden levels of the Guide? The qualification, "reasonably," opens up various possibilities, but charts no clear course for the reader. We are put on our guard in similar fashion by such "small words" in contexts that seem to call for unambiguous statements, e.g., cases of simple counting. Speaking of "lexicographic chapters" (p. xxv), Strauss says that of the first forty-nine chapters of the Guide thirty are lexicographic, "whereas in the whole rest of the book there occur at most two such chapters (I-66 and 70)." Why "at most" when simple counting should settle the issue beyond question. Clearly, because 1-66 does not precisely fit his criterion of what constitutes a lexicographic chapter, since it opens not with a term or terms but with part of a biblical verse. "At most" seems to be an invitation to the reader to check carefully the citations which Strauss lists and to catch him in a mistake. Later on Strauss writes (p. 1) that in 1-68-70 Maimonides "refers to philosophy, I believe, more frequently than in the whole discussion of Incorporeality (1-1-49)... In the exegetic discussion of the divine names (161-67), if I am not mistaken, he does not refer to philosophy at all." Since these are matters which can be settled fairly easily and exactly we must give special thought to the intention of such expressions as, "I believe" and "if I am not mistaken." Is this just a manner of speaking or are these also tests and clues for Strauss' readers?

In certain cases, Strauss raises questions without suggesting any direct answer to them. If there is an indirect answer, it is hidden deeply in the caverns that lie at the end of the tortuous winding paths which Strauss has laid out. Our attempt at an interpretation in these instances is further complicated by our uncertainty as to whether his apparent errors are deliberate or accidental. For example, he makes much of what he calls the "lexicographical chapters" in Part I of the *Guide*. He means by this "a chapter that opens with the Hebrew term or terms to be explained in the chapter regardless of whether these terms precede the first sentence or form the beginning of the first sentence, and regardless of whether these terms are supplied with the Arabic article al- or not" (p. xxv). Strauss goes on to note carefully for us the exact number of each variety of such chapters and then asks why they occur in precisely these numbers and variations; but he never answers the question directly, for he holds that it is of major importance for a student to know which are the right questions, even if he can not yet answer them satisfactorily. What is troubling, however, is that the count which Strauss makes is not accurate. Perhaps he is testing his readers to see if they cheek each detail. Strauss says (p. xxv) that "ten of these thirty lexicographic chapters begin with the Hebrew terms preceding the first sentence." This count seems correct according to the Arabic text used in the preparation of this translation. The ten chapters are 1, 7, 8, 9, 11, 18, 19, 22, 25, 30. Yet, surprisingly, when we consult the Pines translation, to which Strauss has attached his introduction, there appear to be twelve such chapters, rather than ten. In Pines' version, chapters 15 and 21 also begin with the Hebrew terms preceding the first sentence. It is true that there is some ambiguity since in the Arabic text the opening term in each of the other ten chapters is followed by a period, but not in chapters 15 and 21. Is this a trap set for us by Strauss or a mere failure to coordinate introduction and translation, an important clue or an unimportant error?

This same disparity between the introduction, the Arabic original, and the translated text can be found in other places. Perhaps the most striking is in a passage of crucial importance which distinguishes between Maimonides' treatment of the Bible and the Talmud. Strauss claims that Maimonides normally introduces biblical passages with the phrase "he says" or "his saying is." To Strauss this means that Maimonides is anxious to suggest "that in the Bible we hear only one speaker... Yet in the first chapter of the *Guide* 'He' who speaks is in fact first God, then the narrator, then God, and then 'the poor one'." According to Strauss' reading, we should expect to find "he says" or "his saying is" at least four times in Chapter 1. In the translation of Chapter 1, however, the expression "he says" does not occur at all, and "his saying is" occurs only once; but we do find, in addition, the expressions, "Scripture says... it is said," and "the scriptural dictum." These are fully justified as translations of the Arabic term that Strauss renders as "he says." Moreover, Strauss says that in this chapter the "he" who speaks is first God, then the narrator. Three verses are quoted after the translator's expression, "Scripture says." These are the verses which Strauss ascribes to the "narrator." Of these the first, Gen. 39:6, may be thought of as spoken by the narrator. However, the second verse, I Sam. 28:14, is spoken by Saul, and the third, Judg. 8:18, by Zebah and Zalmunna. (For readers who wonder about "the poor one," this refers to the quoted verse, "I am like a pelican in the wilderness" from Psalm 102, which begins, "A prayer of the poor one.") Now what are we to make of this doubly confusing situation? First, the speakers in the text turn out to be other than as Strauss claims. Second, the crucial point embedded in the phrase "he says" is in no way evident in the varied renditions of the translation. Again we are led to wonder whether these are mere human errors, or mysterious clues to secret doctrines.

For reasons which should now be apparent, I have not attempted to give a systematic account of Strauss' interpretation of Maimonides. Professor Strauss can argue, with justice, that an essay entitled "How to Begin to Study *The Guide of the Perplexed*" is literally only a beginning, and that he is not called upon to offer in such an essay final and systematic interpretations. Though it may be justified, this kind of an introduction leaves us unsatisfied. For Strauss exhibits so many brilliant flashes of insight and tantalizes us with so many acute observations that we can only wish that he might be willing to share his secret knowledge with all honest students of Maimonides.

ON THE TRANSLATOR'S INTRODUCTION

Professor Pines has provided a lengthy (seventy-seven pages) and comprehensive historical introduction entitled "The Philosophic Sources of *The Guide of the Perplexed*." While he is in basic agreement with Leo Strauss on how the Guide should be read, Pines has nevertheless, written a straightforward essay. There are here no hidden clues, no secretive allusions, none of the typical devices or apparatus used by Strauss. In assembling detailed information on Maimonides' philosophic sources, Pines has performed a most useful service. Examining in Maimonides' correspondence his statements about the works of other philosophers, Pines turns to a critical and comprehensive survey of those works as they enter into the Guide.

Among the Greeks he gives greatest attention to the influences of Aristotle and Alexander of Aphrodisias, and offers convincing evidence that Maimonides' "personal point of view and his conception of Aristotelianism were decisively influenced by Alexander." But Pines also stresses that with respect to political matters, the ordering of society, and the place of the philosopher in society Maimonides' thinking was primarily influenced by Plato rather than Aristotle. Maimonides also took account in his thought of the various traditions of Arabic philosophy. He had highest regard for al-Fārābī, and was significantly affected by Avicenna and some of the lesser Moslem thinkers as well.

Pines discusses carefully the relationship between Maimonides and his great contemporary, Averroes. In spite of many similarities in their thought Pines argues that "there is no conclusive proof that at the time of the writing of the *Guide* Maimonides was in any way influenced by Averroes' doctrines." He holds that many of their similarities can be explained by their identical philosophic background and their remarkable likeness in philosophic attitude and temperament. The deepest differences between Maimonides and Averroes seem to Pines to result from their contrasting ideas of the best strategy for philosophy in society. "The ideas of the two as to what is prudent and what not in philosophic politics and what is desirable in theological exposition seem to be radically different."

After a thorough consideration of the relationships of Maimonides to the Arabic philosophers and to the kalām, Pines closes his essay with the observation that while Maimonides refers constantly to all the major works in the "official" corpus of Jewish literature, he makes practically no use of the works of earlier Jewish philosophers. From this Pines concludes that Maimonides "evidently considered that philosophy transcended religious or national distinction." His view seems to be that as a philosopher Maimonides was not a Jew tied to a particular parochial tradition, but a man of the world. As a Jew he was not a philosopher. This is what Leo Strauss has in mind when he asserts that the *Guide* "is not a philosophic book—a book written by a philosopher for philosophers-but a Jewish book: a book written by a Jew for Jews... A Jew may make use of philosophy and Maimonides makes the most ample use of it; but as a Jew he gives his assent where as a philosopher he would suspend his assent." Professor Pines clearly concurs in this.

Pines' introduction is far more than a mere catalogue of the sources of some of Maimonides' ideas. He offers us an acute analysis of the way in which Maimonides makes use of those sources for his own specific purposes. Pines shows convincingly that Maimonides was never a slavish follower of his predecessors nor a mere collector of philosophic opinions and arguments. He was a highly original thinker who learned much from his predecessors and contemporaries and then turned their words and ideas to the service of his own goals.

What were those purposes as Pines outlines them and Strauss hints at them? Maimonides sought to pursue philosophic inquiry in complete freedom, while at the same time preserving society from the destructive dangers of philosophy. In Jewish law he saw the ideal instrument for achieving his double goal. Jewish law provided for the best kind of social order, in Maimonides' opinion, while leaving the pursuit of philosophy open to those who qualified. As legislator or interpreter of Jewish law Maimonides was rigorously orthodox; but as philosopher he rejected some of the very doctrines which he affirmed in his legal decisions. He believed that religious tradition is essential to provide for the masses the best life of which they are capable. It also provides for the philosopher conditions under which he can do his work freely. Therefore, the prudent philosopher will do his best to preserve those conditions both for himself and for society.

Both Pines and Strauss have this understanding of Maimonides— a view which would be rejected by those who consider Maimonides one of the pillars of Jewish orthodoxy. Since the deliberate ambiguities of the *Guide* leave room for different and even contradictory interpretations, we must expect that Maimonides will be represented as everything from a fully conventional Orthodox Jew, to a crypto-heretic, to an outright denier of the faith. To decide among these possibilities is beyond the limits of the present essay.

Pines closes his introduction with this explanation of the social desirability of Maimonides' scheme. "Qua philosopher he had the possibility to consider Judaism from the outside. From this vantage point he could discover the justification that, if one takes into account human nature and condition, can be adduced for accepting the obligations of a strict member of the Jewish community and could apprehend and try to eliminate or mitigate the dangers inherent in philosophic truth and trace the task of the philosophers-statesmen, one of whom he was." Strauss summarizes the philosophic advantages this way: "The official recognition of philosophy in the Christian world made philosophy subject to ecclesiastical supervision. The precarious position of philosophy in the Islamic-Jewish world guaranteed its private character and therewith its inner freedom from supervision."[8]

This work by Pines and Strauss must be recognized as one of the most important contributions to the study of Maimonides in the present century. The translation is of a quality unequalled in any modern language. The introductions are controversial, but they are also stimulating and provocative. Every serious reader will be instructed by Professors Pines and Strauss. Some will follow their lead; others will be driven to refute them; and all will profit from the experience.

MARVIN FOX
Ohio State University

NOTES

[1] In the examples which follow, P = Pines and F = Friedländer. Page references to F are, to the second edition, revised throughout, seventh impression, 1942, Geo. Routledge & Sons, Ltd. (London) and E. P. Dutton & Co. (New York).

[2] The volume is handsomely printed and bound and produced with great accuracy. The following misprints should be noted: p. lxxvii, line 9 from bottom: for 1-15 read II-15. p. lxxxiv, line 4 from bottom: for Mutakullimun read Mutakallimun. p. cxxxi, line 11: for antecedents read antecedents. p. 73, footnote 6: for B.T., Sukkah 42b read B.T., Sukkah, 45b. *Ibid.*: for 13.T., Sanhedrin, 43b read B.T., Sanhedrin 97b.

[3] Leo Strauss, *Persecution and the Art of Writing* (Glencoe: 1952), pp. 38-94.

[4] P. xliv. Italics mine.

[5] Ibid., pp. 56-58.

[6] *Ibid.*, p. 39.

[7] *Ibid.*, p. 78..

[8] *Ibid.*, p. 21.

8

MAIMONIDES AND AQUINAS ON NATURAL LAW*

Classical Judaism and classical Christianity have profoundly differing views of natural law. In Judaism there is no natural law doctrine, and, in principle, there cannot be, while in classical Christian thought natural law plays a central role. Little has been done to explore the grounds of this difference or to explain its significance. In this essay I shall address myself to the problem. After commenting on the general Jewish approach to natural law as exhibited in Biblical, Talmudic, and philosophic sources, I shall turn to an examination of the teaching of Moses Maimonides, the greatest of the medieval Jewish philosophers. I shall then try to explain the contrast between the absence of any natural law theory in Maimonides with the major role assigned to natural law in the philosophy of St. Thomas Aquinas.

The history of the *nomos-physis* conflict in Greek thought lies far beyond the limits of our present discussion, though we shall have occasion later to make some reference to it. However, it is important to have some clear idea of what we mean by "natural law", and this can best be gotten by considering some classical versions. Whatever the earlier view of law in Greek thought, by the time of Euripides we already find reference to "the Law that abides and changes not, ages long, the Eternal and Nature-born." [1] More than fifty years later this conception of law had begun to take root, as we can see when Plato speaks in defense of law and art, "as things which exist by nature or by a cause not inferior to nature, since according to right reason *(kata logon orthon)* they are the offspring of the mind..." [2] But it is in Stoic philosophy that natural law achieves its fullest and most influential form, and it is basically this conception of natural law that we are considering in our present discussion The versions of Cicero are the most familiar and most frequently cited as typical statements of the Stoic position:

183

> True law is right reason in agreement with nature (*recta ratio naturae congruens*); it is of universal application, unchanging and everlasting; it summons to duty by its commands, and averts from wrongdoing by its prohibitions...
> We cannot be freed from its' obligations by senate or people, and we need not look outside ourselves for an expounder or interpreter of it... one eternal unchangeable law will be valid for all nations and all times.[3]
> But if the judgments of men were in agreement with Nature... then Justice would be equally observed by all. For those creatures who have received the gift of reason from Nature have also received right reason, and therefore they have also received the gift of Law, which is right reason applied to command and prohibitions.[4]

This conception of a law of nature which dictates principles of justice and morality, which is derived from reason and is in accord with nature, which is universal, eternal and unchanging, exercised enormous influence on Christian thought. Yet, though the main centers of Jewish learning were in contact with Hellenistic philosophy and with Roman thought, Judaism never adopted a theory of natural law, while Christianity did.

I

In the Hebrew Bible men are thought of as subject to direct and specific divine commandments. It is through God's revelation, mediated by the prophets, that men know what is right and wrong.

Moreover, the vast majority of the biblical commandments are addressed specifically to the Jews. Only the smallest part of biblical legislation (as we shall see later) is universal law, intended for all mankind. All the rest, the hundreds of other injunctions and prohibitions, bind only the children of Israel. There is nothing in the Hebrew Bible which even approximates the Ciceronian idea of a natural law, addressed to men by way of reason, and prescribing right modes of human behavior.

In principle, there could not be such a conception in the Old Testament, since there is no idea of nature, nor even a word for nature in that book. The Hebrew word *teba*, when it is understood to mean "nature", does not occur in the Bible or in the *Mishna*, but makes its first appearance in medieval Hebrew usage, particularly in the works of the philosophers.[5] The idea of nature only arises with philosophical reflection, as Leo Strauss rightly points out. "The discovery of nature is the work of philosophy.

Eight. Maimonides and Aquinas on Natural Law

Where there is no philosophy, there is no knowledge of natural right as such. The Old Testament... does not know 'nature'... There is, then, no knowledge of natural right as such in the Old Testament."[6] Aristotle taught us to think of nature as that which is endowed with its own internal principle of motion. The natural world is, thus, self-developing and self-explanatory. In the Hebrew Bible the world and man are seen as created by God, sustained by him, and subject to his will, and intelligible only in this way. Biblical man has full powers of reason, but, contrary to Cicero, the Bible does not teach that once a man has reason he also has knowledge of the moral law. In ancient Hebrew thought there is only one source of the knowledge of good and evil, the commandments of God as they are revealed to man.[7]

In the post-biblical rabbinic texts there are a few passages that are frequently pointed out as supposedly showing some conception of natural law. Properly interpreted these passages in no way justify any claim that the sages of the Talmud advocated a natural law theory. They, regularly and as a matter of course, maintain the classical biblical teaching that divine commandment is the only ultimate source of law. Even positive human legislation is seen as legitimate and binding only insofar as it is an application or extension of rules or principles set forth in the divinely revealed law. It is in this clearly set framework that we must see and understand such a rabbinic comment as the following: "Ye shall keep my statutes' (Lev., 18:5). This refers to those commandments which if they had not been written in Scripture, should by right have been written. These include the prohibitions against idolatry, adultery, bloodshed, robbery, and blasphemy."[8] There is no suggestion here that human reason could have known by itself that these acts are evil, nor is it suggested that they are not consistent with man's nature. What is asserted is only that, having been commanded to avoid these prohibited acts, we can now see, after the fact, that these prohibitions are useful and desirable. It is instructive that the passage goes on to contrast these rules, which civilized men have been taught to value, with other ritual commandments which do not seem to serve any useful purpose. But the conclusion is that both types of commandments bind and obligate the Jews because they come from God, and that ultimately no fruitful distinctions can be drawn between them.

Much the same can be said concerning the passage in which we are told that, "If the Torah had not been given we could have learned modesty from the cat, not to rob from the ant, chastity from the dove, considerate behavior to our wives from the rooster."[9] Those who interpret this statement as affirming a doctrine of natural law seem to me to be missing a crucial point. Rabbi Yochanan, who is credited with this statement, does not say that we would have known morally proper behavior by way of our unaided reason. He seems rather to be saying that without divine commandments we might have learned certain kinds of socially useful behavior by imitating various animals. This view was expressed earlier in a famous bit of biblical counsel. "Go to the ant, thou sluggard; consider her ways and be wise."[10] But neither the Biblical nor the Talmudic statements suppose that man would by himself have known what is good. Rather, man, having been taught by divine commandments to know good and evil, can now look with admiration at certain animals which instinctively live in accordance with some of these same divine patterns. By choosing to imitate these animals, natural man would make his life somewhat more decent and tolerable than it would otherwise have been. He could never have arrived, by such imitation, at ideas of obligations or commandment, i.e., at a theory of natural moral law.

The most important rabbinic source which might possibly be considered as involving a doctrine of natural law is the principle of the seven Noachide commandments. I shall defer the discussion of this topic at present and return to it when we take up the views of Maimonides. Before turning to Maimonides, however, let us consider briefly two major medieval Jewish philosophers who are sometimes thought to hold a doctrine of natural law, Saadia Gaon (892-942) and Joseph Albo (1380-1444), respectively among the first and the last of the Jewish medievals.

II

That so widespread a doctrine as natural law should have had some echoes in Jewish thought in the Middle Ages is not surprising when we consider the extensive and mutual inter-connections among the works of Moslem, Christian, and Jewish medieval philosophers. In fact, what is remarkable is the almost total resistance to the theory of natural law in Jewish thought, a resistance which is emphasized by the small number of instances in which Jewish thinkers even approached such a theory. Joseph Albo is practically the only one of the medieval Jewish philosophers, during the five hundred years or more that separate him from Saadia Gaon, who uses the term "natural law." Saadia, like some others, identifies "tile rational precepts of the Torah" as one of the classes of divine commandments, but he does not use the term "natural law."

Eight. Maimonides and Aquinas on Natural Law

For Saadia, to say that some of the divine commandments are rational is not equivalent to saying that reason knows them independently, or that reason alone can determine what is proper behavior for man. God alone is the source of the law. In addition to creating man, God "also endowed them with the means whereby they might attain complete happiness and perfect bliss... the commandments and prohibitions prescribed for them by God."[11] What Saadia seems to mean then by rational precepts is essentially the same as what we saw in the Talmudic passages which were cited and discussed earlier. They are commandments for which we can produce good reasons from our own purely human standpoint. They have an obvious social utility or can, by reflection, be shown to serve purposes of which reasonable men generally approve.[12] They are contrasted with those precepts which are primarily ritual in character and are in no way endorsed by reason. A man might continue to observe the rational precepts even if he no longer believed in their divine origin. Once he had learned of them, he would see that they are useful and that they help man achieve his own ends. The ritual precepts can only command our loyalty so long as we recognize that "the chief reason for the fulfillment of these principal precepts and their derivatives... is the fact that they represent the command of our Lord."[13] But Saadia, concerned to appeal as far as possible to human reason, goes on to say with regard to these ritual commandments, "yet I find that most of them have as their basis partially useful purposes." This seems to me to be the strongest possible evidence that he identifies the rational with the useful, but that utility does not serve as an independent and universal substitute for divinely revealed commandments. Having received them by revelation, we can now admire God's wisdom in commanding us to live in this advantageous way.

Joseph Albo, coming at very end of the medieval period, is the one Jewish philosopher who introduces the term "natural law" *(dat tib'it)*. His system of classification includes "three kinds of law, natural, positive or conventional, and divine." He goes on to explain that "natural law is the same among all peoples, at all times, and in all places."[14] Yet, even Albo, coming as late as the fifteenth century, and undoubtedly familiar with Christian thought and writing,[15] does not really take natural law seriously. He assigns it to the most inferior place in the hierarchy of types of law and makes clear his adherence to the traditional Jewish view that we are ultimately dependent on divine law. The scope of natural law is too limited to be useful. Its purpose is "to repress wrong, to promote right."[16] But man's reason is not able by itself to spell out what is right and wrong. This is why neither natural law nor conventional positive law is satisfactory.[17] All that natural man can rely on as a guide to good and evil are his own reactions of pleasure and pain, and these are so dependent on individual idiosyncrasies that they are completely unreliable as moral guides.[18] We are thus left only with God's direct instruction, through his prophets, as the ground of the distinctions between right and wrong. Reason cannot teach us to know what is good, nor can feeling guide and direct us. In spite of his minimal recognition of natural law, Albo is still a loyal Jew who can find no place for law without God's revelation.

III

To understand fully this Jewish conception of law and to explicate the principles on which it rests, we must turn to an examination of the views of Maimonides. This great thinker, who is often described as a complete rationalist, is most extreme in his rejection of all claims concerning a natural moral law based on right reason. However wide the extent of reason's dominance may be, it never, in Maimonides' teaching, extends to the realm of morals.

The clearest and most striking instance of Maimonides' approach to the doctrine of natural law can be found in his well-known ruling with respect to the seven commandments of the Noachides. Talmudic legislation had specified that there are seven commandments which are binding on all mankind. Mankind in general is referred to as the "children of Noah", since after the flood all humanity descends from Noah. These precepts include prohibitions against idolatry, blasphemy, murder, adultery, robbery, and the positive commandment to establish courts of justice. These six are considered to have been given to Adam. A seventh was given to Noah, namely, a prohibition against eating a limb torn from a living animal.[19] It is understandable that those who seek a natural law in the classical Jewish sources would seize on these seven commandments of the Noachides as just such a law. They are universal in scope and allow no exceptions, qualities which are usually associated with natural law. However, nothing is said in the rabbinic literature about their originating in reason or being known directly by reason. They are rather treated as divine commandments, on a par with all the other divine commandments.

Eight. Maimonides and Aquinas on Natural Law

We might have expected a philosopher like Maimonides to see in these precepts an opportunity to ground the fundamentals of morality in nature and reason. The fact is that he does just the opposite. In his Code, Maimonides follows the rabbinic ruling that identifies gentiles who observe the seven precepts as belonging to the "righteous of the nations of the world" *(hasidé umot ha-olam),* who are guaranteed a "portion in the world to come," i.e., salvation. So far, he is merely reproducing what had already been said by his Talmudic predecessors. However, he adds another condition which is designed to eliminate any possibility of understanding the Noachide commandments as natural law. Let us study the exact language of the text:

> Any man [i.e., any gentile] who accepts the seven commandments and is meticulous in observing them is thereby one of the righteous of the nations of the world, and he has a portion in the world to come. This is only the case if he accepts them and observes them because God commanded them in the Torah, and taught us through our teacher, Moses, that the children of Noah were commanded to observe them even before the Torah was given. But if he observes them because of his own conclusions based on reason, then he is not a resident-alien and is not one of the righteous of the nations of the world, nor is he one of their wise men.[20]

There are two points here of striking importance. First is the fact that Maimonides explicitly makes the final validity of the observance of the Noachide commandments dependent on a belief in their divine origin as commandments known only by way of God's revelation through Moses in the Torah, so that even the pre-Sinaitic generations are considered to have been directly commanded by God to observe these precepts. What is of particular interest is that Maimonides deliberately excludes the validity of any claim that these laws are known through reason or that they bind us because of purely rational considerations. One might have thought that it would be meritorious for a man to have achieved a basic knowledge of the rules of morality by way of rational reflection. But Maimonides denies to such a man all claims to special merit and in the process denies that there is or can be any natural moral law of the kind that Cicero had defended.

The full force of this denial is evident in the second point which requires our special attention, namely, the final phrase in the quoted passage, "nor is he one of their wise men." Maimonides is here excluding a man who claims rational moral knowledge, not only from the circle of the pious and righteous, but also from the circle of the wise. Much has been written about this last phrase in numerous attempts to show that there is a faulty reading and that the correct reading should be, "but he is one of their wise men." Considering the similarity of the formation of the Hebrew letters in the two words "nor" and "but", *welo-ela,* it is easy to suppose that we are the victims of a scribal or printing error. It is not possible to consider the relevant textual evidence within the limits of our present discussion. It is valuable, however, to note that the reading which we have cited occurs in almost all the printed editions, including the first complete edition printed at Rome in 1480.[21]

A correct understanding of Maimonides will show why he could not affirm a theory of natural law, why he denied salvation to those who believed that they could have moral knowledge on purely rational grounds, and why he considered the latter neither pious nor wise. With respect to the last question, I shall not presume in any way to try to settle the problem of what the correct reading of our text actually is. I shall only give evidence that it would have been perfectly consistent with Maimonides' views, even necessary, for him to have denied that those who hold a doctrine of natural law are wise men, that is to say, good philosophers.

From his earliest youthful work to the great book of his advanced years, *The Guide of the Perplexed,* Maimonides denied that moral rules are based on principles of reason or that they are capable of demonstration. More precisely, he views them, in *his Treatise on Logic,* as not falling under the categories of truth and falsehood at all, so that it is simply a logical error to speak of moral rules as true or false. Instead, he thinks of moral behavior as having to do with the beautiful and the ugly, and these are either matters of subjective taste, or else, as is usually the case, of established social convention. In short, Maimonides holds that moral claims are never open to rational argument or demonstration. They are "propositions which are known and require no proof for their truth." Unlike other such propositions which are indemonstrable, but are certainly true, such as statements about immediate perceptions and the first principles of mathematics, moral rules are only true in the sense that in a well-ordered society they are universally accepted and not subject to any doubt. They are "conventions, as when we know that uncovering the privy parts is ugly, that compensating a benefactor generously is beautiful."[22] Society, properly governed, forms our tastes and patterns of response in such a way that we have no doubt about such matters. However, this is not in any respect a matter of rational certainty or demonstrative evidence.

Eight. Maimonides and Aquinas on Natural Law

That this is a correct interpretation of Maimonides' position, as it is contained in the passage quoted, is borne out by a comment of Moses Mendelssohn. In his gloss on the term "conventions", Mendelssohn says: "These are matters which are incapable of being either true or false, but are only ugly or beautiful."[23] Mendelssohn goes on to argue that Maimonides is not speaking about the -beautiful and ugly in general, but only about modes of human behavior which we consider to be of moral significance and which are so set by convention as to evoke fixed responses from us. These are our reactions to such behavior in which we feel that what we are seeing or contemplating is beautiful or ugly, depending on whether it is socially approved or condemned. The soundness of this way of understanding Maimonides becomes evident when we move from the *Treatise on Logic,* his earliest youthful book, to his treatment of the same topic in his later works.

In *Eight Chapters,* a treatise dealing with moral questions, Maimonides again takes the same position. Moral evil is ultimately a matter of convention when considered from a philosophic point of view, and a matter of violating divine commandments when considered from a religious point of view. In his work on logic there was no proper place for any reference to divine commandments as the source of moral rules. Since that was a work of philosophy, or at least a propaedeutic to philosophy, it would have been inappropriate to introduce into it a purely religious element. Only at the very end of the *Treatise on Logic* does Maimonides give passing notice to the present state of affairs in which we are no longer dependent on the *nomoi,* i.e., the conventional law of the philosophers, since we are in possession of God's commandments. "In these times we do not need all these laws and nomoi; for divine laws govern human conduct."[24] However, in *Eight Chapters,* which being part of his commentary on the *Mishnah* is a religious work, Maimonides deals directly and explicitly with morals as divine commandments. But this does not turn them into rational laws available to man by way of his natural reason.

> The evils which the philosophers term such... are things which all people commonly agree are evils, such as the shedding of blood, theft, robbery, fraud, injury to one who has done no harm, ingratitude, contempt for parents, and the like. The prescriptions against these are called commandments (*mitzvot*), about which the Rabbis said, 'If they had not already been written in the Law, it would be proper to add them.' Some of our later sages, who were infected with the unsound principles of the *Mutakallimun,* called these *rational laws*.[25]

Here we have in a brief statement all the elements of Maimonides' ethical theory. From the standpoint of the philosophers, morals are conventions, "things which all people commonly agree are evils," while from the standpoint of the Rabbis they are divine commandments. One thing is completely clear, namely, that anyone who believes that moral principles can be rational is suffering from a serious intellectual disease. The intensity of Maimonides' feeling about this matter can be seen from the nature of his attack. It is generally agreed that he is directing his criticism especially against Saadia Gaon, whose views we discussed briefly above. In other places Maimonides speaks of Saadia with much admiration. He even goes so far as to say that were it not for him the Torah might have been completely lost.[26] This may explain the veiled reference, rather than a direct attack. Nevertheless, with all of Saadia's merit, the fact that he could speak of rational commandments and open the door even slightly to a theory of natural law is clear and incontrovertible evidence of his being "infected with unsound principles."

This theory of the nature of moral judgments came to full expression early in Maimonides' most mature and most profound speculative work, *The Guide of the Perplexed*. In the second chapter of Part I he answers a question put to him by an unnamed "learned man" concerning the punishment of Adam and Eve after their sin. In the course of his answer Maimonides explains that the true perfection of man is in his intellect and that it is because he is endowed with intellect that man is spoken of as created in the image of God. It is only insofar as he has intelligence that man can be commanded, since commands are never given to animals which have no intellect. "Through the intellect one distinguishes between truth and falsehood, and that was found in Adam in its perfection and integrity. Beautiful and ugly, on the other hand, belong to the things generally accepted as known [i.e., conventions], not to those cognized by intellect."[27] As an example of the kind of conventional behavior which is only bad because of social decrees and commonly developed tastes, Maimonides again cites the case of one who uncovers his genitals in public. For Adam, who was endowed originally with a perfect intellect and was free of all dependence on convention or taste, nakedness was not bad "and he did not apprehend that it was bad." This is evident from the Biblical text where we are told that though Adam and Eve were naked, they were not ashamed. After their sin, when they were robbed of intellectual perfection and reduced to dependence on conventions or feelings, they were embarrassed by their nakedness and covered themselves.

In this model case of man in the state of nature, there is no natural moral law at all, according to Maimonides. Moreover, insofar as there is any law regulating human behavior even in that primal state, it is explicitly a divine command. It is worth noting that in the biblical text Adam is given no reason for the command not to eat of the forbidden tree. He is simply told that "on the day that you eat from it you will die." The force of the commandment rests with the wisdom and authority of God who commands; it is in no way dependent on being grasped as obligatory by human reason. For Maimonides this must be the case, since morals are neither true nor false, while the intellect has as its proper subject matter only that which is capable of being either true or false.

In the light of this it is now clear why Maimonides denied that those who claim a rational knowledge of morality are wise men (if we accept the correctness of the reading in the printed versions). A wise man is one who, among other things, makes proper use of his faculties and understands what to expect from each subject matter. One of the marks of a well trained mind, according to Aristotle, is that it knows how to distinguish between various types of subject-matters, and that it never expects more precision than a subject is capable of yielding.[28] Maimonides knew his Aristotle well and had great regard for the Philosopher. As a follower of the Aristotelian teaching, he quite properly would refuse to recognize a man as wise who could be so confused that he would treat matters of convention or taste as if they were capable of rational demonstration. There is, in addition, a danger to society in such an error, since it rejects authority for pseudo-reason, an error which cannot long be suppressed. Once it is clear that moral distinctions are not rational, and they are no longer accepted on the authority of sovereign or God, there is no longer any ground whatsoever for restraint in human behavior.

This leads us to consider Maimonides' explanation of law, its sources and its purposes. All law must be understood as aimed at directing man toward the achievement of his own ultimate perfection. This perfection consists of the highest development of his intellect, leading to a rational knowledge of the "whole of being as it is"[29] However, no man can achieve this state of intellectual perfection completely by himself. Man is a political animal whose natural habitat is in society. Man cannot survive alone, but requires the help of other people. Moreover, even living in society, a man cannot achieve the fulfillment of his highest intellectual potentialities unless his bodily needs are property provided for. We therefore require a law which will serve two purposes. First, it must order the life of the individual and the life of the community in a way which makes them receptive to correct opinions. Then, it must communicate these correct opinions about ultimate matters so that even ordinary men will have gained a substantial measure of true knowledge of the ultimate things. In a community which is under the governance of such a system of law, the truly gifted individual will emerge with the fullest and most profound grasp of the highest truths with respect to the whole of being as it is. (Such ultimate perfection is intimately connected with immortality in Maimonides' theory; however, that is a topic which lies beyond the limits of our present discussion.)

These two aims of law are not generally achieved by the positive law of secular societies. It is the special merit of "the true Law... which is unique—namely, the Law of Moses our Master" that it is directed toward the realization of both essential human objectives. It "has come to bring us both perfections, I mean the welfare of the states of people in their relations with one another through the abolition of reciprocal wrongdoing and through the acquisition of a noble and excellent character... I mean also the soundness of the beliefs and the giving of correct opinions through which ultimate perfection is achieved. The letter of the Torah speaks of both perfections and informs us that the end of this Law in its entirety is the achievement of these two perfections."[30] Thus, all the commandments of Scripture and the rabbinical tradition are to be understood as aiming at these two goals. This means that every commandment has a reason, but it does not mean that we are necessarily capable of knowing or discovering the reasons of the commandments. Maimonides subscribes to the view that it would be blasphemous to suggest that God, who is perfect, would issue commands which are arbitrary or capricious. He thus makes an intense effort to discover reasons for the commandments which will fit into the general framework which he has set forth. This is, however, only an effort after the fact of our having been commanded, and the force of the commandments does not depend on our having understood them.

This is evident when we consider how Maimonides deals with the commandments in general. Those which are aimed at communicating correct opinions could be known by any man through skillful use of his own unaided reason. Those that are aimed at the propadeutic task of ordering personal and social life so as to make possible intellectual perfection could not be known by reason. Here we are dependent on the goodness and wisdom of God, who graciously taught us how to live in political communities that are properly ordered so that they can bring about the perfection of man. Given this understanding of the nature of the commandments in general, we can then look back at the individual commandments and seek explanations of their utility.

This point is strikingly clear in Maimonides' discussion of the Ten Commandments. Following rabbinical tradition, he says that at Sinai the people heard directly only the first two commandments, i.e., "I am the Lord thy God; thou shalt have no other Gods before me." The remaining eight commandments, like the rest of the Torah, were brought to them through Moses. As Maimonides interprets this, it means that the first two commandments, which deal with the existence and the unity of God, are affirmations which can be known by human -reason. With respect to these demonstrable truths we are not dependent on prophecy for our knowledge, nor does the prophet have any special insight which is denied to other men. "Now with regard to everything that can be known by demonstration, the status of the prophet and that of every one else who knows it are equal; there is no superiority of one over the other. Thus these two principles are not known through prophecy alone."[31] These two principles, known by way of the intellect and open to rational demonstration, are essentially different from the remaining eight commandments. The latter, which are fundamental rules of common morality, are not demonstrable and are in no way derived from reason. Though we are speaking here of such basic rules as the prohibitions against murder, adultery, theft, and the duty to honor parents, Maimonides does not regard them as binding us because we see by way of reason that they are true principles. "As for the other commandments [i.e., the last eight], they belong to the class of generally accepted opinions and those adopted in virtue of tradition, not to the class of the intellecta."[32] it is difficult to imagine a more categorical rejection of natural law theory than that contained in this passage. The most common of the precepts, which are assumed to be essential for the life of any ordered society, are not thought to be derived from reason or in any way available to the unaided intellect. Technically, they are merely conventions which have won widespread acceptance and which are enforced by the power of tradition.

If we were to leave the matter there, the entire fabric of civilized society would be threatened. Secular societies have no other source for such precepts than the will of the sovereign, the tradition of the people, or the conviction that these precepts serve a useful purpose. If this is the only ground of morality, then clearly it cannot bind a rational man. Whenever he feels inclined to substitute his own judgment for that of conventional opinion, there is no good reason for him not to do so. If from his perspective it is not imprudent to violate the conventions, then clearly, as a rational man, he should feel himself free to do so. The laws of such societies are *nomoi,* and there was a long history in Greek thought of opposition between *nomos and physis,* the merely conventional and the natural. Maimonides is faithful to classical Jewish tradition in holding that a merely conventional law is, in the last analysis, no law at all. If precepts do not bind and obligate us by way of our reason, then they can only become fixed obligatory rules as divine commandments. The Jews were favored by God with prophets, and particularly with Moses, the greatest of the prophets, through whom God's commandments were communicated to the people. It is through divine law that we have the principles of an ideal society in which both personal and social needs on the one hand, and correct opinions about the highest matters, on the other, are provided for every man. This law is binding, even with respect to moral matters which are not demonstrable, because it comes to us from God. Only such a law can be effective in leading man to the highest possibilities of human self-realization, "whereas the other political regimens—such as the nomoi of the Greeks and the ravings of the Sabians and of others—are due... to the actions of groups of rulers who were not prophets."[33]

Divine law, as received through the prophets, aims at the double objective of the welfare of the soul and the welfare of the body. The knowledge of ultimate truths is open to any man whose reason is sufficiently developed and who is motivated to engage in intense reflection about the nature of reality and the nature of God. Such men can only arise in a society so ordered that their kind of thinking has a place. Consequently, they too need to have the benefit of the laws which regulate personal and social behavior. For the large mass of men, who are not impelled by nature and talent to metaphysical speculation, it is essential to establish both an ordered society and a system of correct beliefs. Beginning from the base of a properly ordered community and from beliefs which save them from hopeless errors, even ordinary men have some chance of achieving their own proper perfection. Without the divine law, the essential conditions for the movement toward true human perfection are lacking.

Eight. Maimonides and Aquinas on Natural Law

In a key passage Maimonides states succinctly and clearly his views about these fundamental matters:

> It has already been demonstrated that man has two perfections: a first perfection, which is the perfection of the body, and an ultimate perfection, which is the perfection of the soul. The first perfection consists in being healthy, and in the very best bodily state, and this is only possible through his finding the things necessary for him whenever he seeks them. These are his food and all the other things needed for the governance of the body, such as a shelter, bathing, and so forth. This cannot be achieved in any way by one isolated individual. For an individual can only attain all this through a political association, it being already known that man is political by nature. His ultimate perfection is to become rational in actu, I mean to have an intellect in actu; this would consist in knowing everything concerning all the beings that it is within the capacity of man to know in accordance with his ultimate perfection. *It is clear that to this ultimate perfection there do not belong either actions or moral qualities and that it consists only of opinions toward which speculation has led and that investigation has rendered compulsory.* It is also clear that this noble and ultimate perfection can -only be achieved after the first perfection has been achieved. For a man cannot represent to himself an intelligible even when taught to understand it and all the more cannot become aware of it of his own accord, if he is in pain or is very hungry or is thirsty or is hot or is very cold. But once the first perfection has been achieved it is possible to achieve the ultimate, which is indubitably more noble and is the only cause of permanent preservation.[34]

We can see here the end of all true law which is to bring men to both perfections. A true law must be clear about the order of importance and dignity of the two types of perfection, never confusing the instrumental good with the final good. Only the final good is rational. All the rest is aimed at establishing the conditions under which men can achieve the final good, but it has no intrinsic worth. There is no natural moral law. Divine law consists not only of true beliefs, but also of behavioral precepts by way of which man can be brought to the state in which it is possible for him to realize the final good. So important is it to have divine sanction for all the precepts by which personal and social life are ordered that the true law also commands us to accept certain -beliefs without which the precepts might lose their force. "The Law also makes a call to adopt certain beliefs, belief in which is necessary for the sake of political welfare. Such, for instance, is our belief that He, may He be exalted, is violently angry with those who disobey Him and that it is therefore necessary to fear Him and to dread him and to take care not to disobey."[35] This is necessary because reason alone provides no sanction for any set of moral rules.

Maimonides' categorical rejection of natural law does not entail his holding that divine moral rules are irrational or opposed to nature. He is affirming only that moral precepts are not known by way of reason and are not capable of demonstration. Viewed by themselves they would appear to be matters with respect to which one cannot logically affirm either truth or falsehood. So long as man does not live in society, as was the case with Adam, morality can be thought of merely as a matter of taste, and thus as purely subjective. Once man enters society, and historical man is always a social and political being, he can no longer afford to allow morals to be treated as purely private matters of personal taste. For the protection of society, morals are reinforced with the power of convention changing finally into law. But positive law suffers from two defects. First, it is only concerned with man's bodily welfare, while what really matters is the welfare of the soul. Second, it has no real sanction, since one can always question the wisdom or the beneficence of the human sovereign. This reduces the force of law to nothing more than the counsels of prudence. Plato demonstrated long ago that prudence is self-defeating, since the truly prudent man must ask what his true self-interest is, and in the process of this inquiry is led to consider ultimate metaphysical questions.

It is as an alternative to this untenable view of law that Maimonides understands the system of divine law which we have set forth here. What reason cannot do alone is done for us by God through his prophets. What reason can do alone, namely to know ultimate truths is left open to every man, aided by the initially correct beliefs which are provided for him by Scripture. All the commandments, other than those which have to do with true belief, are useful and even necessary for the ideal ordering of the political community. Seen this way, we can say of them that though they are not rational, in the sense of being demonstrable, they are reasonable, in the sense that we can give good reasons for them. With this purpose in mind Maimonides goes to great lengths in his *Guide* to expound the reasons for the commandments. He is concerned to show us that all of the commandments are useful in one way or another as devices for helping us gain the ultimate perfection which is the true end of man.[36] No man could ever come, by way of rational reflection, to the conclusion that there is some particular set of moral rules which is correct and binding. On the other hand, having received the precepts and accepting them as divine in origin, we can, after the fact, recognize how valuable they are. Even in those cases where we fail to find a satisfactory reason for given commandments, we continue to observe them, because having acknowledged the divine origin of the entire structure we can no longer select among the commandments in accordance with private tastes or judgments. Once we are prepared to deny the authority of prophecy to one commandment, however bizarre or obscure it may be, we have effectively denied the binding force of the entire Torah. For this reason, Maimonides lays extreme stress on our obligation to recognize the Torah which we have in our hands as complete and immutable. No one claiming today to be a prophet and proposing to change any law of the Torah can be recognized as legitimate. He is a false prophet who perverts the authority of Moses and in so doing undermines the authority of God's commandments.[37] The Torah was given only once; it is a work of divine perfection; we can hope to see the realization of man's highest possibilities only in that society which submits itself completely to the direction of God's law.

Just as the commandments are reasonable, without being rationally demonstrable, so are they in accord with man's nature without being natural. The law takes account of man's natural qualities and is designed to cope with them. It does not demand that which man is incapable of doing and its commands are framed with an eye to what human nature requires for its own perfection. "The Law, although it is not natural, enters into what is natural."[38] To take just one example, the laws of sacrifice, according to Maimonides, had to be given as a concession to accustomed patterns of pre-Sinaitic worship. To root out certain of these idolatrous patterns required accommodation to man's nature, "For one could not then conceive the acceptance of [such a Law], considering the nature of man, which always likes that to which it is accustomed."[39] In this restricted sense, Maimonides conceives of the law as natural, namely, as consistent with and attuned to human nature. There is no other or more significant sense in which we can find any version of natural law in Maimonides. As I tried to show earlier this extreme position of Maimonides with respect to natural law is a reflection of the normative attitude of the classical Jewish tradition as it is formulated in the Bible, the rabbinic literature, and in the works of the Jewish philosophers of the Middle Ages.

IV

St. Thomas Aquinas provides us with a paradigm case of classical Christian thought with respect to the nature of law. For the purposes of the present discussion we shall base our exposition of Thomas on his Treatise on Law, which is contained in Part I-II of the *Summa Theologica*. We may note at the outset that though Thomas is influenced by Maimonides at various points, and though he quotes him in the Treatise on Law more than a dozen times, he, nevertheless, stands it the opposite pole from him with respect to the question of natural law.

This is immediately evident when we consider the first things that Thomas has to say about law. The first question which he considers is, "Whether law is something pertaining to reason?" and he answers with an absolute and unequivocal "yes". "Law is a rule and measure of acts, whereby man is induced to act or is restrained from acting... Now the rule and measure of human acts is the reason... Consequently, it follows that law is something pertaining to reason."[40] Any law, even that imposed by a sovereign power, is law only insofar as it is rational. "In order that the volition of what is commanded may have the nature of law, it needs to be in accord with some rule of reason ... otherwise the sovereign's will would savor of lawlessness rather than of law."[41] What is true of positive law is true for Thomas of all law; if it is truly law, then it must follow a rule of reason.

All four kinds of law which Thomas distinguishes—eternal, natural, human and divine—have this essential characteristic of being rational. The eternal law is the work of the Supreme Reason and thus fully rational. What is of more immediate interest for our purposes is Thomas' theory of natural law. First, he establishes that there is a natural law. Man is a rational creature and this creature has "a share of the eternal reason, whereby it has a natural inclination to its proper act and end; and this participation of the eternal law in the rational creature is called the natural law."[42] In striking contrast to Maimonides, Thomas holds that the natural law is the source of the precepts of morality and that they are all purely rational in character. "Now, since human morals depend on their relation to reason, which is the proper principle of human acts, those morals are called good which accord with reason, and those are called bad which are discordant from reason... every judgment of practical reason proceeds from naturally known principles... it follows, of necessity, that all the moral precepts belong to the law of nature..."[43] Or, as Thomas puts it in a somewhat different formulation, "all the acts of the virtues are prescribed by the natural law, since each one's reason naturally dictates to him to act virtuously."[44] This natural moral law is universal, the same for all men everywhere, and binding on all men without exception. The natural law is universally known, 'except for some few cases where reason has been "perverted by passion, or evil habit, or an evil disposition of nature."[45] Finally, human law is law only to the extent to which it is derived from the law of nature. Any human law that in any way differs from or opposes the law of nature is not law at all, but is rather a distortion and perversion of law.[46]

In order to appreciate the true significance of the profound opposition between Aquinas and Maimonides in their theories of law, we need to consider the one peculiar exception to his theory which Aquinas introduces. The one instance of law which is not natural and not rational (and, therefore, not binding) is the Old Law, i.e., the law of the Old Testament. Some of its precepts happen to accord with the natural law, and all men are bound to observe these just because they are natural law, but not because they are contained in the Old Law. All the rest is a peculiar kind of law. It is not natural, not in accord with reason, and binding only upon the Jews of pre-Christian times.[47] To continue, after Christ, to observe any of the precepts of the Old Law because one believes them to have deriver their binding force from the fact that they are contained in the Hebrew Scriptures would be a mortal sin. For after the coming of Christ there is no longer any binding force to the Old Law, and to continue to treat it as if it were obligatory is tantamount to a denial of Christ.[48]

What Aquinas has done is to classify the law of the Hebrew Bible in such way that its moral precepts are natural law and are binding exclusively on that score, while its ceremonial and judicial precepts are considered to be a peculiar legislation for the special purpose of prefiguring the coming of Christ. The ceremonial precepts may not be observed any longer under any circumstances, while the judicial may be observed if they seem to be useful, but only so long as they are not considered to have any obligatory element based on their biblical source. The strategy is to introduce a principle of selectivity into the law, so that one can retain, on independent grounds, the moral precepts that are essential for the ordering of society, while rejecting all the rest of the biblical legislation. Maimonides, as we saw, could not admit any such principle of selectivity without undermining the obligatory force of the entire system of biblical and rabbinic law. His philosophy did not allow for a natural moral law. Consequently, he had to argue for the absolute integrity of the whole received law and to treat it all as divine in origin and permanently binding. On theological grounds, it was essential for Aquinas to reject the Old Law. This left him no alternative but to find some principle by which he could retain those parts of the biblical law which were essential while dispensing with all the rest. The theory of a natural moral law, grounded in reason, serves this purpose for him.

In his very elaborate scheme, which we have presented here in only the briefest sketch, Thomas is following closely the method and the logic of the New Testament. It is the inner need of Christianity that brings about not only the rejection of the Old Law, but also the appeal to natural law. The first step is evident in the way in which "Torah" is translated in the New Testament. Torah is not "Law" as the common translations even today render it. Torah is divine teaching, God's instructions for the ordering of human life and the achievement of final blessedness. The key terms in the Jewish tradition are *"Torah" and "mitzvah"*. The former is the whole body of divine teaching as contained in the sacred texts and in the normative tradition. The latter refers to the specific and detailed commandments. As Maimonides has shown, following the classical Jewish teaching, the force of these commandments lies in the fact that they are believed to be God's specific rules for man. The term "law" has a secondary and subordinate place in the entire Jewish system for ordering the life of man and society. The primary place is occupied by "commandment".

Yet, in the Greek New Testament Torah is consistently, and with very few exceptions, rendered as *nomos*.[49] Though *nomos* is the standard term for law, it has a set of associations which are calculated to undermine the authority and force of that which is presented as nomic. Originally, *nomos* is convention or custom which stands in opposition to *physis*, nature and the natural. The latter is fixed, orderly, intelligible, rational etc. The former has about it always an air of arbitrariness, a sense of local peculiarity rather than universal rationality. The shift from Torah to *nomos* is of the highest significance, since it introduces into what were thought by the Jews to be fixed divine commandments a sense of that which is passing, temporary, and certainly not truly divine. Dodd puts the matter with striking clarity when he says, *"Nomos...* is by no means an exact equivalent for *Torah*, and its substitution for the Hebrew term affords an illustration of a change in the ideas associated with the term—a difference in men's notion of what religion is... *Nomos* is fundamentally 'custom', hardening into what, we call 'law'. It does not necessarily imply any legislative authority. It is rather an immanent or underlying principle of life and action."[50] A bit later, speaking of the main elements of Hebrew law, Dodd adds that, "The terms used all imply more or less directly a legislator, and this is true to the Hebrew idea. The fountain of all law for the Hebrews was God, whether the immediate human author of the commandments, statutes, and judgments was judge, king, or priest... But *nomos*, for the most part, as we have seen, renders none of these terms."[51]

Eight. Maimonides and Aquinas on Natural Law

Given the basic presuppositions of normative Christian doctrine, it was important to strip the Old Law of its authority and of its claim to being, as Maimonides saw it, the immutable law of God. It is not my contention here that the translation of *Torah* as *nomos* was a deliberate polemical device on the part of the New Testament authors. Even if they were merely adopting a term which had already come into common use, it nevertheless had the effect of making Torah appear to be the peculiar local customs of the Jews, rather than the permanent commandments of God.

A further element in the New Testament which is calculated to weaken the claims of the Old Law is the representation of that law as having been given not by God but by an angel or mediator. The law "was a temporary measure pending the arrival of the 'issue' to whom the promise was made It was promulgated through angels, and there was an intermediary."[52] Thomas, basing himself on this verse, argues that the old law was clearly imperfect and temporary, a kind of local *nomos*. This is why it was given through intermediaries. "It was fitting that the perfect law of the New Testament should be given by the incarnate God immediately."[53] As *nomos*, the law of the Old Testament can be viewed readily as having been limited to a particular time and place. The change of circumstances which results from the coming of Christ makes that law no longer operative. "But now, having died to that which held us bound, we are discharged from the law, to serve God in a new way, the way of the spirit, in contrast to the old way, the way of a written code."[54]

Since the new law is not a written code, and since it does not explicitly include all the moral precepts of the Old Testament which Christianity wants to retain, these are regained through the device of natural law. The theory that there is a natural law which prescribes moral behavior and binds all men is introduced in the New Testament, to be developed and elaborated in later Christian thought. The *locus classicus* for New Testament natural law theory is *Romans* 2:14-15:

> When Gentiles who do not possess the law carry out its precepts by the light of nature, then, although they have no law, they are their own law, for they display the effect of the law inscribed on their hearts. Their conscience is called as witness, and their own thoughts argue the case on either side, against them or even for them, on the day when God judges the secrets of human hearts through Christ Jesus.

It is hardly necessary, after all that has already been said, to give further evidence that this Pauline statement concerning natural law is far removed from the standard Jewish view.[55] What is of interest is to see where the internal logic of this position leads. Beginning with a rejection of the Old Law, there is substituted for it a belief in a natural law which is written on the hearts of all men. This means that every man knows what is right and, therefore, that every man can be his own judge. The extreme version of this is the twice-repeated statement, evidently approved by Paul, "All things are lawful for me."[56] Clearly, this cannot function as an operative rule for ordering society, so that it is necessary to introduce principles of selection. This moves Paul to add that even though all things are lawful, they are not all wise, healthy, or well-advised. What we need, then, is the capacity to exercise our freedom from the law in a way which will still be good. We need to reintroduce on some new ground the very restraints which were cast off with the old law, and we need to have the positive guides to good behavior which are no longer available to us from the old law. Paul assures his Christian brethren that by offering themselves completely to God they will be so transformed that they will be able directly to "discern the will of God, and to know what is good, acceptable, perfect."[57] On another occasion he prays that, growing in Christian love, the brethren at Philippi will "grow ever richer and richer in knowledge and insight of every kind" and that they will thus gain "the gift of true discrimination", or (in another version) that they will be taught "by experience what things are most worthwhile."[58]

Thus we are led, finally, back to the full development of natural law theory in a Christian thinker such as Aquinas. Here we are assured that all conventional moral precepts are, in fact, required by reason, known to every man, and universally obligatory. There is no room here for purely personal judgment or discrimination, for that would inevitably undermine the foundations of an ordered society. This moves Thomas to affirm that every one agrees about the precepts of the natural law. But what shall we do with those people who obviously do not agree? We simply announce that they are the victims of a reason which has been perverted by passion, or that they suffer from evil habits, or an evilly constituted nature. This is the way he deals, in a paradigm case, with the Germans. "Theft, although it is expressly contrary to the natural law, was not considered wrong among the Germans, as Julius Caesar relates.[59] Thomas explains that since they did not recognize such an elementary principle of natural law, they were obviously possessed of a corrupt and perverted reason. In this way we come back to the fixed norms of the law, while supposedly holding to a theory

Eight. Maimonides and Aquinas on Natural Law

that every man is capable of being his own moral arbiter. All men are equally endowed with knowledge of the natural law which is inscribed on their hearts, but some are apparently more equal than others.

St. Thomas and Maimonides may be thought of as concerned with a common problem. Both need to have a law which will regulate personal life and order communal life properly. Maimonides, finding no rational ground for moral distinctions, avoids the dangers of social chaos by returning to the Hebrew Bible and the rabbinic tradition. Here he finds all that is necessary for man to learn to live in such a way that he can move from the lower perfection of a decent bodily existence to the ultimate perfection of true metaphysical knowledge. This is a scheme of salvation which is dependent on God's law to provide its essential external conditions. That law is viewed as absolutely authoritative because it is divine; it protects men from debilitating bodily passions; it orders the relations between men in society so as to prevent mutual destruction; it implants in even the most simple-minded man correct opinions about the highest matters and protects him from error; and it frees human reason in every man so that all can rise to the highest level of self-realization, to that knowledge of God which is true salvation.

Thomas, on the other hand, must, as a Christian, reject the law. Though he substitutes grace for law, he must still have some regulation of life in ordinary human society, for even Christians are still men. He gains this end through the natural law, which takes the place in his system of Maimonides' divine commandments. It might be thought that there is really no significant difference, since Aquinas holds that, "The natural law is promulgated by the very fact that God instilled it into man's mind so as to be known by him naturally."[60] And he adds the view that "the light of natural reason, whereby we discern what is good and what is evil, which is the function of the natural law, is nothing else than an imprint on us of the divine light."[61] Yet, while he speaks of the natural law as divine, the term has a vastly different force than its meaning in the Jewish teaching of Maimonides. For Aquinas, to call the law divine is simply to say that it is part of the eternal law, a part which he claims is a natural possession of every man by virtue of his being human. When Maimonides speaks of the law as divine commandments, he is relying on the claim of a particular historic event, the revelation at Sinai, as the source of our knowledge of the law.

Neither Maimonides nor Aquinas is prepared to accept a society in which every man is his own judge and feels free to do whatever he chooses.

Each responds to the problem in a way which is characteristic of his own religious community, a way which reflects genuine differences between Judaism and Christianity. If both Maimonides and Aquinas may be thought of as seeking the conditions of salvation, then their differences might be understood in the following way. For Aquinas, the Christian, salvation is neither by works alone, nor by rational knowledge, but by grace. Natural law tells men how to behave, but it cannot lead them to their final and true fulfillment. For Maimonides, the Jew, salvation depends on good works, leading to rational apprehension of the highest truth. There is no natural moral law, only the law of God, which teaches us to live our lives in such way that we are worthy of our claim to have been created in His image. This, in turn, creates the circumstances under which we can develop our intellect in such way as to become as nearly divine as finite men can ever be.